NT

out of joint

Tour includes
13 – 15 Nov
Theatre Royal, York
01904 623568

18 – 22 Nov
Birmingham Rep
0121 236 4455

25 – 29 Nov
Northcott Theatre, Exeter
01392 493 493

2 – 6 Dec
Theatre Royal, Bath
01225 448844

10 – 13 Dec
Live Theatre, Newcastle
0191 232 1232

8 Jan – 1 May
National Theatre, London
020 7452 3000

11 – 15 May
Oxford Playhouse
01865 305305

In 1991, before an election they did not expect to win, the Conservative government made a fateful decision to privatise the railways. Twelve years later we subsidise the industry more lavishly than ever before. David Hare tells the remarkable story of a dream gone sour, gathering first-hand accounts from those most intimately involved – from every level of the system. Funny, tragic, compelling, their voices become an extraordinary parable of British mismanagement and the recent history of the country.

More information:
Out of Joint 0207 609 0207
ojo@outofjoint.co.uk
www.outofjoint.co.uk

Out of Joint and the National

KT-131-624

THE PERMANENT WAY

BY DAVID HARE

DIRECTED BY MAX STAFFORD-CLARK

A must-see for readers of

'THE CRASH THAT STOPPED BRITAIN'

by Granta editor Ian Jack

GRANTA

GRANTA 83, AUTUMN 2003
www.granta.com

EDITOR   *Ian Jack*
ASSOCIATE EDITOR   *Liz Jobey*
MANAGING EDITOR   *Fatema Ahmed*
EDITORIAL ASSISTANT   *Helen Gordon*

CONTRIBUTING EDITORS   *Diana Athill, Gail Lynch, Blake Morrison, Andrew O'Hagan, John Ryle, Lucretia Stewart*

ASSOCIATE PUBLISHER   *Sally Lewis*
FINANCE   *Geoffrey Gordon, Morgan Graver*
SALES   *Frances Hollingdale*
PUBLICITY   *Louise Campbell*
SUBSCRIPTIONS   *John Kirkby, Darryl Wilks, Anna Tang*
PUBLISHING ASSISTANT   *Mark Williams*
ADVERTISING MANAGER   *Kate Rochester*
PRODUCTION ASSOCIATE   *Sarah Wasley*

PUBLISHER   *Rea S. Hederman*

Granta, 2–3 Hanover Yard, Noel Road, London N1 8BE
Tel 020 7704 9776 Fax 020 7704 0474
e-mail for editorial: editorial@granta.com

Granta US, 1755 Broadway, 5th Floor, New York, NY 10019-3780, USA

TO SUBSCRIBE call 020 7704 0470 or e-mail subs@granta.com
A one-year subscription (four issues) costs £26.95 (UK), £34.95 (rest of Europe) and £41.95 (rest of the world).

Granta is printed and bound in Italy by Legoprint. The paper used in this publication meets the minimum requirements of American National Standard for Information Sciences—Permanence of Paper for Printed Library Materials, ANSI Z39.48-1984.

Granta is published by Granta Publications.

Design: Slab Media.

Cover photograph: Nickel Tailings #34, Sudbury, Ontario, by Edward Burtynsky courtesy of Flowers East Gallery, London

ISBN 0-903141-62-0

They've taken us to the **cleaners.**
Now they're all **spun out.**
It's time to **hang them out to dry!**

Pretty **Straight** Guys

Nick Cohen

The savage, witty and spot-on exposé
of New Labour spin and sleaze
from Britain's most feared political journalist.

ff

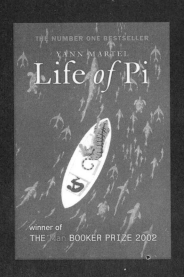

GRANTA 83

This Overheating World

Bill McKibben	**WORRIED? US?**	7
Maarten 't Hart	**MIDSUMMER IN APRIL**	13
Philip Marsden	**THE WEATHER IN MONGOLIA**	29
Wayne McLennan	**ROWING TO ALASKA**	47
Matthew Hart	**THE GREENLAND PUMP**	77
Edward Burtynsky	**THE EVIDENCE OF MAN**	95
Thomas Keneally	**CAPTAIN SCOTT'S BISCUIT**	129
Marian Botsford Fraser	**BONE LITTER**	145
James Hamilton-Paterson	**DO FISH FEEL PAIN?**	159
Mark Lynas	**HOT NEWS**	175
Jon McGregor	**THE FIRST PUNCH**	183
Christopher de Bellaigue	**LOOT**	193
James Meek	**WITH THE INVADERS**	213
Nuha al-Radi	**TWENTY-EIGHT DAYS IN BAGHDAD**	235
NOTES ON CONTRIBUTORS		256

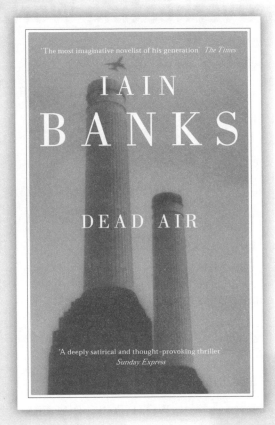

GRANTA

WORRIED? US?
Bill McKibben

Bill McKibben

For fifteen years now, some small percentage of the world's scientists and diplomats and activists has inhabited one of those strange dreams where the dreamer desperately needs to warn someone about something bad and imminent; but somehow, no matter how hard he shouts, the other person in the dream—standing smiling, perhaps, with his back to an oncoming train—can't hear him. This group, this small percentage, knows that the world is about to change more profoundly than at any time in the history of human civilization. And yet, so far, all they have achieved is to add another line to the long list of human problems—people think about 'global warming' in the way they think about 'violence on television' or 'growing trade deficits', as a marginal concern to them, if a concern at all. Enlightened governments make smallish noises and negotiate smallish treaties; enlightened people look down on America for its blind piggishness. Hardly anyone, however, has fear in their guts.

Why? Because, I think, we are fatally confused about time and space. Though we know that our culture has placed our own lives on a demonic fast-forward, we imagine that the earth must work on some other timescale. The long slow accretion of epochs—the Jurassic, the Cretaceous, the Pleistocene—lulls us into imagining that the physical world offers us an essentially stable background against which we can run our race. Humbly, we believe that the world is big and that we are small. This humility is attractive, but also historic and no longer useful. In the world as we have made it, the opposite is true. Each of us is big enough, for example, to produce our own cloud of carbon dioxide. As a result, we—our cars and our industry—have managed to raise the atmospheric level of carbon dioxide, which had been stable at 275 parts per million throughout human civilization, to about 380 parts per million, a figure that is climbing by one and a half parts per million each year. This increase began with the Industrial Revolution in the eighteenth century, and it has been accelerating ever since. The consequence, if we take a median from several respectable scientific projections, is that the world's temperature will rise by five degrees Fahrenheit (roughly two and a half degrees Celsius) over the next hundred years, to make it hotter than it has been for 400 million years. At some level, these are the only facts worth knowing about our earth.

Fifteen years ago, it was a hypothesis. Those of us who were convinced that the earth was warming fast were a small minority. Science was sceptical, but set to work with rigour. Between 1988 and 1995, scientists drilled deep into glaciers, took core samples from lake bottoms, counted tree rings, and, most importantly, refined elaborate computer models of the atmosphere. By 1995, the almost impossibly contentious world of science had seen enough. The world's most distinguished atmospheric chemists, physicists and climatologists, who had organized themselves into a large collective called the Intergovernmental Panel on Climate Change, made their pronouncement: 'The balance of evidence suggests that there is a discernible human influence on global climate.' In the eight years since, science has continued to further confirm and deepen these fears, while the planet itself has decided, as it were, to peer-review their work with a succession of ominously hot years (1998 was the hottest ever, with 2002 trailing by only a few hundredths of a degree). So far humanity has raised the planet's temperature by about one degree Fahrenheit, with most of that increase happening after 1970—from about fifty-nine degrees Fahrenheit, where it had been stuck since the first cities rose and the first crops grew, to about sixty degrees. Five more degrees in the offing, as I have said, but already we understand, with an almost desperate clarity, how finely balanced our world has been. One degree turns out to be a lot. In the cryosphere—the frozen portions of the planet's surface—glaciers are everywhere in rapid retreat (spitting out Bronze Age hunter-gatherers). The snows of Kilimanjaro are set to become the rocks of Kilimanjaro by 2015. Montana's Glacier National Park is predicted to lose its last glaciers by 2030. We know how thick Arctic ice is— we know it because Cold War nuclear-powered submarines needed the information for their voyages under the ice cap. When the data was declassified in the waning days of the Clinton administration, it emerged that Arctic ice was forty per cent thinner than it had been forty years before. *Perma*frost is melting. Get it?

'Global warming' can be a misleading phrase—the temperature is only the signal that extra solar radiation is being trapped at the earth's surface. That extra energy drives many things: wind-speeds increase, a reflection of the increasing heat-driven gradients between low and high pressure; sea level starts to rise, less because of melting ice caps than because warm air holds more water vapour than cold; hence evaporation increases and with it drought, and then, when the overloaded clouds finally part, deluge and flood. Some of these effects are linear. A recent study has shown that rice fertility drops by ten per cent for each degree Celsius that the temperature rises above thirty degrees Celsius during the rice plant's flowering. At forty degrees Celsius, rice fertility drops to zero. But science has come to understand that some effects may not follow such a clear progression. To paraphrase Orwell, we may all be hot, but some will be hotter than others. If the Gulf Stream fails because of Arctic melting, some may, during some seasons, even be colder.

The success of the scientific method underlines the failure of the political method. It is clear what must happen—the rapid conversion of our energy system from fossil to renewable fuels. And it is clear that it could happen—much of the necessary technology is no longer quixotic, no longer the province of backyard tinkerers. And it is also clear that it isn't happening. Some parts of Europe have made material progress—Denmark has built great banks of windmills. Some parts of Europe have made promises—the United Kingdom thinks it can cut its carbon emissions by sixty per cent by 2050. But China and India are still building power plants and motorways, and the United States has made it utterly clear that nothing will change soon. When Bill Clinton was President he sat by while American civilians traded up from cars to troop-transport vehicles; George Bush has not only rejected the Kyoto treaty, he has ordered the Environmental Protection Agency to replace 'global warming' with the less ominous 'climate change', and issued a national energy policy that foresees ever more drilling, refining and burning. Under it, American carbon emissions will grow another forty per cent in the next generation.

As satisfying as it is to blame politicians, however, it will not do. Politicians will follow the path of least resistance. So far there has not been a movement loud or sustained enough to command political attention. Electorates demand economic prosperity—more of it—above all things. Gandhianism, the political philosophy that restricts material need, is now only a memory even in the country of its birth. And our awareness that the world will change in every aspect, should we be so aware, is muted by the future tense, even though that future isn't far away, so near in fact that preventing global warming is a lost cause—all we can do now is to try to keep it from getting utterly out of control.

This is a failure of imagination, and in this way a literary failure. Global warming has still to produce an Orwell or a Huxley, a Verne or a Wells, a *Nineteen Eighty-Four* or a *War of the Worlds*, or in film any equivalent of *On The Beach* or *Doctor Strangelove*. It may never do so. It may be that because—fingers crossed—we have escaped our most recent fear, nuclear annihilation via the Cold War, we resist being scared all over again. Fear has its uses, but fear on this scale seems to be disabling, paralysing. Anger has its uses too, but the rage of anti-globalization demonstrators has yet to do more than alienate majorities. Shame sends a few Americans shopping for small cars, but on the whole America, now the exemplar to the world, is very nearly unshameable.

My own dominant feeling has always been sadness. In 1989, I published *The End of Nature*, the first book for a lay audience about global warming. Half of it was devoted to explaining the science, the other half to my unease. It seemed, and still seems, to me that humanity has intruded into and altered every part of the earth (or very nearly) with our habits and economies. Thoreau once said that he could walk half an hour from his home in Concord, Massachusetts, and come to a place where no man stood from one year to the next, and 'there consequently politics are not, for politics are but the cigar smoke of a man.' Now that cigar smoke blows everywhere.

Paradoxically, the world also seems more lonely. Everything else exists at our sufferance. Biologists guess that the result of a rapid warming will be the greatest wave of extinction since the last asteroid crashed into the earth. Now we are the asteroid. The notion that we live in a God-haunted world is harder to conjure up. God rebuked Job: 'Were you there when I wrapped the ocean in clouds...and set its boundaries, saying, "Here you may come but no farther. Here shall your proud waves break...Who gathers up the stormclouds, slits them and pours them out?"' Job, and everyone else until our time, had the sweet privilege of shutting up in the face of that boast—it was clearly God or gravity or some force other than us. But as of about 1990 we can answer back, because we set the sea level now, and we run the storm systems. The excretion of our economy has become the most important influence on the planet we were born into. We're what counts.

Our ultimate sadness lies in the fact that we know that this is not a pre-ordained destiny; it isn't fate. New ways of behaving, of getting and spending, can still change the future: there is, as the religious evangelist would say, still time, though not much of it, and a miraculous conversion is called for—Americans in the year 2000 produced fifteen per cent more carbon doxide than they had ten years before.

The contrast between two speeds is the key fact of our age: between the pace at which the physical world is changing and the pace at which human society is reacting to this change. In history, if it exists, we shall be praised or damned.   □

GRANTA

MIDSUMMER IN APRIL
Maarten 't Hart

TRANSLATED FROM THE DUTCH BY

MICHIEL HORN

That year I heard the first blackbird sing on New Year's Day, and the marsh tits were singing before the start of February. Just over two weeks after the new year began I saw the coltsfoot flowers open on their naked stems, and a little more than a week after that the pale yellow of lesser celandine shimmered among the green leaves along the ditches. During Eastertide, which—how could it have been otherwise?—came early that year, the cuckoo flowers were in bloom, and the fruit trees in the garden were in full flower. The night before Easter Sunday I was stung by mosquitoes for the first time, and on the Sunday itself honey bees and bumblebees zoomed through the garden as though it were midsummer.

At first I thought, everything is early this year, strangely early. But on Easter Sunday morning, when I sought shade under an already flowering laburnum, I felt dull and languid because of the oppressive, summer-like warmth, and it seemed to me that something had gone wrong, either with my capacity for registering changes in time, or with nature itself. A premonition of approaching calamity deepened in the course of March to an unease that drove me almost crazy.

The kind of unease that troubled me so greatly resembled a feeling I occasionally had in my youth. From time to time I would become convinced that Christ would soon come again and that the days of the great tribulation, which would precede that event, would not be long delayed. Standing in the small unlit room in our house, aiming the splashing jet at the middle of the toilet bowl, how often had I lifted my head to look out through the small window at the crescent moon in order to check whether it was covered with the 'sackcloth of hair' that heralded the arrival of Judgement Day. Only recently did I notice that I used to remember that Bible verse incorrectly: 'the sun became black as sackcloth of hair, and the moon became as blood.' But back then I looked for sackcloth around the moon. A few times, as a grey cloud drifted in front of the moon, I clearly saw the outline of a sack, and I ran into the living room shouting, 'He's coming, He's coming!' But neither my father nor my mother would believe me. Only once did my mother come with me to the toilet. She looked at the moon and said, 'That's a cloud.'

As Christ did not come, not even after I saw sackcloth around the moon on five separate occasions, my fear of the Second Coming receded over the years. But every time I walked along the river with

15

just one friend, I thought of the words of Jesus: 'Then shall two be in the field; the one shall be taken and the other left.' I was convinced I would be left, and my heart shrank at the thought of what would await me: I would be consigned to outer darkness, where the worm shall not die, neither shall the fire be quenched.

So that year, in the nights after Easter I dreamt of the Second Coming again and again.

Usually it began in a train, in a freight car. After a journey of several days we arrived in a large station. He, Christ, stood on the platform and, after we got off the train, motioned with His thumb to separate the sheep from the goats. Each and every time I was unable to get off the train. I wanted to scream but my throat was clamped tightly shut. Then I woke up and looked at the slowly swaying curtains and raised my head because I thought I heard noises, the sound of trumpets that announced His coming. I went back to sleep, I rode in the train again, I couldn't get off, I couldn't scream, I woke up, and my heart pounded as though it would break.

On the Tuesday after Easter a female colleague arrived from England. She had written to ask whether she could work in our laboratory for a while and use our surplus sticklebacks. She had a pike, she wrote, which she had taught to eat sticklebacks, and she had heard about the sticklebacks that we had bred for aggression. She wanted to test whether they would be better able to defend themselves against the pike than her own sticklebacks. Her curious letter increased my unease further: a woman who was coming over from England with her trained pike—how peculiar! I replied that I usually fed the surplus sticklebacks to my rats, but that I was willing to save them up for her. So, after some fitful correspondence about when she would arrive and where she would stay, she stood in front of our house, at dusk on the Tuesday after Easter. All day long I had been in a state. What would she look like? The malaise I felt, the result of the acceleration of time I thought I had detected, might all too easily lead me to become infatuated with her. Not that I was hoping for that: absolutely not. The sort of gnawing pain over a woman you see every day and with whom you talk and laugh as a matter of course and who is nevertheless unattainable: for God's sake, not that.

Trembling, I opened the door of our house. There she stood, next to her car, framed by the leafy green of the lime trees in front of the house. She was a tall blonde, a woman to look up to, with a big voice that said, '*Hello*,' and that agreeably affecting awkwardness which can cling to women biologists. When I opened the door she was staring up at the dark blue of the evening sky. I followed her gaze and saw the small bats that rapidly appeared above the roof of the house, so rapidly that it looked as if they were being shot from catapults, one after another.

'*Bats*,' she said and followed me inside, and I showed her the way to the guest bedroom. After that we took her pike to the laboratory. It was a young fish that to all appearances adapted itself quickly to the artificial ditch in there.

It soon became clear that she was passionately interested in field biology. As a result, that year I observed several phenomena I might not have noticed otherwise. I took her to the dunes at Meyendel to show her something of the work that people in our lab were doing with wolf spiders, click beetles, cinnabar moths, sow bugs and a number of other humble animals. We walked along dune paths, the white sand glistening brilliantly in the sun. The scent of wild honeysuckle was everywhere, and the sea buckthorn was in full bloom. It was very summery, and it didn't seem right to hear a curlew calling and to hear the song of willow warblers, blackcaps and finches. At a copse she suddenly halted and said, '*Chiffchaff*,' and I heard the surprise in her voice but didn't grasp the reason for it. I listened; aside from the penetrating sound of the chiffchaff I also heard the clear song of the willow warbler.

'*Strange*,' she said, and still I didn't know what she was driving at. I tried to find the chiffchaff but could not see the little bird. The sound came from near the ground and I knelt down to have a better look. As I was kneeling I suddenly understood why she had said '*strange*'; a willow warbler high in the trees and a chiffchaff down by the ground. Normally it is just the other way around. I was on my knees in the sand, I heard the bird but did not see it. Sow bugs were walking slowly over the sunlit white sand. I opened my eyes wide, yes, they were sow bugs all right. 'How can that be?' I muttered. And of course it couldn't be: most of the sow bugs dried out and shrivelled during their ramble in the sunshine; they can move only at night when it is warm and moist, they are like crayfish who suffocate when it's dry. Only the occasional sow bug managed to reach the flowering tansy ragwort that fringed the path.

'Ragwort can't be in bloom already,' I said softly to myself. I looked for the cinnabar moth's zebra-striped caterpillars that are often present on ragwort, but I couldn't see any. I began to mumble to myself. The words were incantations, more or less, as I sought to ward off a growing feeling of panic, and I sensed that she was regarding me with amazement. I hardly dared to look at her, but when I raised my eyes to hers I saw the expression of someone asking herself whether she was in the company of a madman. I got up hastily, slapped the sand from my trousers, and we walked silently towards the field laboratory. There, too, I heard about the strangest facts: bird-cherry ermine moths that belonged on the spindle trees were on the hawthorns instead, hedgehogs weren't rolling themselves into balls, tansy ragwort plants weren't being visited by the larvae of the cinnabar moth, and a pair of cuckoos had built their own nest.

'This year there's almost three times as much helleborine as last,' one of the ecologists said.

I tried to interrogate them, gingerly, about all these irregularities in nature; they were very much surprised, yes indeed, but they were not afraid. They seemed to regard the aberrations as a consequence of the extraordinary climatic conditions and had thrown themselves fanatically into the study and description of the strange phenomena. They were cheerful rather than downcast because so many unusual things were happening and because the weather kept on being so gorgeous. I could not put up with their good spirits for long. I left the field laboratory and, breathing heavily, halted in the shade of the mixed trees that stood in the hollow in the dunes near the assembly tent. I heard the twirling song of the goldcrest and I saw a few whitethroats. That's strange, I thought, usually you don't get to see a whitethroat. While I pondered this, I tried to discover the goldcrest. It is almost always found high up in spruce trees, and since there was a good deal of spruce around, I looked intently at the upper branches. Unable to locate the goldcrest, I walked towards the sound. By chance I looked at an oak that stood nearby and saw the goldcrest, perched in the oak. 'That's okay,' I half shouted, 'they are not married to the spruces,' but I clapped my hands over my eyes. I'm going crazy, I thought, goldcrests in oaks, whitethroats that show themselves, midsummer in April, and the ermine moths that belong on the spindle tree are on the hawthorn instead.

Early in the morning after the nights when I did *not* dream about the Second Coming, I could hardly imagine why something as insignificant as seeing a goldcrest in an oak tree had upset me so much. But almost every day during that month of April, something happened to interfere with my sleep. I didn't dare talk about it with anyone; as soon as I opened my mouth it struck me as so ridiculous to make a fuss about wolf spiders or click beetles that I retreated into silence. As a result I was all alone with my strange premonitions, my absurd fears. Once I tried to discuss it with Priscilla, my English colleague. Over breakfast I said, 'Everything is very early this year, don't you agree?'

'Yes,' she said, 'it really is a splendid spring,' and after that I was unable to say another word. A splendid spring? Spring? It was midsummer! During breakfast, swarms of wasps tried to steal our sugar, and if you opened a jar of jam, within minutes there would be dozens of wasps inside. Those wasps became an intolerable plague, and our April breakfasts were mostly devoted to waging a dogged warfare against them. They managed to get inside the house even though we kept all the doors and windows shut; they had to, because where else would they have been able to find sustenance? Food in the form of ripening fruit was not yet available. Day after day, when dinner was finished, as long as the light lasted, I did nothing but search for wasps' nests. The first nest I discovered was under the eaves, and on four consecutive evenings I sat on a ladder, holding the nozzle of a vacuum-cleaner hose. The vacuum cleaner stood on the window sill in the second-storey bedroom, and I vacuumed up wasps that came back to the nest for the night. No other method of combating the nest came to mind. It was jammed so closely between the downspout and the eaves that I could not reach it, and if I had poured kerosene over it and lit it the whole house would have gone up in flames.

On the first evening, after I had spent forty-five minutes vacuuming up wasps, my wife looked out through the bedroom window.

'Having any success?' she asked.

'Some,' I said, 'but you can turn it off now. I'm going to quit; my left leg has gone to sleep and hardly any more wasps are coming.'

'Okay, I'll go and turn it off.'

She disappeared. I climbed down a few rungs of the ladder and went in through the open window. My wife was already gone but I still heard a muffled humming noise. She's left the vacuum cleaner on, I thought. I pulled the plug out of the socket; the vacuum cleaner kept on humming. It sounds like the motor is running at half speed, I thought. I pushed the knob. No change. Even the appliances are out of kilter, I thought, and the malaise that had already bothered me for so many days surged through my body again. I stood motionless in the half-dark bedroom. I listened to the threatening sound of the vacuum cleaner, and only then did it sink in that the sound was being made by wasps still buzzing inside it. I murdered them with ether and that evening was one of the few evenings in April that I felt happy. It's all an illusion, I thought, nothing is the matter, it's simply that I'm fool enough to make a big deal of everything, even wasps in a vacuum cleaner.

It was an unforgettable evening, a summer evening full of the heavy scent of lilacs. I listened to one of the most beautiful compositions I know, the nocturne from *Béatrice et Bénédict* by Berlioz: '*Nuit paisible et sereine*,' peaceful and untroubled night. It was as if he had composed that unbelievably beautiful music for that very night.

The next few evenings were also sublime. I destroyed one wasps' nest after another. I poured kerosene into the nests that had been built underground and then I set fire to them. Oh, how they burned! They were made of paper that the wasps produce themselves; drenched in kerosene, they went up like a torch. Still, there was one nest I couldn't get rid of. I had located the hole all right, but even though I poured several litres of kerosene down the hole and threw in one lighted match after another, the nest would not catch fire. I'm going to have to dig it out a bit and then spray it, I thought. And so on one of those summer evenings in April I went into the garden with a shovel and a barrel of kerosene. I wore leather gloves and canvas rainwear to protect myself against possible stings. Even before I had put the shovel into the ground, the sweat was pouring down my body. Some wasps flew past, and I had such a strong sense that it was a warm summer evening late in August that, on my way to the nest, I stopped for a moment to pick a ripe pear. I acted without thinking, but when I tried to grab the pear and found myself riffling through the leaves in vain, I became aware of what I was doing.

'Things are not *that* early,' I said. I had developed the habit of talking out loud when alone; it was as if I were two people, a half-crazed wasp hunter and an observer who regarded the hunter with amusement. I stopped for a moment, gripped my shovel resolutely to suppress my fear. I walked on until I reached the nest and drove my shovel deep into the ground. I prised the soil halfway up. Then, suddenly, thousands of wasps rose out of the earth in a flash. It was a yellow-black cloud, and the oddest thing was that the upper surface of that cloud was completely flat. I stood there in the evening light, staring in fascination at that mass of wasps which seemed to be held down by an invisible ceiling. But the sound coming from the cloud contained a tremendous threat; a very angry buzzing that rapidly gained in volume. I turned around and ran away, but the wasps caught up with me at the pear tree and stung me in five places at once. By the time I reached the house my body was nothing but an organism burning with pain, yet I was still able to open the kitchen door and quickly close it before I lost consciousness.

For more than two weeks I lay in bed with a high fever. Right after my assault on the nest they even feared for my life. I had been stung 142 times in all, as the swollen lumps on my body showed. I suffered uninterrupted pain and had continuous visions of the Last Judgement. I was in hell and was being tortured: they were sending thousands of wasps to sting me. And even when I was able to think a bit more clearly, the pain was so intense that the visions of hell that came with it did not entirely disappear. Only after two weeks did I begin to sleep normally again, and that night I dreamt a new version of the Second Coming. I was walking in a vast plain, all alone. I had been raised from the dead and Christ had judged me, and now I was on my way to hell. I had to go even though I didn't want to. There were neither shrubs nor trees on that plain, nor any animals. I was walking barefoot through the very sharp grass. My feet were bleeding, the sun burned low in the sky, and on the horizon I saw tiny figures. When they came closer I saw that they were horses, red, white, black and pale ones, who seemed to be approaching slowly under the red sky. But they weren't walking slowly, they were galloping rapidly towards me and I could already see their manes. Oh, what gorgeous hair, I muttered, it's just like a woman's. But I had not yet seen the tails. Only when the horses were very close and slowly began to enclose me did I see those tails. They were black stings, and the horses turned their hindquarters to me, raised their stings and approached me. When the first horse pierced me with its sting, I tried to scream but couldn't utter a sound. The horses whinnied, I woke up, and again I heard the whinnying. At first I thought the sound belonged to my dream, but then I heard it for a third time, and it frightened me so much that I hardly had the strength to throw off the covers. As I walked to the window I heard the sound of horses' hoofs on gravel. I opened the curtains. By the light of the full moon I saw horses walking on the gravel path alongside the lawn. Occasionally they stopped to graze for a moment, then they raised their heads again and whinnied. I heard my wife's voice, 'What's going on?'

'Horses in the garden,' I said.

'Horses? How can that be?'

She was already at my side, she looked at the horses, so pale in the light of the moon, and said, 'Oh, those are the horses from the riding stable, they got out, of course, and now they're doing the rounds of the gardens; I'll go and phone.'

She left the window. But I was in no condition to move, it felt as if I were no longer alive. I'm going crazy, I thought, I've got to see a psychiatrist, I've got to get treatment. I moved the curtains so as to cool my burning forehead. But I couldn't bring myself to close the curtains, I had to look at those horses that walked so quietly and peacefully through the garden. They were the horses of the Apocalypse, they stood there grazing, the white horse, the red horse, the pale horse, the black horse, the horses with the curved stings of scorpions.

Perhaps I really would have gone crazy if I hadn't had Mozart and if Priscilla's husband had not shown up. I had always loved Mozart's music with a passion but until those days of my wasp fever when I was still oddly light-headed and couldn't do anything except listen to music, I didn't fully realize how unbelievably profound the music of Mozart is. Every time the memory of fever-dream visions became too much for me I put a black disc labelled 'Mozart' on the turntable. As soon as that music, melancholy, cheerful, ever perfect, resounded in the room I felt calm again. I was being addressed by someone who had also gone through terrors of the kind I had felt but had risen above them. Strange that something as incomprehensible as music—aerial vibrations that reach the ear—of which you can say only hesitatingly what it actually expresses, can mean such an enormous amount to you. During my convalescence, how would I have managed without Mozart?

I was still taking the Mozart cure when late one evening and completely without notice, Priscilla's husband George suddenly stood before us. By then I was almost over my wasp fever, though still a bit light-headed, and he began to talk about the accelerated movement of time of his own accord. He was a tall, sinewy man who spoke nonchalantly about the telescoping of spring and summer. He associated it with processes of decomposition in the polluted oceans.

'Because of that,' he said, 'not only does the air above the oceans warm up as a result of the heat released by decomposition, but the water also becomes warmer. The temperature in the warm Gulf Stream rises and so our winters become milder, and occasionally there is a chance that spring may fade away. In fact, the seasons are disappearing.'

He talked about his work. He was an algologist and did measurements in the Atlantic Ocean of, among other things, the oxygen production of algae. I don't think I exaggerate in saying he was obsessed by the oxygen economy of the world.

'The world's deserts are spreading,' he said, 'effect: fewer forests to produce oxygen. Now they've sold the timber on Borneo to Japanese timber companies; they drive bulldozers into the forest and systematically cut metre after metre. So the fertile topsoil is exposed to erosion, the soil washes away, nothing grows there any more, and then no more oxygen gets produced by plants.'

He spoke tersely, and both for that reason, and because of course he spoke English, I can't remember his remarks all that clearly, but 'less oxygen' has stuck with me, so often did he repeat it. He calculated for me how much oxygen there was on the globe, how much was used by cars, humans, animals, plants, industry, and how much was won back by oceans and rainforests. It made for a gloomy picture. He himself became visibly downcast in the course of our conversation. But his comments cheered *me* up tremendously. What I had seen in nature was brought about by developments in the oceans, it seemed, not by developments within myself.

A few days after he had arrived, I suggested to him and Priscilla that we should go and have a look at the bluegrass wetlands along the Wijde Aa river. Most of all I would have liked to cycle with them along the Ruige Kade, something I always do in the spring to count the orchids in the marshes and bluegrass lands. Unfortunately neither of them knew how to ride a bike. In their car we drove as far as the small bridge over the branch of the Wijde Aa, and moments later we walked across the bridge to the narrow path on the other side. A pair of grebes swam under the bridge. They did not dive, so I stamped a few times with my right foot. Why did they still not dive? Once again I felt my old surprise at the unusual, and I shivered for a moment. Surely *this* couldn't be the consequence of decomposition in the oceans? It was as though I heard the noise of horses' hoofs. But I forgot my fear when I saw the first orchid. It stood on the same spot along the path where I had seen the first orchid a year earlier. In memory I went back a year; it had been the first fine day in what was otherwise a cold and windy spring. I pointed to the orchid. I related how a year earlier I had spotted sixty and as I said this I realized that I was a year further along, that this year spring had not been cold and windy but had in fact not happened. We agreed that we would count the orchids this time as well and walked on, looking for the purple torches of the southern marsh orchid.

It was a strange day. An autumn-like smell hung in the air under an overcast sky, penetrated in just a few places by hazy, light-red sunlight, and not a bird was to be heard. There was not a ripple in the Wijde Aa; two garganeys flew by soundlessly in the windless air, and far off in the distance I saw the silhouette of a cormorant being pursued by two gulls. Here and there along the path stood untidy clumps of mushrooms. We counted the orchids and found that their number was amazingly large. Especially on the gentle slope of the dyke along the Wijde Aa, a lot of them were in bloom among the sorrel and the buttercups. Along the edge of the grass, tall horsetails raised themselves high, alternating with flowering black sedge, and in a few places we could see the small pale-blue flowers of lamb's lettuce. When we reached the copse of willows at the far end of the grassland we had counted 172 orchids. We sat down in the grass near the copse. My voice sounded high and shrill as I said, 'Strange, last year sixty, this time one hundred and seventy-two, I don't get it at all.'

'That's possible, isn't it?' said Priscilla.

'Yes, why not,' said George, 'not all years are the same.'

'But I've been counting them for ten years now,' I said, 'and there have never been this many. Usually there are between sixty and eighty, and now suddenly one hundred and seventy-two.'

'Be glad there's been so much progress,' my wife said.

'I find it strange,' I said, 'it's just like everything is exuberant for one last time...like a TB patient just before he dies.'

'What nonsense,' said my wife.

'Maybe not,' said George, 'the same thought has crossed my mind a couple of times this year.'

He fell silent, we looked at each other, I resumed speaking, calmly at first, then gradually more agitatedly and rapidly, with many gestures which I tried to restrain, making them seem awkward. I spoke about everything I had seen, about the sow bugs, the ermine moths, the goldcrest and all those other apparently so insignificant phenomena. I felt relieved to have my say, and he listened to me without even a moment's disparagement or scepticism.

When I had finished he said, 'And now it's almost like autumn.'

I looked out over the meadows. I had often sat there in springtime, usually on April 30, the holiday for our Queen's birthday, and suddenly I remembered how much I had enjoyed seeing the common swifts flying high. I looked up to the sky. There were no swifts at all.

'The swifts haven't come back,' I shouted. 'What's going on anyway?' I hardly dared to look at the ditches in the meadows before me. But if I didn't want to see that no barn swallows or house martins were flying around either, I would have to close my eyes.

'Maybe they're still on their way,' Priscilla said.

'They should have been here by now,' I said, 'especially since everything else is so early.'

'Swallows don't bother themselves about an early spring,' said George, 'but it is funny they aren't here yet. Perhaps it's got something to do with all those strange climatic phenomena, as well.

We've calculated that if the oxygen production of the oceans declines to forty per cent of the original level, there will be no way back any more. Then everything in the oceans will rot, something that's already happening on a large scale. At a certain point oxygen will no longer be produced, it will only be consumed by the process of decomposition. The rainforests won't even be able to produce enough oxygen to supply the process with the oxygen it needs. And then it will be game over for all life on earth.'

He spoke without showing any emotion. I could never have done that. I wanted to ask him: what percentage did you come up with this year? But I didn't dare: I was simply scared to hear that magical number forty again. The others didn't ask either, and he didn't say anything. I thought of a verse from the book of Revelation: 'And the second angel poured out his vial upon the sea; and it became as the blood of a dead man: and every living soul died in the sea.'

We got up and walked back along the path under that flaming-ashen sky. I kept an eye out for house martins but saw none. For a moment I thought: they left before I could see them. I haven't been unconscious for several days as they said I was; I've been unconscious for several months. I have been 'hibernating' all summer and now it's autumn and everything that frightened me so much during the spring didn't really happen but was something I dreamt during my summer of sleep. I cherished this thought. It wasn't so hard; in spite of the fact that the leaves weren't falling yet, it was so autumnal that more and more I believed in my summer of sleep. But I took care not to ask my wife, 'Have you all been deceiving me, have I been unconscious for several months?' for I didn't want to wake up from my dream. It happened all the same. After dinner we sat in the garden until it was quite late. The sky was dark blue, the bats like black specks. The intoxicating scent of the almost overblown lilacs blended with the deep fragrance of the philadelphus. George smoked a pipe, the smoke curled up slowly, hung in the windless air. He was talking with Priscilla, a simple dialogue, fleeting words spoken casually, apparently without significance or implications.

'How was it this time?' Priscilla asked.

Without taking his pipe out of his mouth he asked, 'How do you mean?'

'With the ocean. The tests.'

'How much oxygen in the algae, you mean?'

'Yes.'

'Less than forty per cent, for the first time since we started.'

'So the situation is hopeless now?'

'I think so.'

'How much time before...?'

'I have no idea, but it won't be very long.'

'And then what?'

'I'm afraid we'll suffocate.'

By this time it was about to turn ten. I was waiting for the tawny owl. It had the habit of dropping by around ten every evening, seating itself in the alder. First it would let us hear its shrill cry and then it began its doleful hooting. It had been doing this for years, and even this year it had not diverged from its customary behaviour, thank God. I heard the living-room clock strike ten and at the same time I heard the owl's sharp cry. I saw it sitting in the tree, an inverted equilateral triangle with a round base. Suddenly it pounced, and we heard the death cry of a sparrow. That terrifying shriek abruptly made the implications of George and Priscilla's conversation clear to me, and I said, 'We've got to warn people.'

'Pointless,' he said, 'they won't believe it, they think it's enough to cut back a little on industrialization, energy use and solid waste.'

'We've got to warn people,' I repeated.

He shrugged his shoulders.

'You want to be a Cassandra?' he asked, and continued: 'As far as I am concerned, I don't much care about humans disappearing from the earth. What *does* bother me is that all plants and animals will become extinct too, except for a few organisms such as sulphur bacteria that don't need oxygen.'

'But humans...' I said.

'After the calamity has finally come to an end maybe new forms of life will emerge from those bacteria, and evolution can begin anew. But,' he said, raising his voice, 'it is to be hoped that no other species like the human race emerges. It's a good thing, the extinction of a species that has so shamelessly destroyed other animal species and plants, and that has plundered the earth with such complete lack of care or scruple. Maybe that extinction balances out against the fact that all other forms of life requiring oxygen will also meet their end.'

'Yes, all right, but...but...' I said.

'Without humans there would be no concentration camps, no wars, no torture, no dreadful traffic accidents, no..., well, just try to enumerate all the horror.'

I tried desperately to think of an argument that would justify the continued existence of the human race. The tawny owl hooted mournfully at the bottom of the garden, and George looked at me expectantly. I wanted to contradict him, to defeat him with powerful arguments. I felt that in that way I could still postpone the threat of the coming destruction of all life. The owl took wing, and the only thing I could come up with was, 'Then there won't be anybody left to listen to Mozart.' □

GRANTA

THE WEATHER IN MONGOLIA

Philip Marsden

Narmandakh Baatarjambyn, 2001

The Weather in Mongolia

The weather in Mongolia is a constant presence—cruel, beautiful and extreme. Climatically, the country belongs to the category known as 'harsh continental'. In Ulanbataar, the world's coldest capital, the temperature can drop as low as minus forty-five degrees Celsius. There are places in the country, and not just in the Gobi desert, where you can experience a temperature range of thirty-seven degrees Celsius in a single day. Winds race across the treeless steppes like an invading horde, cruel and sudden and full of face-lashing grit. They are either very cold or very hot or very dry.

But Mongolia also has one of the sunniest of the world's climates. On average, it receives more than eight hours of cloudless sun every day. Far from the influence of the oceans, blocs of intense high pressure build up over the country, particularly in winter. Unhindered by cloud cover, the land's residual warmth disappears into the atmosphere. It is an atmosphere almost entirely without humidity, leaving the sky so blue that if you fired an arrow up into it, you would get the sense that it might just stick there.

Blue is everywhere in Mongolia. The flags that fly at *ovoo*s, the cairns erected to propitiate the spirits of significant places, are blue. In the herds, you can often spot certain animals with blue tags tied around their necks. *Khatag*s are the blue scarves sold at monasteries, presented to the various representations of the Buddha or used for more earthly purposes, draped over the tops of televisions in Ulanbataar's apartments, or stuffed for protection inside the windscreens of cars—it is the few metalled roads around the capital that are most dangerous; as they are increasing, so are the fatalities. And the supreme presence in the traditional Mongolian pantheon is blue. Even after a savage half-century of Stalinist repression, even after a half-millennium of imported Buddhist rites, Mongolians have never really relinquished the animistic reverence in which they hold *Kokh Mongke Tenger*, the Blue Eternal Sky.

For me it began as an indulgence. During a desk-bound year writing fiction, I developed a hankering for wide open spaces, landscape, movement, physical exhaustion at the end of the day—in short, a ride across the Mongolian steppe. But such formless impulses have a habit of taking on their own shape. I began to read. I read about the timeless habits of Mongolian pastoralists, about the country's recent history which during most of the twentieth century had mirrored that of its parent state, the Soviet Union. I read about the chaos of the 1990s—the same pattern of unemployment, insecurity and inflation that had dogged all those living between Belgrade and Vladivostok. And I read too about the enduring, poetic world of Mongolian belief.

The Mongolians' cosmology expresses both the extreme severity of the environment and their absolute dependence on its forces. Thus the word for 'god', 'sky' and 'weather' is the same—*tenger*. Beneath the *Kokh Mongke Tenger*, the Blue Eternal Sky, are ninety-nine lesser *tenger* who each control an important aspect of the herding life. They include the *tenger* of heroes, *tenger* riding on the clouds, cattle *tenger*, eggs *tenger*, billy goat *tenger*, *tenger* who increases the fruits of the field and *tenger* who makes the rain fall. If there is a moral aspect to the traditional Mongolian belief system, it has to do with *tegsh* or 'balance'. Misfortune arises from imbalance—whether for an individual, a group, a herd or within the wider environment. As to restoring it, the use of a blue scarf can help, as can a visit to a holy mountain, or to an *ovoo*. In extreme circumstances, a shaman can be called on to intercede.

In the spring of 2001, I noticed reports from Mongolia in the British press: 'White-outs threaten Mongolia's herds... Snowstorms play havoc with Mongolian Pastoralists.' The reports talked of the *zud*—the winter famine—and were invariably illustrated with a foreshortened picture of a dead animal, stretched out on the steppe; the unseasonal covering of snow had prevented it from feeding.

In Mongolian lore, winter lasts precisely eighty-one days: nine periods of nine days, each signified by particular conditions (first nine, the drink *koumiss* congeals; second nine, *arak* congeals; third nine, tail of three-year-old yak freezes; fourth nine, horns of four-year-old yak freeze, etc.). But recently this pattern has been disturbed. The weather in Mongolia is changing. The rains in summer are lighter. The permafrost is melting. Spring is capricious. Violent weather has become more frequent and more widespread. Heavy snow is now falling as early as September. *Zuds*—traditionally a three-times-a-century occurrence—are now disturbingly regular. Every March great dust storms sweep south over China. A couple of years ago they affected 130 million people; at times the air was so clogged with Mongolian dust that the people of Beijing found themselves wandering blind through it.

Few other places on earth retain such an ancient way of life over so wide an area, and one so precariously sensitive to the weather. Of course, the threats to Mongolia's herders are not just climatic. The country has been thrown out of sync by the withdrawal of Soviet support. But the change in weather is emblematic of a more general malaise, a sense that something is not quite right, that *tegsh* has been damaged in some profound way.

In May, I contacted Graham Taylor, an Australian whose lone five-month ride through Mongolia a few years earlier had had such an effect on him that he stayed on. He set up a tour company in Ulanbataar and called it Karakorum Expeditions. I emailed him: could he provide me with a guide?

'Sure,' he replied. 'No worries.'

So, after an all-night flight from Moscow, I stumbled into the arrivals hall of Buyant-Ukhaa International Airport and spotted a handwritten cardboard sign: PHILIP MADSED. Behind it was a tall, lithe-looking figure who smiled when he saw me. It was a charming smile, one that I came to know as characteristic of him, a smile that made his eyes disappear completely.

Narmandakh Baatarjambyn was twenty-four. He had been born and brought up in Ulanbataar. He had spent his childhood summers, like many young urban Mongolians, with his grandparents, helping out with the herds and living in *ger*s, the white, conical-roofed tents that dot Mongolia's steppe. He was now studying tourism at Ulanbataar's university. He had a wife called Lkhagwadelger and a three-month-old son called Dulguun. Over the coming weeks he proved the best of companions—good-natured, competent and with an infectious love for Mongolia's wilder places. With people like him, I thought, Mongolia's future was brighter than it appeared. It was only a week since he had contacted Graham Taylor for the first time, looking for work—and here it was, stumbling into the airport, shaking his hand.

He took me straight to the market where I bought three saddles (a Mongolian saddle, a pack saddle and a Russian cavalry saddle), three hobbles, three stakes, fifteen metres of leather strap, a quantity of food, and a silver bridle studded with tiny pieces of turquoise.

Next we called in on the National Agency of Meteorology, Hydrology and Environment Monitoring. The director sat in an office trailing with flowering succulents. Every day he received a mass of information from meteorological stations around the country. But when I started to ask him about the changes in Mongolia's weather, he held up his hands.

'Excuse me—but everything is in here,' he explained, patting the cover of the agency's own book. When we left him he was watering the roots of his plants with a miniature watering can. I took the book back to my hotel.

Climate Change and its Impact in Mongolia makes disturbing reading. No single statistic dominates the picture but each detail contributes to an alarming overall impression. For every degree that the temperature rises, water resources decline by up to six per cent; this reduces the pasture land, pushes herds into a smaller area and results in further overgrazing. Meanwhile the desert is projected to grow by more than three times in the next fifty years, by which time nitrogen levels in the grasslands will have diminished by sixteen per cent and permafrost will be less than half what it is now. The shrinking of the permafrost will convert good pasture into marsh. It will also undermine the foundations of roads, bridges and the high-rise apartment blocks that ring the skyline of Ulanbataar.

Seventy per cent of Mongolia's grassland is already overgrazed, one third of the country's water resources is deemed 'highly vulnerable'. The production of fodder has diminished by two thirds since the withdrawal of Soviet support fifteen years ago; in the same period the number of livestock has increased from twenty-five million to thirty-two million. It is also estimated that by 2020, Mongolia's human population will have doubled to five or six million, thereby placing a greater strain on her natural resources.

The province of Dzavhan, to the west of Ulanbataar, had been particularly hard hit by the winter's *zud*. Its herders had lost about twenty-three per cent of their livestock. That evening, fresh from the state department store, Narmandakh arrived with a map of Zavkhan. We traced a route east from Uliastay, the capital of Zavkhan, up across the mountains and into the neighbouring province of Arhangay.

The shading darkened across the spine of the Khangai mountains and at one point was dabbed with white—the peak of Otogen Tenger.

'What does '*otogen*' mean?' I asked.

'Younger sister,' he said. 'A sacred mountain—the younger sister of the sky.'

The plane dropped through islands of thin, scattered cloud. A man was pointing through the window. 'Look! Look!'

Rising from their seats, the passengers crowded the aisle to see—and for a moment, in its approach to Uliastay, the small plane wobbled. Between them, some fifty miles to the north, I glimpsed the snowcap of Otogen Tenger.

Sitting on my other side was a doctor. He was pointing through the window on his side. 'Every year it gets closer.' Beneath the bronze treeless hills, to the south, a tongue of desert sand was stretching towards Uliastay.

The weather station for Zavkhan was at Uliastay's airport—a low, concrete building. Most of the rooms were empty. The director was not there but we did manage to reach him on a crackly phone.

'Zavkhan? Yes, we are one of the coldest places in the world... also we have one of the highest barometric pressures,' he said proudly. 'Over the last fifty years average January temperature is minus forty-two C... last ten years it has dropped by one or two degrees... rainfall has been falling also... the Gobi is now only forty miles away—' Then the crackles took over and he was gone.

Uliastay was a two-horse town and neither of them was for sale. So we took a jeep and followed the course of the Bogd river up into the mountains. Three times we stopped at clusters of *gers*—but no one had horses to spare. In the end, the driver lost patience. He dumped us beside the river. 'Maybe here you will find your horses.' We watched him go. He turned back down the valley, the jeep disappearing into nothing before a pale parachute of dust. The wind soughed in the grass. A mile away was a group of *gers*. It was getting dark.

We collected dried dung and made a fire. After a meal of noodles we crawled into our tent and I rolled out my sleeping bag. 'Where's yours, Narmandakh?'

'It's okay.'

'What do you mean? You'll freeze!'

'It is the Mongolian way. I have my *del*,' he fingered his knee-length cloak, the serge uniform of the herders. 'If I am to be a good guide, I must make myself tough.'

In the end, neither of us slept much. At about two, the wind freshened, the tent collapsed and we had to struggle out through billows of canvas. Low clouds were racing across the moon. The ground was cold underfoot but we were laughing as we fetched rocks from the river, re-erected the tent and weighed down its rim with the rocks.

'Perhaps we fly in it!' shouted Narmandakh above the noise of the wind. 'Up to Otogen Tenger, like in a balloon!'

Word travels fast in these high valleys and at dawn a man rode up to the tent leading three horses. Two of the horses stood with their heads down. Ribs striped their sickly-looking flanks. The third was a lively bay gelding and when we tried to saddle him, he reared up and showed his teeth.

'What do you think?' I asked Narmandakh.

'He is an angry horse.'

'I can see that.'

'An angry horse is good.'

'Really?'

'He is a good horse.'

'Okay—we will take this one,' I told the man. 'But not these two.'

He looked at me sadly. 'Please?'

'No. They're practically dead.'

'I am getting married. I need to buy a flat in Ulanbaataar.'

I shook my head and we watched him hobble the horses—though it was hardly necessary—and ride off. He would collect them later, but now he was going to the Naadam Festival.

Staking our new gelding, we made our way over to the *gers*. There too they were preparing to go to the Naadam, the annual festival of Manly Sports. They were grooming a palomino, quiffing up his mane and tying it with a red ribbon. The family were champion herders. Three herding medals were nailed to the *ger*'s lintel, dated 1981, 1983, 1987—the good years.

We sat in the *ger* and talked. We talked about the dry summer and the snowy winter. They had lost a good number of animals in the desert and when we asked if we could buy a horse, they said: 'We are sorry—we have no horses to sell.'

So we walked back across the steppe to our tent, towards our mound of equipment and our one angry horse.

'Don't worry. Something will happen.' Narmandakh smiled. His optimism was unfailing.

We lit the fire and made tea. Then came a distant, insect-like whine. A motorbike was bouncing towards us from the *gers*. Its rider had been sitting in the corner of the *ger* we had just visited.

'I have made a decision,' he said, propping his bike on its stand. 'I will sell you my mare.' She was his last horse. He was an accountant in Uliastay. His son was doing a teaching diploma and he needed money to pay the fees. In previous summers he had kept twenty horses and forty cows up here with his brother. That winter they had gone to the Gobi and the snow came early and the horses tried to eat but their muzzles had frozen and they died. He pointed across the river to a group of a dozen horses. 'That is her, on the left.'

'Aren't you sad to sell her?'

'Look—she is fat. In the autumn she might be stolen and killed for her meat. Then I would have nothing.'

In the early afternoon we left the main valley and headed south-east—towards Otogen Tenger. With only two horses, we loaded the mare with our equipment and Narmandakh and I took it in turns to ride the gelding.

Narmandakh was wearing a denim baseball hat, embroidered with the name SHIVA, and his pale-blue *del* with an orange sash belted around it. He looked around him. He began to sing. He sang a great deal during our journey. 'It is the countryside,' he said, 'I cannot stop myself.' He sang 'The Beautiful Deer of Khangai' and 'The Tall Brown Horse'. He used to perform the songs in Japan where he had worked for a couple of summers.

'The Japanese loved those songs. Too many come now to look at our land—they say that Japan is a very crowded place and they like to look at our empty steppe!'

We heard the riders long before we saw them, the beating of hoofs behind us and the dust and we climbed the slope to let them pass. Thirty horses and their child-jockeys galloping up towards the finishing line. Three races passed us by the time we reached the Naadam crowd, sitting on the grass at the head of the valley.

The wrestling had just begun. Dressed in boots, coloured trunks and ornamental sleeves, the participants lumbered out into the circle of spectators. They were big and bull-necked. Lips of fat spilled over their trunk tops. Before each bout, they performed a dance—the *devekh*, the eagle dance—and for a moment these two thugs, swaying and dipping with outstretched arms, seemed as weightless as steppe eagles.

It was already late afternoon when we left the Naadam to walk and ride the ten miles to Kokh Nuur, the Blue Lake. We ate a meal of bread and dried fruit and put up our tent in the dark.

In the morning the sun rose and filled the tent with its buttery glow. Narmandakh was still asleep in his *del*, head propped on his saddle in the Mongolian way. Outside it was very cold. I peeled away frosted socks from my frosted boots and walked out to the lakeside. For two miles the water stretched north, a flat sheet of grey in the morning sun. Smoke rose from a group of distant *ger*s but otherwise nothing moved in that vast arena of mountains.

In the gers above the lake was a man named Baatar Tsimbingsereng. He was a young grandfather who lived with his extended family. Normally they spent the summer close to Uliastay but in recent years the number of other herders had forced them higher. They had a horse for sale, a light-stepping ginger mare.

'Her mother was a very beautiful horse.' Baatar patted her neck. 'She had one blue eye and a white streak down her face and a walk like a limousine.'

She proved the best of our three horses. She never slipped or stumbled. She was the easiest to coax across girth-deep rivers, the easiest to lead through boulder fields, or down narrow cliff-paths.

We closed the deal with Baatar in his *ger* with a bowl of tea. He spoke slowly: 'We asked the lamas: "What can we do to stop the animals dying?" and they said you must choose one animal in each of the herds and tie a scarf on it and this animal must not be slaughtered, and as long as he lives the herd will have good luck.'

In September they had arrived on the edge of the Gobi desert. One morning they felt a blast of cold air from the north and saw the first spots of snow against the mountains. They had not even started wearing winter clothes. They lost half their horses within a couple of months, half their goats and sheep and every one of their yaks. But it was the black *zud* that did for them. The white *zud* was the blanket of snow and it didn't last too long. Then the snow went and in its place was the black *zud*. The earth was black, he said, black as the night with not even a 'foal's hoof' of grass to cover it.

Baatar looked out of the open door. 'Yes, I know why it is. I have heard there is a big hole in the north and that is what is making it different. It is because of a big hole in the sky.'

Wherever you go in this half-continent of a country, you can walk into a *ger* and everything will be in exactly the same place—kitchen and food to the right, saddles to the left, the stove dead ahead. Beyond that, on the left, is the guest area and you must make your way there at once and drink the bowl of tea given to you. Even if you are a complete stranger, even if you have already placed your saddlebags inside the door for the night, only then might you attempt some sort of introduction.

As Mongolians worship the land and sky around them, so *ger*s, their shelter against the climate, have become microcosms of these elements. At the apex is the *tono*, the smoke hole through which can be seen *kokh tenger*, blue sky. From there radiate *uni* or roof supports, painted orange to represent the rays of the sun (itself one of the eyes of the Father of Heaven, the other one being the moon). Because *ger*s always face in the same direction, you can tell the time simply by seeing on which of the *uni* the sunlight is falling. When the country's holiest statue, the enormous bronze Migjed Janraisig in Ulan Baatar's Gandan monastery, was recently rebuilt—the original was smelted down for arms during the 1937 purge of the lamas—a *ger*, with its furniture, was placed inside it.

As the *ger*s have come to represent the larger cosmos above, so the sky itself is seen as a great tent. The Milky Way is the seam while the other stars are light-holes in the canopy. Meteors occur when the gods open the tent to peep inside; winds come through gaps in the horizon, when the foot of the tent is not completely fixed to the ground.

Anyone who sees the *ger*s and spends enough time with the herders to witness just a little of their harsh nomadic life, comes away astonished by their toughness, their ability to live without superfluous possessions let alone luxuries. But the herders' way of life is not as robust as it seems. They have been unable to develop the Darwinian virtue of adaptability. Shift the tent poles of their life, shift any of the parameters on which they depend, and these often heroic pastoralists look distinctly exposed.

That evening, Narmandakh and I took the new mare and the gelding up to the local *ovoo*. Baatar stood with his back to the lake and raised his arm. 'Follow that slope and you will see it, on top of the hill.'

Shortly below the top, we hobbled the horses and continued on foot to the shrine. The summit was flat and broad, a field of frost-shattered rock. Each slab wobbled as we stepped on it, and let out a hollow knocking sound. The *ovoo* itself was a pile of stones and several ragged blue *khatag*s. Broken vodka bottles lay between the rocks.

It was dusk. Muddy-brown cloud had brought the day to a premature end. A cold wind brushed at our ears. As we turned back, I saw something moving.

'Look!' I pointed.

'What is it?' asked Narmandakh.

'I don't know. Maybe a dog.' It was already gone.

But it wasn't a dog. When it reappeared there were others, five of them, five wolves padding across the rocks. One of them stopped suddenly and looked at us. It remained there for several seconds. I could see its silvery, fibrous coat and its eyes and the dark line of the mouth. It turned away. One by one the pack dropped down below the skyline, down towards the horses. Normally a wolf is no match for a horse. Wolves catch plenty of foals each winter but a grown horse can easily outrun a wolf. Unless it is hobbled.

We ran. It took too long, much too long. We leapt from slab to slab. But when we cleared the ridge, the horses were there, happily grazing. There was no sign of the wolves.

For days afterwards I thought of those wolves. We both did. They coloured everything we saw—their threat, their constant invisible presence. It wasn't so much fear that I felt towards them as a strange attraction. They above all were what animated these bare mountains.

Genghis Khan, shared spiritual ancestor of the Mongolians, was said to be descended from a blue wolf and a red deer. The Huns, too, used to wear wolf masks in battle. The wolf is a common guise of Mongolian and Siberian shamans; the switch of identities between the human, sacred and animal worlds is a feature of Mongolian belief as it is of countless other folk religions. The three great monotheisms resist it vigorously. Islam has a taboo against animal depictions and Genesis is one of the few creation myths where man is created as separate from the animal world and given dominion over it, and where God does not at some time appear in the form of a bird or a lion, a tiger or a wolf.

The next morning we left Kokh Nuur early. We hoped to reach lower and warmer ground before nightfall. It was late in the afternoon before we saw another rider. He galloped over to us as though bringing important news from the front. He wore a maroon *del* and a hat of imitation straw. On the hat's ribbon was printed: FOORBAL—SOUTH KOREA 2002—MORLC DUP! For a moment he said nothing.

'Have you seen three horses?' he asked.

'No.'

'Two brown and one with a white stripe on his chest?'

'No.'

He spat on the ground. 'A yak and her calf?'

'No. But we saw a camel in that last valley.'

'That camel belongs to some people from the south.'

We rode with him up a shoulder of stony ground to a col. A chest-high *ovoo* had been erected there. Visible for the first time, little more than half a dozen miles off, were the cliffs of Otogen Tenger.

The man said: 'You used to be able to see the plane from here.'

A Chinese plane had flown into the mountain about thirty years earlier and until recently when the authorities went to remove it, the tail had been visible, sticking out of the ice.

The man grinned. 'They found one of those Chinese men still sitting in his seat—but his head was a hundred metres away!' He pushed up his MORLC DUP hat and the wind flicked at his hair.

'Do you see that big rock—just below the ice, on the right?'

We squinted and could see a bulbous shape at the edge of the ice.

'Three years ago you could not see that rock. Then we saw it for the first time through binoculars. Now the ice is down even more. This summer we can see it with our eyes.'

We left him squatting by the *ovoo*, his hat pushed up, scattering matches on the ground. He would find his animals. The matches, the *ovoo* and the distant peak were going to point him towards his lost animals.

It was late the next afternoon when the rain caught us at the top of a high valley. We cantered down through freezing cloud to the first *ger* we could find. Inside was an elderly man in an orange check cap, sitting on the *ger*'s carpeted floor, filling the bowl of a long soapstone pipe with powdery tobacco. Briefly he glanced at us, before returning to the important business of smoking his pipe.

For two days we stayed with Damdinsuren and for two days it rained. It wasn't good rain, useful rain, but a light spitting rain that was too cold to make the grass grow. Most of the time Damdinsuren sat in his orange checked cap, patiently smoking. His right arm was crippled from half a lifetime driving Soviet-made trucks, a job that he had abandoned a decade earlier to spend his later years herding. Behind him, in the place reserved for the most valued possessions, was a yellow-painted chest and on it a frame full of photographs. They were arranged in ascending order of importance. There were family groups at the bottom, tightly swaddled babies, dazed-looking national-service portraits and a black-and-white picture of a younger Damdinsuren (in the same checked cap) unloading the *ger* frames from camels, at the beginning of winter, on the pale edge of the Gobi desert. Above all these was a large photograph of the Dalai Lama and beside it Mongolia's President Natsag Bagabandi, who was born in Zavkhan. A reproduction of the famous Yuan dynasty portrait of Genghis Khan was inset in the top of this photograph. But above them all, at the summit of this private pantheon, was a picture of the mountain, Otogen Tenger.

On the third day when I woke, Damdinsuren was already up, already preparing his pipe. Bright sunlight dropped through the hole at the top of the tent and shone on his orange cap.

'*Kokh tenger*,' I said. 'Blue sky.'

'*Kokh tenger*.'

On the floor, Narmandakh was just stirring.

'It's cleared,' I told him. 'The cloud's gone.'

He grunted. Narmandakh was not a morning man; horses, the

cold, the long days and long evenings talking among strangers—these things he took in his stride, but the early morning foxed him.

An hour later, the three of us were riding across the river, splashing out of the shallows and up the far bank. Light snow remained on the ground where the sun had not reached it. We zigzagged up a grassy ridge and between the green of the ridge and the blue sky appeared the white tip of Otogen Tenger. Damdinsuren dropped down from the saddle. He plucked a handful of thin, ankle-high grass. 'We used to cut hay up here. Now look at it.'

Hobbling his horse he turned away to open the front of his *del*. 'If you need to do pissing, do now! After this place, it is holy ground.'

Topping another ridge we came out into a vast, open stretch of ground. The ice cap of Otogen Tenger glowed to the north. Miles and miles of featureless moor ran down from it and in the middle was a tiny splash of colour—closer to an Yves Klein blue than sky blue.

'The *ovoo*,' announced Damdinsuren.

It took us another two hours to reach it. The structure itself was a timber, pyre-like frame but the blue *khatag*s on it were tied so thickly that it was hard to see it beneath them. Damdinsuren raised his arms and prayed. Narmandakh clasped his hands in front of him and bowed his head. The scarves were restless in the wind. Above them all a long pennant flicked its frayed edge against the sky.

'I was a lama here,' said Damdinsuren. 'For one day.'

A few years ago a film had been shot at the *ovoo*—*Tsaagan Dugani Mokhol*, 'Destruction of the White Temple'—about the religious purges of the 1930s, and the crew had dressed Damdinsuren as a lama. He had also been up here more recently. Four days earlier he had come with a group of herders and they had walked round and round the shrine. They had hung it with scarves; they had prayed for rain. The rain had come—we had witnessed it—but it was too light and too cold and anyway now it was over. The sky had reverted to its clear and infinite blue.

Back at Damdinsuren's *ger* we had a bowl of noodles and left. There were no goodbyes; there never really were goodbyes in Mongolia, no polite greetings, no long farewells.

'What a beautiful man!' said Narmandakh as we rode on down the valley, and he began to sing.

Philip Marsden

For the best part of a week we rode north-east. In the Buyant valley, the grass thinned, the soil dried and dust collected in the manes of the horses. To the south the brown hills became lower, dropping down towards the desert. The heat haze rose from the valley floor and the far-off *gers* seemed to be floating on water.

'It looks like autumn,' said the herders, but it was only July.

'This type of land is not pleasant,' said Narmandakh. He had stopped singing.

Pushing towards Zavkhan's eastern border we reached those who did not winter in the Gobi but at the end of the summer crossed the high pass into the province of Arhangay. That year in Arhangay there had been no white *zud*, nor a black *zud*. But so many herds had come from Zavkhan that they trod the grass to mud and caused a *torrai zud*, or 'hoof' *zud*.

We ourselves left the last *ger* of Zavkhan on a cold and sunny morning and headed up the Bukheet river towards Arhangay. Pass the rock looking like a man's head, they told us. When you see the rock of a sitting rabbit, turn up the valley and at the top you reach the table rock where in the Manchu dynasty they used to put people on trial. Carry on until you see the hill shaped like a woman's breast and there will be an *ovoo* and that is Arhangay.

It was exactly as they said. We crossed into Arhangay and saw the breast-shaped hill. High up, at the pass, the land was green and lush. We could see the course of the Terkhiin river far below.

'Now you can start singing again,' I told Narmandakh. He grinned—and sang a song about a bay horse with hoofs of gold, and we began the long descent.

But the land changed again as we lost height and Narmandakh fell silent. It was nearly midnight when we reached the river. We had been riding for fourteen hours and we needed water. But the pebbles chinked beneath the horses' hoofs. The river bed was completely dry.

An hour later we reached a spring. The moon shone on a vast platform of ice; from beneath it, audible in the darkness, trickled a tiny stream.

For a couple of days we followed the dry course of the Terkhiin river. Its valley was wide and flat, almost desert. The wind came scouring across it and made the horses nervous. One morning we reached a group of two shabby-looking *gers*. The children were listless; an old woman was sitting on a rock. That winter they had lost everything: every horse, every sheep, every cow, all of their camels. They lived now by herding for other people.

'What happened happened,' said the woman. The early sun was shining on her face. She looked out across the bare steppe. 'Of course it was bad—but you cannot control nature.'

Back in Ulanbataar, we went to Narmandakh's flat on the fourth floor of a grey, Soviet-style block in a crowd of other Soviet-style blocks. Outside in the yard, boys were playing football. An old man in a maroon *del* sat looking at his boots. Narmandakh lived with his wife and son in one room of his parents' flat. He took his son from his wife's arms and held him up high above his head. The boy squealed and smiled—it was the same smile—it was his father's smile.

Returning from Mongolia, I sent Narmandakh photographs of our journey. He emailed me back—he was going to the Altai Mountains for a couple of weeks. 'It is my first trip with a group! Please, Philip, could you send some tourist journals? It is for my dissertation.' I made a selection of travel and trekking magazines, one of which had a feature about walking in Mongolia. Then I went to Spain for a month. On my return, there was an email saying the trip to the Altai had gone well. He had passed his audition. When not studying, he would work as a regular guide with Karakorum Expeditions.

A week later another email came in from Mongolia:

Dear philip marsden
My brother Narmandakh and my father, there are both died in
traffic accident on 21 September, last friday
We will bury them in monday morning
Narmandakh's sister Tsatsral.

☐

From Mexico to the streets of Seattle everyone's looking for Chano Salgado ...

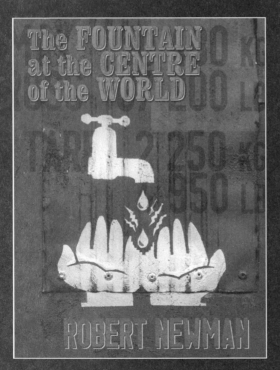

Political apostate Chano goes on the run just as the brother he's never met comes looking for him, and the son he thought he'd lost forever reappears.

In an extraordinary epic novel by Robert Newman, which takes us from Mexico to the streets of Seattle where, amid the tear gas and rubber bullets, the destinies of Chano, his brother and his son will be changed forever.

The Fountain at the Centre of the World
Published September 2003 by Verso
Price £10.99
ISBN 1 85984 573 8

VERSO
www.versobooks.com

GRANTA

ROWING TO ALASKA
Wayne McLennan

Juneau, Alaska

The rain came down so thickly that the water-pregnant clouds that carried it were camouflaged and hidden high above. The bare, breast-shaped hills that were pockmarked with tree stumps became muddy and slick. Streams appeared, gullies formed. A cold and miserable greyness shrouded the landscape, suffocating optimism.

Doug appeared two metres to my left, his thick glasses and wet straggly moustache his only recognizable features above his covering of yellow wet-weather gear. His movements were slow and precise as he climbed upwards. Every second moment his right hand, which held a long wooden-handled mattock, would slash down through the wetness and gouge a hole into the soft ground, while his left hand plucked a spruce plant out of a soaking mud-weighted bag that was strapped to his back. In one movement the plant was rooted into the ground and held in place by dirt that Doug would wheel in. He would then take three steps forward and repeat the planting. And I would attempt to do the same.

The beer tasted sour and weak, but I drank it anyway. They only sold beer in the tavern. Doug, who drank cautiously, spoke in the same way, 'You warmed up yet? It's no way to start your first day of tree planting with slick boots and no wet-weather gear, not up in this country where it rains more than it shines. You looked like a walking drowned man. I ain't never seen anybody shaking so much.'

I had found the job the day before through a man who had picked me up hitch-hiking outside Portland, Oregon. We had driven together to Olympia in Washington State, and I was now working for his brother-in-law, John Mulverhill at Forest Renewal Management, for $4.75 an hour.

Doug stood by the bar staring at the pool table, wondering about his last shot, not understanding how he had missed. 'Not such bad country up here?' he finally asked after his long contemplation of the balls that he had just played. He seemed to be speaking to somebody else. I looked around before I answered. The jukebox was flashing light and filling the bar with a Dr Hook tune, the cigarette smoke united and became a blue-grey mist held by the low ceiling. Drinkers who looked like bikers, but who I knew to be woodsmen either killing trees or planting them, crowded the bar and occupied the pool tables, swilling their Budweisers from the bottle, dry and happy. Young women wearing tight jeans flittered in and out with trays of beer, occasionally rubbing against you, giving you hope.

'She'll do, mate,' I finally answered, 'she'll do.'

I worked two months planting spruce saplings in country that climbed so high it pushed through the low-slung clouds. Cold rain was thrown at you constantly like pebbles at a stray dog. We lived in mud. But on occasions the sun would shine and the warmth would lift the wetness from you in a vapour, light would be refracted from the dampness and the world would begin to sparkle, deer would walk near as if they were just part of the work crew. Men would laugh.

Doug became a good mate during this time. He taught me the planting technique, hole, plant, bury, three paces, repeat, and he showed me how to hide trees under fallen logs to keep production up and convince the foreman—who screamed a little too much instead of watching more closely—that we were damn quick workers. At midday break when the weather allowed we would light a fire and heat water for coffee. Tree bags which weighed thirty pounds were downed for an hour and the crew would fall around the fire to warm. The foreman drank his coffee alone. He wasn't welcome.

It was during one of these breaks that Tommy, a grey-bearded, middle-aged drifter who always spoke with eyes pointing downward, slurped his too hot coffee and told us a story about the Alaska gold rush. 'Men became mad, crazy for gold,' he began, 'they came from every state in the Union, wharf labourers and clerks from New York, Boston, farmers from the Midwest, or south of the Mason–Dixon Line, cowboys from Montana, Wyoming, Texas, poor men, adventurers, thieves and profiteers. They came from all walks of life, all heading to Alaska. Some crossed the continent from east to west, others caught ships that sailed down the East Coast, and passed through the Panama Canal before heading north to San Francisco or Seattle. Everybody was heading for Skagway, from where they could cross over the mountains to the goldfields and fortune.

'For men with money it wasn't a problem getting to Skagway, but for others it was a desperate time. Food supplies, tents, blankets, mining equipment, bars, shovels, gold-pans and mercury had to be bought, and the prices had been pushed sky-high by the gold seekers crowding the stores. Tickets going north were expensive, boats had to be shared with cattle, horses and freight. A lot of men were forced to try it on their own. Small boats were built or bought. Sailboats, canoes, rowing dories. Some were worm-riddled, rotting, unseaworthy, and the men that set out never had a chance of arriving. Others were good boats handled by men who understood tides, weather and charts. These carried their passengers all the way to Skagway. The sailboats could make it in a month, but the rowers took two and a half months to pull the one thousand two hundred miles. Sometimes a line would be thrown from a passing ship and they could hook a ride, but that wasn't often.'

I can't remember whose idea it was, whose heart first beat faster, who made the other excited, but at some point during our time working as tree planters in the forests of Washington State, Doug and I decided to row a boat to Alaska.

The planting had finished and now we sat slowly sipping tin-tasting Budweiser beer in the small prefabricated home of Jack Waterman, our lead planter and hero since he had told the foreman 'to go fuck himself' the day before. Jack's Nez Percé Indian wife Charleyne stood frying pancakes for everybody on their two-burner gas stove.

'What's this I hear about you rowing a boat to Alaska?' asked Sid Beachworth, the father figure in our crew, as he carefully measured and poured our first glass of after-dinner Jack Daniel's. 'It don't make sense.'

'What don't make sense?' answered Doug defensively.

'Well,' continued Sid, who had a fierce drinking face gouged with lines that could only have come from laughing, 'it will take you a long time, time that you could be using to work, to start a career, getting on with life, not wasting it. Besides it's been done before.'

'That was a long time ago and not by an Australian,' I said.

'Wish the hell I was going,' yelled Jack from the other side of the room where he had been changing a country song for another country song. 'As far as I see it, it don't have to make sense.'

Sid smiled, deepening his face ravines. 'I guess I'm just getting old,' he offered in his good-natured way, raised his glass of Jack Daniel's and wished us the best. We all drank.

Seattle was built on a neck of land between the Puget Sound and

Lake Washington. To the west climb the Olympic Mountains, protecting Seattle from heavy winter rains that race in from the sea. To the east, the Cascade Mountains shield it from the great heat and cold that breeds in mid-continental America. It is completely married to the surrounding wilderness. A pearl in a blue-and-green shell. It was born as a mill town, but its protected harbour and geographical location allowed it to blossom as a centre of trade to the Orient and Alaska. The harbour is constantly full of large ships, emptying and loading, or just swinging around on their anchor lines waiting their turn at the dock like milling cattle needing to be milked. The clean, tall, modern city stands gazing down. Seattle was the place we chose to start our trip.

We found a small basement apartment at an address downtown, close to the water. The bad part of Seattle, or so we were told. The apartment block was managed by an ex-army colonel, who wore a goatee beard and played saxophone in a band. He walked with a crippling limp, the result of being blown up in Vietnam. He had no regrets he told us, for him the threat of a communist sweep through South-East Asia was real and worth defending against. He gave us the apartment without a bond, he thought Doug looked trustworthy.

There are many considerations when you decide to row a boat to Alaska, and we had considered very few of them, but when you consider too much it often becomes too much. Off we went. Doug, who was from Colorado with a bachelor's degree in biology, found a job changing truck tyres, and I, working under the imposition of having no green card, became head dishwasher at Steve's All-Night Broiler, a restaurant owned by three Greek brothers: Stefanos, Costas and Georgios.

We found a boat builder called Mr Polak who had large thick hands and a short-sightedness that left him stumbling and tripping like a newborn foal. He worked from a town named Carnation, a Dutch immigrant community nestled in dairy-farming country thirty miles to the east of Seattle. We settled on a price of one hundred dollars a foot. Mr Polak would build us a Grand Banks dory, twenty-two feet long, made from Douglas fir and powered by ash oars. It would be beautiful and unsinkable, he assured us, and if we wanted to row it to Australia, he would guarantee it, but would not accompany us.

By day I would be filling a steaming stainless-steel machine with egg-splattered, meat-soiled, mayonnaise-glued dishes, and at night we would be looking for the right food to take on the voyage, attending sales talks on newly produced dry goods, scouring the papers for second-hand camping equipment and safety gear. We bought books on currents, tides, charts of the passage, books about mammals, birds, we read about bear, whale, deer. We learnt to use a compass, a camera, and we played. Or rather, I played. Doug was a one-woman man, solid and old-fashioned, somebody who respected tradition, correctness, he stayed loyal to his girlfriend who was still studying at his old university, 3,000 miles away in Denver, Colorado.

Steve's Broiler ran all day and night. The three Greek brothers would each manage one of the eight-hour shifts, always there, watching. With thickly accented English and a powerful first-generation work ethic, they were calmly, completely in control. Each shift they employed one dishwasher, two short-order cooks, and three waitresses. At the back of the restaurant they had opened a cocktail bar that was gloomy and comfortable.

At Steve's, the coffee refills were free and the long counter always full. The cooks dressed in white, pulled orders, fried eggs—over easy or sunny side up—crisped bacon, browned hash browns, toasted bread, sizzled sausage—three orders at a time. The waitresses, dressed in their short pink-checked skirts, moved around and between the fake red-leather covered booths, serving food at a pace that mesmerized their clients, and I rinsed and rinsed, before stacking my machine with dishes, cups, pots and pans, and stared through the opening by the sink at madness.

At times, as in all public business, there was trouble. The bacon was not crisp, the order would be wrong, the egg not exactly right, the coffee cold. Sometimes people just want trouble. In the worst cases the police were called, at other times the cooks and dishwasher were sufficient, but mostly the waitresses took care of the problem. They would pet the troublemakers like doting mothers, cajole them like a schoolmistress, or scream and threaten them like a shrewish wife. One evening Cheryl, a half Sioux Indian with wavy, thick black hair, deep dark eyes and the bewitching beauty of a tropical flower in a weed garden, was serving coffee to a man who had left his penis hanging out of his pants as an invitation. Without a word she poured the hot coffee directly on to his balls. That night only an ambulance was needed.

We had decided on dried food for our trip. It was light, affordable, and the salesman assured us it was nutritious. Just add water. Bulk was a problem, space a premium, we needed so much that it was impossible to carry it all. We solved this by arranging to have three boxes of food flown to a town at the northern end of Vancouver Island in Canada, and another load to Ketchikan, Alaska. We bought a second-hand tent, new sleeping bags, pots and pans, cups, a small gas-burner, gas bottles—we planned to cook as much as possible on open fires—one survival suit, they were just too expensive, and a radio receiver, no sender, the same reason. Rain gear, ropes, jackets, knives, fishing tackle, chain and anchor. Doug taught me to cook chilli con carne with cornbread, heavily spiced.

Every few weeks we would check the progress of our boat and we would always find Mr Polak stumbling around, hammering this, screwing that, heating struts to bend, or shaving timber, the cold air in his unheated shed heavily polluted with wood dust. He would rush over to us, excited and proud of how the boat was coming along, his large hands almost breaking ours with his welcome.

In the beginning the *Renee Blue*, as we had named her, looked inelegant and flimsy, a large animal that had been picked clean of flesh. But over time Mr Polak built in a strength and pride. You could see her taking shape, like a hollow-chested boy turning into a man; the double ends that were characteristic of a Grand Banks dory rising high and fine, the ribs filling in.

On one of these inspections we bought a gun. We had thought a lot about it, we had talked to many people. 'Would we need a gun?'

'Where there is bear you need a gun, and if you don't fire it, it's still damn nice to know that you could have if needed,' so explained Mr Polak, who liked guns.

The gun shop was next door to the boat building shop. For 250 US dollars, no identification necessary, we bought an Ithaca twelve-gauge pump action shotgun that fired eight cartridges. We were advised to alternate the cartridges with slugs for bears and shot for birds. We did.

We were constantly unpacking and repacking our equipment, making the size and order right. We had bought waterproof bags that could be packed away in storage space that Mr Polak was building at the front and back of our boat. We were getting nearer.

The preparations were expensive, much more than we thought. I took another job as a cleaner in the Bell Telephone Building, inventing a social security number and a history to explain my Australian accent. I worked almost three months under this lie and each week I received my pay cheque and pay slip with my name correctly spelled and my fake security number printed neatly above, all tax deductions listed. Near the end of my employment I considered applying for a tax rebate, but was advised by Doug that that might be pushing my luck.

By the middle of June the *Renee Blue* was finished. Mr Polak had sanded and joined his last timber, his paintbrushes were stiff, hard, used and useless, his tools lay scattered on benches or half hidden amongst discarded wood and half empty paint and varnish tins, unwanted and ignored. The *Renee Blue* rested on low scaffolding that in turn rested on a bed of sawdust. She had been painted bright red and her name had been drawn on each side of the bow in white. The ash oars that had been coated three times with varnish leaned against the far wall waiting to go to work.

The *Renee Blue* was wrapped in ropes that were run through pulleys and then raised until her bed of scaffolding could be knocked out of the way and a trailer reversed under.

Once sitting comfortably, she was pulled through the streets to the cheers of beer-swilling villagers who had come to watch, and then down to the river which passed beside the town to begin her journey, first to Seattle harbour and then to Alaska a thousand miles away.

We drove to our apartment and back to the now floating *Renee Blue* in Mr Polak's dodge pickup, loading and unloading. By midday she was packed, our anchor was tied on, our goodbyes were said, and we solemnly accepted the good lucks offered to us. Down we sat, side by side, and away we pulled, and pulled. Mr Polak and a few village people watched, smiling and waving. But something was wrong; the *Renee* would not row straight. I thought it must be Doug pulling too hard and he thought it must be me. As we sat next to each other, each in control of one oar, each pulling harder and harder, snarling, Mr Polak started screaming from the shore, 'It's the ballast, we forgot the ballast.'

The *Renee Blue* was unloaded, the floor hatch pulled up and gravel from the shore shovelled in.

'More weight on top of the one thousand two hundred pounds we already have to pull,' groaned Doug, wiping raindrops from his face with the back of his hand, smiling crookedly. It was deep into the afternoon when we finally rowed out of sight of our gang. It was dark and still wet when we stumbled ashore exhausted, pushed our boat out to anchor and set up camp that first night. We pegged our tent out on the beach, laid out the sleeping bags, primed and lit the gas stove, cooked our first dry food meal, a chewy beef stroganoff, sipped our coffee, and I smoked. We felt content and confident heading towards Alaska. That night we were washed out of our tent by the incoming tide. But we were lucky, the weather was gentle, and we only lost a little food.

The next days brought blisters and beards. My hands had become so scarred that I could barely hold the oars, and my arse little better as it skidded across the seat in time with the rowing motion. I remembered a home remedy that I had used to harden my hands when I was boxing a few years before, so every morning before taking up the oars I would piss on them. Doug was in no better shape, but it was hard to tell because he complained a lot less.

We moved slowly, pulling in time with each other across the gentle rain-flattened water towards the north. The Juan de Fuca Strait, a tongue of water separating Vancouver Island and a slip of mainland, threw the Pacific at us in swells one after another. The *Renee Blue* rode up and down, balanced and sturdy.

Further we went, snaking through the San Juan and then the Gulf Islands, heading for Nanaimo on Vancouver Island. Tall evergreen-smothered inlets, with rock-strewn sandy beaches, became our home, splashes of painted wild-flowers surrounded our tent. The *Renee Blue* waited patiently, riding on water as smooth as oiled steel.

Sometimes we would get lost in the greyness because the rain would not stop and the islands that were as thick as roosting gulls would never match the islands on our charts, then we would ask a cruiser because we saw many small boats on this part of our trip.

'Where are you going?' they would always ask.

'Alaska,' we would shout back. A smile always came to their faces. Doug always called it a smirk.

We passed on good terms through the Canadian Immigration and Customs, which was just a small office built on a low cliff overlooking a rock-spotted cove on an unspectacular island. Our inspector, a small round man in a sharply ironed uniform, had visited Australia in 1954 with the Canadian navy. It had been during the visit of our newly crowned Queen Elizabeth II, and he was a fierce believer in the Commonwealth and a great admirer of Elizabeth. I convinced him that I was too, and that we were brothers under our queen. Our boat was never checked and the shotgun we had decided not to declare was never found.

We reached Nanaimo after eight days, but rowed uncaringly past. From the sea it looked large and unloved, and we had grown used to astounding beauty. We would wait until the town of Campbell River for the pleasures of civilization.

Clouds smothered the sun, but it had stopped raining. Our blisters had broken and hardened and my beard had thickened. Doug continued to shave. We were pulling next to each other as if born with an oar in our hands. The *Renee Blue* cut a reasonably straight line through the sea as she headed north. At the end of each day we would fight the waves that came with the change of weather, struggling to keep the boat from being bashed on the beach by surf as we unloaded our gear. Afterwards, Doug or I would strip, and swim the boat out beyond the surf line to anchor her. Before making camp we would light a fire from the driftwood that lay everywhere and dry ourselves. We began to eat more and more.

We had planned on harvesting shellfish but they had become polluted. A red tide, a bad bacteria, had invaded the coast. We trailed a line behind us as we rowed hoping to entice salmon but our pace was too slow and we caught very few fish. In the evening we were too tired to fish, or too lazy. When we reached Campbell River we were low on food.

It was at Campbell River that we had arranged to have some of our dry food flown in. We picked up three boxes from the office of Northern Freighters, a small transport company that delivered to Canada and Alaska. Later, when the food was packed away and our hunger unbearable, we found a small cafe decorated with two mounted salmon and a stuffed, medium-sized black bear, and sat at tables covered with plastic green-checked tablecloths. When the waitress, a plump middle-aged woman with dyed-red hair and deep cleavage, brought our order of bacon, eggs over easy, hash browns, pancakes and syrup, she hovered around us like a worried mother, filling our coffee cups and listening to our stories of seas and storms. When we ordered the same again she had the cook pile on the food so high that the pancakes slipped from the plate, dribbling syrup on to the check tablecloths. That evening we found a bar, its dark lighting forcing us to squint as we entered. Old, stale beer smells assaulted us. Drinking noise echoed, smothering familiar conversation. Heat from the wool-clad drinkers warmed the air. We drank Molsen beer with the locals and wobbled out at closing time.

'Watch out for Seymour Narrows,' was their warning as we wished them goodnight.

'Good sense and judgement are necessary qualities to use when making a trip through the Northwest Passage to Alaska,' or so we had read. But at times undependable emotion makes the important decisions. There are tools provided for people boating to Alaska that help you make qualified decisions: charts and compass for navigation, information about tide changes, directions of currents. These things are most important because there are places along the way where twenty-foot tides rush through narrow passages, moulding violent whirlpools that can suck a small boat under. If you move through these dangerous waters at slack tide, when it is not coming in or going out, then there is no danger.

We woke hung-over and restless. The Canadian beers which tasted of chemicals had soiled our stomachs and boxed with our heads, leaving us uncoordinated. Doug checked the tide tables. It was another three hours to slack. Seymour Narrows, a mile-long tunnel of water that at the wrong time sped between steep cliffs at fifteen knots, waited for us three miles further up. To leave now meant we would be travelling at the most dangerous time.

'We can eat and take it easy,' I suggested.

'I'm damn sure hung-over,' Doug answered after a long pause, 'Let's get out of this town.'

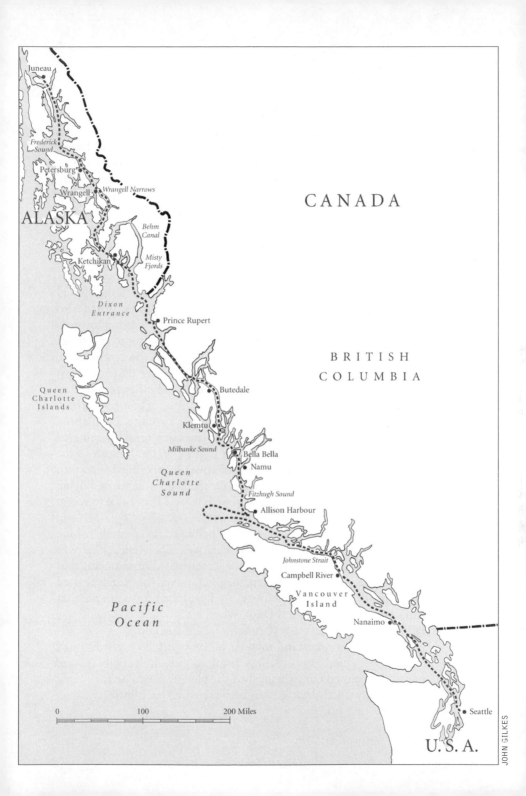

We loosed our lines and started moving quickly towards the narrows, at five knots. There was no need to row, we used our oars only to guide the boat. It was still early morning and it had begun to rain heavily. We found the entrance amongst the confusion of islands and reefs. Trees growing on the cliffs on both sides were entwined with clouds that hung like grey lace shawls, shutting out light. The black-and-white water in the narrows was jumping, twisting, bumping like a crowd in a busy city, limiting our view. We could see that the sides were calmer, the water had more room, it flowed quickly, but composed. We pointed the *Renee Blue* and headed into the passage, moving faster and faster.

The freighter appeared through the downpour as a large animal sometimes appears in the night before your headlights. It had also chosen the side of the narrows. It towered over us, pushing towards us against the rushing current, forcing a wall of water to stand out on both sides of the bow. We were jostled towards the centre of the passage, towards the whirlpools. The wall of water that stood ten feet high crashed down on us as we hung on. The *Renee* filled, an oar washed overboard, we had lost the last piece of control we had. The white circling pools that were as large as a room sucked at the boat and spun her round and round, at the same time thrusting us through the passage. All we could do was sit on the bottom of the boat and cling. The *Renee Blue* was thrown from one whirlpool to the next, finally slowing and turning like the last pirouette of a dying ballerina. Our oar had made the trip with us and I was able to scoop it up as we were spat out at the end of the ride.

We rowed heavily to a dock that belonged to a small fishing community built at the end of the narrows. The *Renee Blue* was three quarters full of seawater but the watertight compartments that Mr Polak had built in her structure had saved us. Gear floated around in the bottom of the boat. As I searched for a smoke that hadn't been soaked, I asked Doug why he thought we should have tried the passage when it was running at its quickest.

'Well, I don't understand myself,' he thoughtfully replied, 'I just needed to get going, probably just drank too much the night before. Besides,' he pointed out as he pushed the plunger down on the plastic pump and watched thick gushes of water dive back into bay, 'you could have said no.'

'But I drank more than you did, Doug,' I answered, shivering.

A sharply angled white boat with two powerful outboard motors raced toward the passage, saw us bailing and swung violently towards us. It spun to a stop, its wake banging the *Renee Blue* against the dock. It flew a large Canadian flag and COASTGUARD was clearly written in red on one side.

'Did you see anybody sink in the narrows?' he screamed down at us, from his position high up behind the wheel of his boat. 'We got a message from a freighter that they had sunk somebody.'

'No, mate,' I replied, continuing my bailing.

'We didn't see a thing, sir,' added Doug, who was always more formal.

'Where did you two just come from then?' he asked suspiciously.

'Seymour Narrows,' answered Doug, not looking up from his pumping.

Canadians are famously more paternal than Americans. Like their colonial parents, the British, officials take a much greater interest in the personal safety of their people. They make laws to discourage risk-taking. The police were infamous during the Alaskan and Yukon gold rush for stopping miners from setting out to the goldfields during the winter months, or from travelling the rivers before the spring floods caused by melting ice had slowed. Our coastguard man felt the same responsibility and lectured us about the stupidity of what we had just done and the dangers that lay ahead. Better quit, was his advice.

'Is there a law to stop us from going on?' I asked, stopping my work for a moment to relight my cigar that was still damp.

'No,' he replied quickly, 'but my advice is to quit.'

'Then we'll go on,' answered Doug, losing his formality, 'We're sorry you were called out, but we didn't make the call.'

The bay was full of logs jammed together. In the woods behind the shoreline, nestled among the towering timbers, were wooden houses. They were spread out in no formal order but their design was specific, they were built to shelter large numbers of people. A tiny man stood on the jetty waiting for us. As we neared, he reached out and took the rope that I had thrown out to him. His name was Peter Connelly. He was four feet nine inches tall and moved with a low-to-the-ground quickness that dazzled you. Peter was a logger. He was guarding the camp while the rest of his crew took a break, and his round cheery face showed just how happy he was to have company.

'I'm forty-four,' he told us as he served up our second helping of steak and mashed potato. 'I've been working in logging camps since I was thirteen, so that would be,' he thought a moment, 'thirty-one years.

'I've done about everything in a logging camp, that is except climb the trees, couldn't ever take the heights. But now this belly of mine starts to get in the way so I do a lot of odd jobs around the camp, the kitchen, keeping the place looking a bit civilized, that sort of thing.'

'What do you do when the camp is empty?' asked Doug, still digging into his mashed potato like a starving man.

'I read,' replied Peter. 'Only learnt when I was thirty, but now look at this.' He showed us a thick book, a Louis L'Amour cowboy story, 'I love 'em.'

That evening, sitting at the long dinner table before an open fire that dominated the canteen, we drank coffee and sipped from the whisky bottle that Peter had brought out. Peter played sad Canadian ballads on his harmonica, leaving us feeling warm and safe, and strangely reminding us of faraway places.

'What about women, Peter?' I asked as his music died away. Doug looked at me and moved his head ever so slightly left and right. Peter scratched at his unshaven neck. 'I had a girl once,' he told us, 'but she drank, so did I in those days, a lot. We would always end up fighting, throwing things. Once she called me a worthless little imp and pulled a gun on me. I had to hit her, I never went back. Now I just pay for my women. It's a little sadder but a lot safer. Nanaimo has a lot of women who take care of men like me.'

The next morning after a breakfast we rowed quietly away. Peter sat on the jetty, short legs teasing the water, waving us seaward.

We moved slowly along a stretch of water called the Johnstone Strait, fighting the wind that blew at the *Renee Blue*'s nose. We were in choppy sea, not rough, but it hid our view of the dolphins until they were almost on top of us. Even when they were surrounding the boat their black bodies disappeared into the darkness of the water, but every now and then as they butterflied past, you could glimpse their white undersides, you could see two black streaks running from their eye down into the whiteness below. There were over thirty of them.

'Striped dolphin,' said Doug, without being asked. I acknowledged his answer with a nod and a grin and we rowed on.

The small inlet looked full wine-glass calm as we pulled out of the strait after noticing huts built just back from the water.

'Must be another logging camp,' muttered Doug.

'Good food,' I answered. 'Let's have a look, test the hospitality.'

There were no logs jamming the water; Doug thought they had probably hauled them away. The men who stood around the shore watching us row in were work-muscled and rough-looking. It was a warm day out of the wind and most wore T-shirts and almost all were heavily tattooed. There was no jetty and no other boats. As we moved closer we called out a greeting but got no reply. As I stepped ashore the men moved back to let a man through who had just arrived. He was heavy-set, but seemed less threatening than the others. His full black beard almost hid the large smile he gave us in welcome. 'My name's Jacob,' he offered, and then, 'Where's your boat?'

'This is our boat,' replied Doug, pointing at the *Renee Blue*. He turned to look at the other men, and then back to us as if somebody was playing a trick on him. 'Where are you coming from?' he finally asked.

'Seattle,' I replied, grinning at their confusion.

'You rowed two hundred miles?' asked one of the tattooed men.

'Yeah,' I answered, 'took us two weeks. Got a cigarette, mate?'

The tattooed man threw me his tobacco pouch. Jacob and the others wandered closer to look at the *Renee Blue*. Finally Jacob turned back to us, 'You must be hungry, let's eat.'

As we walked up the hill towards the metal huts that had been built on a large dust-layered clearing, Jacob, towering over us, spoke, 'Did you know this is a corrective work-camp?'

'A jail,' translated Doug, more for himself than me.

'But don't worry,' Jacob continued, 'the worst we got here is an armed bank robber, and he got caught easy.'

Over a lunch of cold meats, salads and potatoes, Jacob explained to us that it was a low-security corrective centre. 'These men are here to be rehabilitated, they thin young trees, chainsaw work, and they get paid nine dollars a day.'

'What about escapes?' I asked, perplexed at the lack of confinement.

'Well, there's a dirt road out of here, but we are in the middle of nowhere. I've got the only vehicle, and besides Vancouver Island is just that, an island. We would always get them and they know it.'

'Are you the only guard?'

'I'm not really a guard,' he explained, 'I'm more a work foreman. They police themselves, and yes, there are two of us. Norman, he's in Nanaimo buying supplies.'

As we sat eating, a tall thin man with long, stringy brown hair and daggers and hearts tattooed on both forearms came to our table. 'A few of us have been talking,' he began without introducing himself, 'we're gunna build you a mast, make a sail.'

We spent three days in the work camp. We slept in our own tent but ate all our meals with the inmates. The cook, who was a little older than the rest and seemed more at home with his role as prisoner, served us crab, steak and even lobster. His breakfasts were as good as those in Steve's Broiler, and like all good cooks he would flutter around the tables demanding approval of his meals. He was the bank robber. Daggers and hearts, we found out, was there for robbery and assault. Newfy, his mate, a shaven-headed Newfoundlander, who always put me in mind of a grinning bear, had been in and out of jail since he was a kid. He was sewing the sail. There were three others in the group; along with the cook they were at top of the camp hierarchy. They sat at the head table, received food first, worked on the easiest slopes. Once, before I understood, I sat without thinking in a seat used by a group member. I was quickly warned out. I also had to play by their rules.

It was the rules that kept the peace, the rules were made by the strongest but that was no different than other places I had been. I saw no aggression, but was told by Jacob that fights occurred. 'As long as they don't kill each other, we stay out of it.'

Our trip became very important to a lot of the prisoners. We would go over the places we had been, the weather conditions, sea conditions, what lay ahead. Our charts would be pored over in detail, and dangers pointed out. When we mentioned a town we planned on visiting, we were told where to drink and where not to, the quality of the girls and the trouble involved in catching them. It seemed important to them that we not run into problems, that we reach Juneau, that we succeed. We were never given an address to stay.

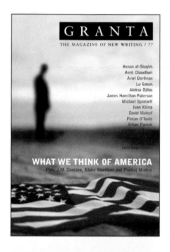

SAVE OVER 40%!

Each quarterly issue of *Granta* features a rich variety of stories, in fiction, memoir, reportage and photography—often collected under a theme, like those shown overleaf. Each issue is produced as a high-quality paperback book, because writing this good, deserves nothing less. Subscribers get *Granta* delivered to them at home, at a substantial discount. Why not join them. Or give a subscription to a friend, relative or colleague? (Or, given these low prices, do both!)

GRANTA **'ESSENTIAL READING.'**

OBSERVER

ORDER FORM

I'D LIKE TO SUBSCRIBE FOR MYSELF FOR:
- ○ 1 year (4 issues) at just £26.95
- ○ 2 years (8 issues) at just £50
- ○ 3 years (12 issues) at just £70
- START SUBSCRIPTION WITH ○ this issue ○ next issue

I'D LIKE TO GIVE A SUBSCRIPTION FOR:
- ○ 1 year (4 issues) at just £26.95
- ○ 2 years (8 issues) at just £50
- ○ 3 years (12 issues) at just £70
- START SUBSCRIPTION WITH ○ this issue ○ next issue

MY DETAILS (please supply even if ordering a gift): Mr/Ms/Mrs/Miss_____

_____

_____ Country _____ Postcode _____

GIFT RECIPIENT'S DETAILS (if applicable): Mr/Ms/Mrs/Miss_____

_____

_____ Country _____ Postcode _____

03HBG83

TOTAL* £_____ paid by ○ £ cheque enclosed (to 'Granta') ○ Visa/Mastercard/AmEx:

card no: __ __ __ __ __ __ __ __ __ __ __ __ __ __ __ __

expires: __ __ / __ __ signature: _____

* POSTAGE. The prices stated include UK postage. For the rest of Europe, please add £8 (per year). For the rest of the world, please add £15 (per year). DATA PROTECTION. Please tick here if you don't wish to receive occasional mailings from compatible publishers. ○

➠ **POST** ('Freepost' in the UK) to: Granta, 'Freepost', 2/3 Hanover Yard, Noel Road, London N1 8BR. **PHONE/FAX:** In the UK: FreeCall 0500 004 033 (phone & fax); outside the UK: tel 44 (0)20 7704 9776, fax 44 (0)20 7704 0474 **EMAIL:** subs@granta.com

'We only know people as bad as ourselves,' Newfy once told me.

The mast had been carved with care. Newfy had used old, colourless canvas for the sail, he had gouged eyeholes and attached the sail to the mast with ropes and a crossbeam. More ropes had been attached for the positioning of the sail. We packed it securely down the side of the boat before saying our goodbyes. Daggers gave me a parcel—'Tobacco and food for the trip,' he grunted. Cook stood a little up the hill, arms folded, smiling. We received a warning from Newfy not to use the sail in big winds. A lot of the boys had come to watch us leave. They squatted down, waiting until we had rowed out into the chop of the channel and out of sight.

After the prison we crossed over to the mainland, dancing through the small islands that still crowded the Johnstone Strait, and then hugged the coast to start our pull up the Queen Charlotte Sound.

We fashioned a new system for anchoring out. The anchor and its rope and chain were left sitting on the bow, another rope was fastened to the anchor. After unloading we would push the boat out past the tideline. The anchor was then tugged from the *Renee Blue* with the second rope. At times we misjudged the distance. One morning we found the *Renee Blue* standing vertical against a large boulder as if leaning patiently on the bar waiting to be served. Twice we woke just in time to see the tide trickle past her sides, leaving her rock-stranded for six hours.

Thick fog; a grey wet wall sat around us. Water flooded our faces, Doug licked his moustache continually. I squeezed droplets out of my thick beard until they formed a stream and then fell, cascading to my chest. We had been rowing blind for two hours when we finally agreed that we should lay out the compass to check direction. We had been rowing to Japan.

Along the Queen Charlotte Sound we camped much of the time in inlets, coves when we could reach them. Calm peaceful places that usually had good driftwood for fire, and sometimes a stream to fill our water tanks. At other times we were left to the open beach, our boat bobbing upon waves that had already travelled thousands of miles. During those nights we slept in the *Renee Blue*, careful that she wasn't washed away.

Mornings were often damp and hazy but it cleared in the

afternoons when the west wind cleansed the sky and made rowing rough, thumping water into us until our shoulders burned and our backs cramped. When you looked to the shore the trees came down to the sea edge. Two powerful natures resigned to stalemate.

Once we saw an Alaskan ferry racing by, and once a stumpy, thick-shouldered tugboat pulling loaded barges, parting the water as if it were a sharpened knife slicing paper. But the small pleasure boats were gone. Sea otters with heads like old men stretched out of the waves to look at us. Eagles hunted the shores.

We bounced around Cape Caution, shoved and pushed in many directions by a confused sea that became more so when the strong winds and ebbing tide fought, past Allison Harbour and into the Inside Passage, a great piece of open sea behind us. Our hands had callused and our bodies were lean and fit. We had been travelling for a month.

It was like standing in a gallery admiring a painting for a very long time and then moving to the next. You could clearly see it was the same artist, the familiarity was unmistakable, but it was as if one had been painted with the left hand, and the other with the right.

The forest that crowded the shoreline and the rocky headlands, and that appeared black and secretive, started climbing. Mountains loomed, some fringed in green, others still capped in frozen white.

My hands had started to cramp during the cool of the night. Each morning I would have to pry my fingers open one by one. Doug had started mixing egg powder, flour and water together to make dumplings to add to our packaged food. Each evening after our gear was unloaded, one of us would swim the *Renee Blue* out in freezing water to anchor. We had given up on the two-rope system.

We rowed on past the Haida Indian village of Namu, past the fishing boats that bobbed at the docks waiting to unload at the cannery that employed the town—which had been built high on wooden legs to protect it from the tides. It was low tide when we passed and all the buildings stood uncomfortably in rubbish-polluted mud. An Indian boy wearing a Yankees baseball cap came down to the dock and waved us past.

The channel was narrow and we were protected from westerlies and southerlies, but the currents forced us to row in a rhythm, to follow the moon. Doug talked with yearning about growing old and having a good rocking chair and fine memories. My tobacco was almost finished.

We reached Bella Bella, another Haida community, as daylight faded to late afternoon dimness. But there was no store. As we walked along the dock towards the neatly spaced wooden houses that perched on higher ground amongst the timber, a man called out from his seat on his front steps that my blonde hair would make a good scalp. He touched a knife that he wore on his belt as he spoke, others became caught up in the joke, their laughter ate away the quiet. We walked slowly around the town, uncomfortable about being white amongst a people who had complaints about their treatment in history. Many men were drinking, some were drunk, others unconscious.

'A plane landed with alcohol.'

I looked behind me to see a heavy, serious woman wearing a spotless white T-shirt and pressed blue jeans.

'Normally this is a dry town,' she continued. 'Drinking can be a problem here. If you want supplies, row across the bay. It's a white-run store,' she added, dropping her head in embarrassment. After buying cigarettes we rowed quietly out of Bella Bella. We preferred to camp in peace.

The bear was only fifteen feet away, her cinnamon colour blending into the shadows thrown by the tall firs, blurring her, disguising her. We were gliding by on a glass backwater, she could hear us, she followed a few metres, stood and glared at the water. She was not big—black bears seldom are—but she was powerful and curious. We pulled a little harder, putting distance between us, watched her drop back down to her four feet and lose interest.

The southerly was steady and solid, the waves rolling but even. Today the Milbanke Sound was kind. Doug spat a glob of chewing tobacco from the side of his mouth, staining his chin, missing the water. It fell solidly, landing at his feet on the bottom of the boat.

'Let's try that sail,' he said, giving me a wink and a brown, mushy grin. We set the mast, laid up the crossbeam and quickly unfurled it. We tied off on one side and hand-held the other sail rope to position it to the wind. We lashed our two oars together as a rudder and began to fly. They had made us a square sail which could be tilted to catch a following wind, but one which you could not tack with. We used it only once, the wind was never just right again.

Past the village of Klemtu, past Butedale, past cascading waterfalls dropping through the trees, foaming, spitting out fine white spray, splashing rainbows in the air. Between mountains that loomed down on us on both sides like powerful, old, white-haired men, amused at our travels. Past valleys that had been ripped out of the mountain by glacial meanderings, and out into the sea before the town of Prince Rupert.

There the roar of fast cars, souped-up engines and shortened exhausts drifted down to the docks where we were busy tying off the *Renee Blue* and packing away loose gear. This was the first town with a road leading somewhere since Campbell River on Vancouver Island and the last one we would come across as we headed north.

When we first pulled in it had been drizzling, now the rain began to have more weight and purpose.

'Where are you guys planning to sleep tonight?' came a deep, friendly voice from above. I looked up at a man with thick dark hair.

'In the boat,' I answered.

'It's real wet, bro. Come and stay up at the house, it's not much but it's dry.' That night in a weatherboard house at the back of town, we drank with Robert and his mates. Some were Indian like Robert, some white like us. Later, we walked through town towards a bar area looking for another drink, stepping around sleeping, staggering, screaming, fighting people.

'Lot of drunks in Prince Rupert,' said Doug to no one in particular.

'Yeah,' answered Robert with exasperation, 'mostly Indians, disappointed angry Indians.'

'Robert gets a bit pissed off with his own people,' explained one of the other men in our group.

'They're always so fucking bitter,' complained Robert.

'Yeah, well there's a lot of cultural confusion out there, not much confidence or self-respect.' It came from one of his white mates. Robert just shook his head.

The strippers in the bar were a bit clumsy, sometimes a zipper would stick, or a button catch. Some looked bored, others embarrassed. None was beautiful, but each time a piece of glittering clothing fell to the ground, or a painted hand was dragged slowly over a breast or left to linger between legs, whoops and yells filled the room. Men reached towards the stage that was all flashing lights, chrome and wetness.

I was told the story between performances. A tall black girl had just finished seducing dollars from the crowd, the music had been lowered and the patrons had settled back to drink.

Robert sipped at his Jack Daniel's before he began. He told us he was fishing for halibut in the Johnstone Strait on his boat the *Sea Eagle*, a thirty-foot hand liner, black hull, high wheelhouse. He had anchored for the night in the channel, port and starboard lights burning, two lights on the radio mast. It was a clear evening, stars filling the sky. There was a dark edge to the night but it was far away. He saw lightning but couldn't even hear the thunder. When the boat started to lift and drop in the undetermined early morning he knew that the storm had caught them. He felt his boat nose into the wind and drift across the waves. Robert had a good anchor and a lot of chain and rope out, so he wasn't worried. He checked on deck and could only see white foam splashing on a black canvas. Nothing to do. He went back to his bunk, lay down, and a few minutes later he was flailing and choking in the cold, wild water. He could hear his deckhand screaming across the wind. He rose with the next wave and caught sight of the man clinging to a part of the *Sea Eagle*. The tanker that had sliced through their boat continued to drive straight ahead, its lights becoming dimmer, its wake adding to the confusion of the angry water. They both managed to crawl on to part of the dead boat. The storm passed. They were picked up next morning by another fishing boat, very cold and pissed off.

'No broken bones?' Doug asked in a soft respectful voice when Robert had finished.

'They kept us a day or so in Nanaimo hospital, we were almost blue,' answered Robert.

'And your boat?'

'Insurance paid up, I'm an organized Indian.'

Dixon Entrance pounded, rolled and thumped us as we headed for the Alaskan border. The thirty-five knot winds raised the water around us until we were forced to run and hide like cockroaches in a kitchen. Some days we would row five hours and make one mile.

We were wet and chilled for days on end. One time when it was too rough to go out we built a large fire under a rock ledge that let you look over the frantic water but still stay dry and warm. We swelled our bellies with food, and drank cup after cup of sweet black coffee. As I smoked a long dark cigar that I had bought in Prince Rupert, Doug retrieved the shotgun out of its canvas case and started to rub grease in as a protection against rust. 'What about those waitresses at Steve's Broiler?' he suddenly asked. 'Did you sleep with any?'

Doug never talked too much about sex. Once, a little unfairly, I even asked him did he think about it. He assured me he did but always with this girl in Colorado. 'Well?' he pushed.

'Sure I did,' I finally replied.

'How many?' he asked.

'All of them,' I answered, 'Well, all except Mary.'

'Why not Mary then?'

'Strict Catholic and a grandmother.'

'And Anne from upstairs?' he continued.

'You know I did.'

'But she was only eighteen!'

'Yes, but she knew more than I did about sex.'

'And Sharon?'

'I was with her for two months.'

'Well?'

'Well nothing, I found her sleeping with another man. It didn't matter, it wouldn't have worked anyway.'

'But she went to Shore College, that's one of the best schools in the country, and she was beautiful.'

'Yes, she was,' I nodded.

'Have you ever thought of staying with one girl?'

'Sure, Doug, I even tried, but when they were going right I was always turning left.'

'What's that supposed to mean,' he pushed.

'Just that I haven't found one yet that's going the same way, one who wants to live the same life.'

'I think you're full of shit,' he said, rubbing more grease on the gun, 'you're never together with anybody long enough to find out, you just like fucking around. Do you know how much time you're wasting chasing all the time? You'll end up alone.'

It was not far out of Ketchikan on a finger of the Misty Fiords, before Behm Canal, early morning. The water reflected like polished wood. Flossed clouds floated by, the *Renee Blue*'s red hull mirrored itself, weaving a passage over drowned green trees that pointed downwards.

There were three jet-black dorsal fins scything through the reflections, moving in the same direction as the *Renee Blue*, parallel. It was a father, mother, baby. When you looked deeper you could clearly see the mass of the black body, the white daubing above the eye like a painted warrior, the broad flippers, the blunt nose, the white belly reaching up unevenly into the black. Masses of teeth. We thought that the killer whales were going to pass when the male turned towards us. Just before collision, he slowed, wheeled, and lay beside us, watching, his dorsal a yard higher than the gunwhales, his length much greater than the *Renee Blue*. He swam with us a while, the mother and baby watching from a distance. I had seen a drawing of a killer whale taking an Eskimo from the ice, he could easily do the same to me. I was scared, but at the same time enchanted by his nearness. I could almost lean out of the *Renee Blue* and touch him. Doug assured me that they mistook the Eskimos for seals, I should not be worried, it was obvious I was not a seal. The whale had seen enough, he shot back to his family. Doug removed his glasses and wiped his itching eyes with the back of his right hand. He then placed it on my shoulder and we watched the whales silently leave.

We rowed among the boats of the Ketchikan fishing fleet looking for a moorage. Green mountains loomed at the back, shunting the town towards the water, forcing it to stretch further along the channel. The buildings had been constructed over the water on posts because that's where the commerce was, and all the room they had. Timber felling by lumbermen left the lower mountains disfigured and scarred like a wounded face. We collected our food box from the office of Northern Freighters, ate a huge meal as we always did in town, and left. Ketchikan seemed like a metropolis and we were more comfortable in the bush where we could take care of our gear and ourselves.

We spent that night in a log cabin built among tall grass and wild flowers by a hunter, or fisherman, or nature lover. There was tinned food which we did not touch. We replaced the firewood that we used to light the stove and warm the room. Mice ran about unconcerned as if they had built the place. The *Renee Blue* bobbed serenely in the protected cove. We lingered next morning, walking the pebbled beach, watching the tide, trying to decide whether to stay or leave.

The deer came down to lick salt off the rocks, it had not expected us. I waded to the boat and freed the shotgun, moved as close to the animal as I dared and fired. The cartridge caught her in the flank, she fell crippled, turned her head to look at me, her large brown eyes in panic. I raced towards her, ejected the empty cartridge, ejected the next which was birdshot, and fired the third into her head, crushing it, killing her quickly.

I had never skinned a deer.

'Can't be too much different than a kangaroo,' Doug encouraged me. I started from the back hoof, slitting the heel and working up, hand ripping the skin as I cut. When all four feet were done I gutted her, joining the cut to the legs and peeling the skin off her body. The head I severed with a machete. It was a rough job but I had saved most of the meat, the heart and liver were laid on a rock ready for immediate frying. Doug, who made fires as he did all other things— slowly, precisely—started gathering small, larger and still larger twigs. He fashioned them into a tepee, small twigs first, blew to make sure there was enough oxygen, then carefully built up the heat by adding new fuel until the fire ate upon itself and roared. All the wood was damp. I tied rope around the deer's skinless back legs, hoisted the rope over a branch and hung her to bleed. Later we salted her with coarse salt that we had brought along for that purpose. We ate the liver and heart slowly, chewing each mouthful, letting their juices wash around our mouths before swallowing.

The current in the middle of the channel ran strong and pulled the light aluminium boat tight against its anchor line. As we rowed closer we could see that it was piled high with empty traps. There were no oars. Small bubbles appeared around the motor shaft, soon a head appeared covered with goggles and a snorkel. A sandy-haired diver threw a rubber-handled knife into the back of the boat before hoisting himself over the edge, landing, sitting in one motion on the seat closest to the motor. He hadn't seen us. As he reefed at his mask, he twisted and caught sight of us, a smile filled his smooth face. 'Geez, who are you guys?'

The diver's name was Todd, his motor had been snarled with floating rope. Todd was a lightly built, fifteen-year-old crab fisherman. He was working alone. We were fifty miles out of Ketchikan and forty before Wrangell with nothing in between except water and bush.

As he towed us back to his camp, which turned out to be a large canvas tent set up on flattened scrub on the inner lip of a small cove, he explained that he had been working with three other men but they found it too lonely and had returned with the boat that comes to pick up the catch.

'It's a pigsty,' apologized Todd as we carried our gear up from the boat. I looked around: the tent was large, four cot beds, a gas refrigerator, a fold-up table. Clothes littered the canvas floor, half-eaten foods covered the table, filthy dishes were piled high in a bucket near the entrance, garbage had been thrown together in a pile, traps lay strewn about outside. Todd told us that at night, black bears came down to the edge of the light thrown out by the kerosene lamps. Seduced by the filth, I thought. Tod kept a thirty-aught-six hunting rifle upright by the entrance in case they came further. That evening we washed a few dishes, boiled crab and fried deer steak and shrimp on his gas stove and sipped the whisky that I had bought in Ketchikan.

Todd told us that he was born in Wrangell. His light blue eyes and pale skin colour suggested, like so many inhabitants of the area, a Scandinavian history. When I asked him about his work he seemed surprised.

'Just working my school vacation,' he answered shyly.

'Yeah,' replied Doug, 'but most kids wash cars or cut lawns for extra money. I worked at a 7-Eleven.'

Todd didn't seem to understand the compliment. 'My girl might come down the next time they collect the crab,' he happily told us, 'guess I got to clean the place up a bit.'

Before we left next morning we watched Todd pull traps, straining with the effort, hand over hand, alone, the current rushing by. Then we slowly rowed away.

The next few days we gorged ourselves on deer. We had left a big piece with Todd and wanted to finish the rest before it began to rot. Each evening, because it had rained and the wood was wet, Doug with his infinite patience lit the fire, and the deer was fried and eaten with dumplings. Afterwards it was built up until it burnt away the dampness that seemed to be constantly with us now, and we would lie back on logs counting the stars in the clearness between the dark travelling clouds. One evening Doug pulled out the fishing line, sat on a rock in the drizzle and fought a small salmon. Next day we gave what was left of the deer to a passing fisherman, we could not finish all of her. It had been six days since I had shot her on the beach.

I had read that Wrangell began as a fur-trading settlement. Otter, seal, mink and lynx were traded by the Tlingit Indians. It had been settled by the Russians, the English and Americans, but those days are long past. As we rowed in, a large Japanese freighter that had come to collect lumber from the mills stood under cranes that were readying to load her. Tugboats, seaplanes and seine trawlers filled the moorings and salmon and shrimp canneries worked noisily along the waterfront.

It had started to rain heavily, incessantly, and we had started to argue pretty well all the time. We were nearing the end of the trip and it had begun to resemble a marriage breaking down. All we remembered were the difficult parts, all we recognized in each other were the annoying things. We were meant to row into Wrangell quietly, unnoticed, buy tobacco and leave. There was no need to linger, we had no money to buy a bed, but I wanted to drink, I needed company. Doug never needed it, he hardly ever spoke. Along with the tobacco, I bought whisky. We left still arguing.

If you look to starboard as you row out of Wrangell, not forgetting that you are rowing backwards and therefore facing the back of the boat, you would see a great mass of brown-coloured water. It is river water pushing silt and mud out into the tideline. Brown churning into aqua-green. Where it slows, there's bound to be fine gold but it's almost impossible to retrieve. The river is the Stikine and its gold is carried down from upper British Columbia 400 miles away. It was along this river that Americans travelled into British Columbia in the latter part of the nineteenth century to make their fortune; it was because of this river that Wrangell ceased to be just a fur-trading outpost.

Towards Petersburg, reaching closer and closer to Juneau, arguing more and more. The rain pounded down. I asked Doug once if anything I did annoyed him, 'You never rinse the soap off the dishes,' he replied immediately.

Knife-sharp peaks stood at a distance looking over the neatness and bustle of a town built on muskeg meadows by Scandinavians and known as Little Norway. Petersburg is a fishing town. A passage of water known as Wrangell Narrows fronts the town. Twenty miles of tricky navigation, marked with coloured lights, flashing beacons and bobbing red buoys that point out the danger. Fishing boats, tugs and tankers bunched up trying to get through. We rowed along ignoring the warnings, safe with our shallow draught and self-propulsion. We never visited Petersburg, we were pulled by the fever of arriving at the end.

In Frederick Sound small blue-white, white-blue shapes of ice floated around on the feisty little waves, reminding you of young girls in ball frocks dancing and curtsying. Whales flew high out of the water ahead of us, fell back, pounding the sea, dived deep, turned and shot again towards the sky, and again fell. Spray surged upwards spreading like a glass curtain. The sun burnt through making colours. As we came closer we saw that they were humpback whales, black and thick, fifty foot long, a pod, they were feeding in a circle, mouths open. We sat drifting in the *Renee Blue*, watching the frenzied feeding, the cliffs of water, marvelling at the power needed to propel the heavy mass so high. Doug used a strip of plastic as a cover against rain, set our small gas cooker underneath, primed and lit it, and then started boiling coffee water. He pulled out his chewing tobacco, lay back against the side of the dory, let one hand fall soaking into the sea, and with the other began to fill his mouth, never taking his eyes from the whales. I brewed and poured the coffee, lit a cigar and did the same.

'I've decided to stay in Alaska,' Doug suddenly, unexpectedly told me, still mesmerized by the spectacle. The light wind burned my cigar ash a fierce red, the rain made it soft and spongy.

As we rowed along the last part of Stephens Passage, the wind stinging our backs, the rainwater filling the boat, nearing Juneau with every stroke, I understood completely, that it was over. I felt a sudden, unreasonable pride, and then later, anxiety, and still later, a deep nostalgic sadness. Feelings I recognized that come with the end of something, before a beginning.

We had been living together more than six months. All our thoughts, our energies, our money had gone towards the trip. We had rowed through daunting beauty, wild, breathtaking country, and because of our noiseless, slow progress, we had come closer to animals than we had thought possible. We had drifted on seas so calm that they could have been ponds in a backyard, and suffered through weather that made rowing so heavy it left our bodies burning with pain. We had run low on food and on tobacco. The last month we had woken only to morning cold and rain that soaked our humour and made uncramping our hands almost impossible. Tension had run high, insults were spat out without thought, but just once did we almost start swinging, and then only because exhaustion and frustration had smothered anything resembling good sense. And now it was over.

We rowed past under the metal coat-hanger bridge that joins Juneau to Douglas, and tied up among the small fishing fleet. It was raining. It had taken us four and a half months of preparation, and two and a half months of rowing. In the end we understood that it had nothing to do with old-time gold miners heading north, it was only about doing something.

The trip had strong, opposite effects on both of us. I saw it as a beginning, the first cold beer on a hot Friday night after a week of hard work. It became my catalyst to a sometimes unreasonable need to see strange places, and do different things. My life would never be settled again. For Doug it was the end. A magnificent, frivolous taste of adventure. When we reached Juneau he decided that that was enough. Life must now become uncomplicated, conventional, settled. We both understood that it was the end of our time together, for always.

I found a job on a salmon-fishing boat, and returned to Australia three months later. Doug worked for a while in a fish processing plant, and then moved to Anchorage, where as far as I know he still lives. For months afterwards I would have to knead my fingers to start them working in the mornings, for years afterwards beer glasses would drop without warning through my hand and crash, spilling glass and precious liquid around the feet of my drinking pals. They would never believe it had nothing to do with drunkenness, but came from rowing a boat to Alaska. □

GRANTA

THE GREENLAND PUMP

PUMP

Matthew Hart

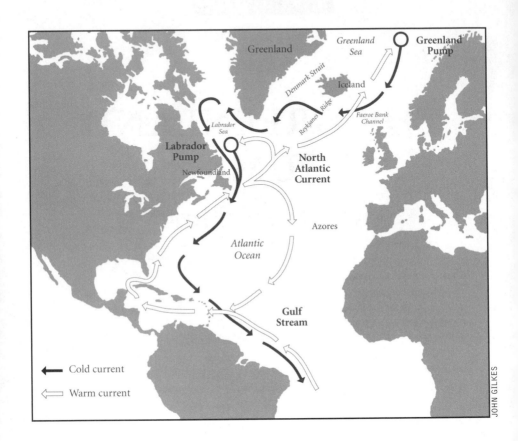

Greenland

Greenland
Sea

Greenland
Pump

Denmark Strait

Iceland

Reykjanes Ridge

Faeroe Bank
Channel

Labrador
Sea

Labrador
Pump

North
Atlantic
Current

Newfoundland

Azores

Atlantic
Ocean

Gulf
Stream

Cold current

Warm current

JOHN GILKES

The Greenland Pump

In the cold water at the bottom of the Faeroe–Shetland Channel, in the months of December and January, lie shoals of a tiny animal called *Calanus finmarchicus*. *C. finmarchicus* is a species of copepod—translucent crustaceans a quarter the size of a grain of rice, with long, graceful paddles that propel them through the water. In the midwinter months the copepods drift in the current, in a kind of hibernation known as diapause. In the spring they ascend the water column and get eaten. Forty years ago these little creatures made up seventy per cent of all the summer supply of zooplankton in the North Sea; now the population has collapsed by half.

The fate of this brisk little swimmer is connected to deep-water flows through a narrow gap in a line of sills that stretches across the whole of the North Atlantic—the Greenland–Scotland Ridge. The gap in this ridge is called the Faeroe Bank Channel. It is a key part of a scheme of circulation that imports warm water from the southern oceans, up the Gulf Stream to the British Isles, where the water heats the air and helps to bathe the entire region, islands and continent, in a climate far warmer than the latitude would otherwise permit. This circulation system may now be failing. If the failure is accomplished, the human population of the region could be swept up in a catastrophe of climate change, heralded by falling temperatures. It is an image begging a moral—the least and the greatest of creation inextricably whirled together by the engine of fate.

Low, grey clouds were streaming across the Grampian hills when I came down through Aberdeen to join the research ship *Scotia*. She sat at the quay, a gleaming blue-and-white vessel with the blue-and-white flag of St Andrew snapping at her bow. Christmas lights hung in the town and a solitary trumpet player stood on Union Street blowing carols down the hill, and the ship looked like a large, bright Christmas present herself, floodlit, festooned with white cranes like bows on a ribbon. I tramped up the aluminium gangway, banging the rails with my bag—laptop, thermal gloves, Wigwam socks: everything needed to record the end of the world.

After breakfast the next morning, a chemist named Pam Walsham entered the mess with an armload of tinsel and began to decorate a little tree. Mick Williams, the steward and second cook, a small, round man from Teesdale in the Pennines, came into the lounge to roll a cigarette. He carried a dishcloth on his shoulder and began to share, just like that, his boundless affection for the avian world. 'When we get near the Faroes you'll see puffins. *Fractercula arctica*. That's the proper name. They eat them in Iceland. I couldn't. Not the puffin. There's nowt else this time of year except the gulls.'

Then the chief scientist, John Dunn, a grey-bearded, blue-eyed Scot in jeans and a fleece, arrived and led me to his cabin and tossed me a sheaf of xeroxed charts. Lines of black dots marked the seas around Scotland and the Scottish islands, the Faeroe–Shetland Channel, and the Atlantic Ocean south of Iceland. 'We're going to run a health check on the water column,' Dunn announced. 'We'll go out and investigate some currents.' He then launched into an ardent catalogue of the qualities of the ship, an object, it soon became clear, with which he was besotted. We left, and ranged through the whole vessel from the kitchens to the trawl deck to the immaculate engine room. Then, climbing through one hatch after another, we came to a small compartment with a hole in the deck. A well dropped twenty feet straight down. Hanging from a massive chain was a seventeen-and-a-half-ton, yard-thick slab of steel, eighteen feet high, poised above an open slot in the hull. Like the centreboard of a dinghy, *Scotia*'s drop keel would be lowered at sea to help steady the ship in the delicate work of deploying instruments overboard. The keel was also fitted with acoustical sensors and, when lowered, would allow these probes to operate beneath the turbulence created by the hull of the moving ship. We leaned on the rail and peered down the length of this paragon. Oily peaks of harbour water yapped around in the opening. 'I'm very proud of this keel,' murmured Dunn. At noon we slipped our lines and went out of the River Dee.

Scottish scientists have been going to sea since the end of the nineteenth century. Fishing was crucial to Scotland's economy and the export of herring was an important source of wealth, for Aberdeen in particular. Ocean knowledge was part of the technology that supported this bonanza and Scotland began to acquire, through exploration, data that described the sea around it. It was only natural that mariners would become swept up by the more adventurous seafaring projects of the day, and in 1902 the Scottish National Antarctic Expedition bought and refitted a 140-foot barque-rigged, auxiliary-screw Norwegian whaler, rechristened her the *Scotia*, and sent her off to the Southern Ocean.

It was a purely Scottish venture. The Coats brothers, thread manufacturers, supplied not only money but bales of Fair Isle sweaters, which the sailors wore in layers, adding sweaters as they proceeded into the polar seas. The expedition was fiercely resented by Sir Clements Markham, president of the Royal Geographical Society in London, who accused the Scots of a 'mischievous rivalry' with Robert Falcon Scott's first *Discovery* voyage, which had sailed the year before.

But the first *Scotia* had no plan of polar conquest. She spent her time in the sensible activity of sounding the Weddell Sea and setting straight mistakes on British Admiralty charts. She fished the sea to see what was in it. Almost 200 trawls were hauled aboard, one from three miles deep. Twenty months after leaving the port of Troon, *Scotia* returned, bringing back a collection of Arctic marine invertebrates that remained unmatched for many years. This was the tradition that produced, a century later, a ship costing £24 million and the £10,000 a day it takes to keep her at sea.

We went up the North Sea in a nasty chop until we reached latitude fifty-seven degrees and seventeen minutes North, opposite the tip of the Orkneys. It was the middle of the night. Dunn and the scientific party bundled up in orange boiler suits and fanned out on to the hangar deck. Pam Walsham wore a Santa Claus hat pulled down over her plastic helmet. Sarah Hughes, an oceanographer, scowled at a rack of bottles. An engineer named Martin Burns, a man with seraphic aplomb, poked a screwdriver at a troublesome fluorometer. A fluorometer pays its way by emitting rapid-fire bursts of green light that excite the phytoplankton into a reciprocal fluorescence. Phytoplankton is the base plant-matter of the sea, and the measurement of its fluorescence allows an extrapolation of the total biomass. The fluorometer was bolted to a white-painted metal cage with a carousel of twelve grey plastic cylinders. The cylinders snap shut at either end to capture water samples to be tested later for conductivity, temperature, and density—hence the device's name, CTD.

That night and the next day we made our way along the stations of a sampling line that has been monitored for forty years. Ocean scientists parse the sea along scores of such transects. The data collected is freely available and often the product of international cooperation. We were one of a trio of ships acting in concert to investigate the possible collapse of the Atlantic thermohaline circulation. 'Thermohaline' defines a system driven by both temperature and salinity—the critical drivers of the ocean's circulation. The other two ships were the *Hudson*, a Canadian oceanographic vessel at work in the Labrador Sea, and *Discovery*, a British ship out of Southampton that was having her legs kicked from under her by weather in the mid-Atlantic. Our mission lay in the seaways of the north-east Atlantic, and two days out of Aberdeen we steamed past Fair Isle and made a course for the Faeroes.

The ocean is composed of different masses of water distinguished by temperature and salinity, and therefore density. These masses are amazingly discrete, and can slide over and beneath and between each other without yielding their characteristics, like the blobs of a giant lava lamp. It is a system of some grandeur. Water from the North Atlantic, for example, may find its way into an abyssal drift that will channel it here and there in the deep ocean so that, by the time it surfaces in the North Pacific, its journey will have taken a thousand years. In other places, huge volumes of water pour through the ocean at astonishing speed. The Gulf Stream moves along the surface at sixty-five million cubic metres per second—a flow equivalent to one hundred times the water disgorged by the Amazon river as it drains the greatest watershed on earth. When the Gulf Stream reaches the Flemish Cap, an ocean feature east of the Grand Banks, it divides into two currents. One of these, the Azores Current, turns west towards Newfoundland and Labrador, while the other, the North Atlantic Current, continues northward past the British Isles at twenty-five million cubic metres per second, delivering, as it has for 10,000 years, a trillion kilowatts of heat into the air. As warm water flows north, a mass of cold water called the North Atlantic Deep Water flows south through the dark ocean at depths below two kilometres. This exchange of warm water for cold is called the meridional overturning circulation, and if it stops, God help Britain; the islands' supply of benign weather is generated by an engine of winds and ocean currents of which this mighty loop is a crucial part.

There are two places in the ocean where warm water changes into cold—the Labrador Sea and the Greenland Sea. Oceanographers call these sites 'pumps', because they drive the overturning circulation. What happens is that warm water flows in at the surface, cools and becomes more saline, and is thus made denser. This denser water sinks, piles up behind the dense, cold water that is already there, and ultimately pushes that bottom water southward over the sills of the Greenland–Scotland Ridge and into the deep Atlantic, ventilating the abyss with a fresh supply of salty, cold water and driving the overturning circulation. Now there is evidence that the Greenland Pump is failing. If it is, proof will be found in the Faeroe–Shetland Channel, and late one night we began a sampling run across the strait.

The Faeroe–Shetland Channel is an intensely studied waterway. In its currents the ocean is printing news about our future, and we must keep up on the latest bulletins. The channel also provides an example of how swiftly changes in the ocean can affect life—in this case, a hardy little water bug whose antecedents have been sleeping in the channel for 10,000 years.

A link between the copepod *Calanus finmarchicus* and the cold water flowing south to the abyss had been hypothesized but unproven until 1993, when an Aberdeen marine biologist named Mike Heath took up the offer of free ship-time from a German colleague, and they hurried out into the strait and lowered a plankton net. 'It was very exciting,' Heath recalled, 'because we thought that's where they wintered, but you never know until you find them.'

Because *Calanus* eats phytoplankton, it must rest in the winter, when there is none. It cannot remain in the warmer surface water, where its metabolism would continue to fire away at its normal, frenetic speed and burn up all the animal's stored fat. So the copepod must find a cold place to sleep away the winter months. The deep water is that place.

It is impossible to sail on a ship where people study copepods without becoming fascinated by the creatures. Take the way they mate. After slumbering through December and January at a depth of 800 metres, the animals begin to stir. 'The first ones to wake,' says Heath, 'moult [physically alter] to adult males and start to swim upwards, but they stop at around 400 metres below the surface and sit there in a layer. As time progresses, an increasing proportion of the animals that wake up moult into females, and these swim right on up to the surface—through the layer of males. We assume that the males are lying in wait for the females and ambush them on their way to the surface.'

By March, hosts of *Calanus* drift through the Faeroe–Shetland Channel into the north-east Atlantic, completing a month-long ascent to the surface waters. At the surface the animal meets different currents. One of these is the Continental Slope Jet Current, which, together with the North Atlantic Current, carries warm water north. Branches of the Continental Slope Jet peel away into the North Sea. A copepod lives for only six months, so it is a swarm of newborns that rides the current into the North Sea food chain—or used to ride it.

Mike Heath's theory was that given the collapse in the North Sea population of *Calanus*, there should be a correspondingly smaller number of them upstream in the bottom waters of the Faeroe–Shetland Channel. This proved to be so, inviting a further hypothesis that the drop in numbers might mean that their habitat had shrunk; that there was less cold, deep water in the channel than there had been before. That too turned out to be true, encouraging the supposition that declining copepods in the deep strait spelled the failure of the ultimate source of their habitat water—the Greenland Pump.

Since distinct water masses are found at different depths, and copepods prefer, depending on the time of year, only one of these water masses, it is important to know where you are getting the creatures from if part of your interest lies in knowing how much of that water there is. This requirement—getting planktonic animals out of the ocean and knowing where they were when you caught them—demands quite complicated plankton-capturing rigs, and it was one of these, called ARIES, that *Scotia*'s deckhands swung out into the water of the Faeroe–Shetland Channel.

One night I stood with John Dunn on the trawl deck, waiting for ARIES to be hauled back up. A fifteen-foot sea was running through the strait. Rigs on the Western Frontier oil field glittered in the distance. ARIES burst from the sea, streaming water as the crane swung it up and on to the deck. Dunn quickly stripped away bits of gear to get to the heart of the apparatus—a reel loaded with tiny nets, rigged to open and close in sequence, gulping in mouthfuls of plankton at regular intervals. He unbolted the reel and carried it inside to the lab. The nets were fastened on with Velcro, and one by one we pulled them off.

Dunn shook his head at the poverty of the catch. Each net is about the size of a two-year-old's sock, and even looks like a child's garment, silky and soft and white. As net after net came off the reel empty, the pile of discarded nets began to look forlorn. Finally we found a net stained with the pale pink jam of copepods. 'There, now,' rumbled Dunn, 'that's typical copepod. Nothing, nothing, nothing, then a whole layer of them.'

He finished rinsing the nets, loaded the reel again, and went back on deck to prepare the sampler for the next station. Dunn invented ARIES, and I asked him why he'd called it that. 'Auto-Recording Instrumented Environmental Sampler,' he reeled off.

'Quite a mouthful.'

'Aye,' said Dunn, his hands shoved into the pockets of his greasy boiler suit. Another wave rolled by on its way to Norway. 'Actually,' said Dunn, stroking a steel brace with his palm, 'if you want to know the truth I named it that because it's my birth sign.'

ARIES is an open frame of large and small plankton nets, water-sampling bottles, fluorometer, optical plankton-counter, and a thing called a transmissometer that counts every speck of matter it can find, and gives you the total. ARIES looks clumsy, but is not. The moment it hits the waves it straightens out, like a diver suddenly remembering to point his toes, and buries its face in the sea for a perfect ten. Dunn's pride in it is natural. But the best invention of Dunn is Dunn—chief scientist on a cruise that will cost £140,000, yet he has no science degree. He has no degree at all. He dropped out of university, took a train to Aberdeen, and the first job he saw in the paper was at the Marine Laboratory. He's been there ever since, inventing masses of gadgets. It's what you'd expect from a man whose hobby is fixing steam tractors, and who once drove a twelve-and-a-half-ton Foden steam lorry from Aberdeen to Chester-le-Street, in County Durham, a distance of 398 miles. The journey took two days, a ton and a half of coal and 9,000 gallons of water.

The plankton-capturing game requires a similar attachment to the arcane. It is full of minutely specified demands, such as porosity. Plankton nets have a very fine mesh, and the size of this mesh must remain the same even when the net is being stretched by the pull of water. The nets on ARIES are made of a polyester so rigidly specified that the supplier is a Swiss medical-equipment manufacturer. The porosity is regularly checked by a machine that examines every rectangle of space between the polyester strands, measuring it to the thousandth of an inch.

On the morning of our third day out the Faeroes hardened into sight to port. We were steaming north along the east coast of the islands. As we drew past a headland, the lights of Torshavn, the capital, winked into view along the shore. An hour later we reached the first station in a sampling run that would take us back across the channel towards Muckle Flugga, the northernmost tip of Shetland.

The day was marvellously soft. A seaman appeared on the hangar deck in shorts. We were sixty miles from the Arctic Circle, yet the temperature was five degrees Celsius. At these same latitudes, we later learned, the Canadian ship *Hudson* was turning out all hands to chop away sixty tons of ice that had formed on the superstructure. The Canadians were in the Labrador Sea while we were in the balmy climate of the North Atlantic Current.

The Marine Laboratory in Aberdeen possesses an important set of ocean data. For a hundred years its scientists have monitored the ocean at hundreds of points, including sampling lines, weather buoys, the cruises of a succession of oceanographic ships, and instruments placed in the ocean. An array of four such instruments lies across a deep channel south-west of the Faeroe Shelf, between the shelf and a height to the south called the Faeroe Bank.

This small, deep gap is of great interest to oceanographers, because through it passes most of the cold water flowing south into the Atlantic from the production of the Greenland Pump. The instruments placed on the bottom are summoned to the surface twice a year by means of an acoustic signal, and their data collected. In 1995 a pair of oceanographers—Bogi Hansen of the Faeroe Fishery Laboratory and Bill Turrell of the Aberdeen lab—noticed changes in the water below 800 metres. The water was warming and freshening.

For the pump to work, extremely large volumes of salty water must cool and sink. If the water is not salty enough, it will not be dense enough to sink. Salinity and cold operate in tandem to give the water density. The seabed sills of the Greenland–Scotland Ridge present a barrier to the movement of cold bottom water south into the Atlantic. Even the Faeroe Bank gap, although deeper than elsewhere on the ridge, is not as deep as the basin north of it. For cold water to leave this basin and exit south into the Atlantic, it must have enough force of dense, sinking water piling up behind it to drive it over the sill into the Atlantic. Although some cold water slops over the ridge in the Denmark Strait, between Greenland and Iceland, and a smaller amount gets through the seaway between Iceland and the Faeroes, the deep, narrow channel of the Faeroe Bank gap is the principal drain for bottom water from the northern seas. When Hansen and Turrell noticed the declining salinity in the gap, then, they naturally wondered whether the drop signalled a weakening of the pump. They would have to measure the flow of water to find out.

This is not as easy as it sounds, because the cold, dense water produced by the Greenland Pump needed to be identified and measured separately from the rest of the water moving in the channel. Warm water, for example, would be flowing north in the upper layers while cold flowed south below. Moreover, other cold water masses *not* produced by the pump would also be moving through the gap. On repeated voyages, Hansen and Turrell and their team took samples from the water column at many points in the channel. They developed a detailed cross section of the current, as if they had taken slices out of the moving water. This gave them the area in square metres of the different water masses at several points in the gap.

Multiplying the area of the bottom water by the current speed in the channel, they established that 1.5 million cubic metres per second of the cold, salty water produced by the pump was flowing through the gap. Five years later, in 2000, that flow had dropped by five per cent—in ocean terms, a very swift plunge.

It was a thunderclap of a discovery, but an enormous 'if' hung over it. The trend would be significant (for north-western Europe, catastrophic) *if* the decline in cold-water production was a steady drop over time, and not just a five-year blip soon to be reversed by another heave of the ocean's shoulders. Turrell and Hansen had a mass of data at their disposal, including, most importantly, fifty years of salinity records from Ocean Weather Station Mike, a weather ship at the edge of the Norwegian Basin. Hansen designed a mathematical model based on Mike's salinity measurements from 1950 to 1990, and asked the model to predict what would happen in the next five years. The result of the model almost perfectly matched the actual measured decrease in flow, pointing to the conclusion that the decline in the Pump's production over five years was part of a longer trend, and not an anomaly. Underlining this, the model indicated that since 1950 the flow had declined by twenty-five per cent. In the scale of planetary time, events were moving at a blur.

As the Canadian vessel *Hudson* hacked away ice and returned to Nova Scotia, the *Scotia*'s other partner, the *Discovery*, was having trouble keeping her feet in the seaway. Gales swept the mid-Atlantic stations she was sampling and in the rough conditions the crew dropped several hundred thousand pounds' worth of oceanographic gear over the side and could not retrieve it. 'Ach, that bloody boat,' a *Scotia* crewman snorted at the news. 'She rolls in wet grass.' Because of *Discovery*'s difficulties, she could not complete her sampling, and it fell to the Scottish ship to run out into the Atlantic south of Iceland and make her way along the stations of a line called the Atlantic Transect.

The next morning we came into the broad ocean. The sky cleared and the waves rose and we batted along at thirteen knots. 'Did you see those juvenile glaucous gulls?' asked Mick at breakfast. 'They have the lovely gold flakes all along their backs. There's always some of the glaucous about. You can pick 'em out from the herring gulls because they're so white you can see right through 'em. That's how you know they're the glaucous. *Larus hyberboreus*. All the gulls are *Larus*. It's the Latin. The kittiwakes are *Rissa tridactyla*, on account of they have three toes.'

The sampling line lay on a west-south-westerly course from Faeroe Bank out into the Iceland Basin. On the morning of December 13, the sixth day of our voyage, we were steaming across a calm sea, with a pale blue sky and scattered cloud. Porpoises appeared to starboard. They leapt along in bursts of white spray, about thirty of them keeping up with the ship for five minutes, and then diving off through the green Atlantic. *Rissa tridactyla* hurtled past on a bombing run. I left all this and went down to the lower deck to visit Sarah Hughes, the lone crew member banished to the hold. The ocean hissed by on the other side of the hull as I stepped from a companionway into the oily, echoing space. Hughes's portable steel lab stood by itself, an outpost of bright light in the green fluorescence. The sound of Ladysmith Black Mambazo spilled out as I opened the door.

Hughes was a short, irrepressible woman in her early thirties, with flyaway, dark-blonde hair and blue eyes. A pair of oval spectacles perched on her nose. She had a large arsenal of opinions, such as on what people should eat, a subject rich in opportunity on a ship whose cooks sent out a steady shuttle of deep-fried food, and where no meal was complete without the final, thudding appearance of some peculiarly British kind of cake, made of bread or sponge and set adrift in a bowl of yellow custard. Watching her shipmates wade into this while she picked at a plate of withered grapes, Hughes would happily proclaim, 'You're going to *die*.'

Hughes sat for hours at a time in her steel container in the hold, processing the hundreds of water samples collected along the way to see how much salt they contained. The machine for reading salinity needs a constant, cool environment, and Hughes bundled up in fleeces against the draught from the air conditioning. The little pump that pulled salt water through the machine made a steady whee-whee-whee sound. 'It drives you crazy,' said Hughes. 'It sounds like that character in *The Fly* going "Help me! Help me! Help me!" I usually have on louder music, like Stone Angel or Pixies, and I yell away along with the beat. No one can hear me in here.'

Salinity is described in parts per thousand, and the variations are small. The freshening of deep water southward through the Faeroe Bank channel was .02 in twenty years. Put another way, it took twenty years to lighten the load of a litre of water by .02 milligrams of dissolved salts. I sat there with Hughes's clipboard as we talked, and jotted down the numbers she called out. Bottle 481: 34.8967; bottle 482: 34.8881; bottle 483: 34.8978. At sea, Hughes spent hours staring into the salinometer and filling page after page with rows of pencilled digits. It is a far cry from the image of the oceanographer as Jacques Cousteau, splashing over the side of a white yacht into a turquoise bay. Yet Hughes's own passion for the sea comes from exactly that kind of experience. Her parents ran a diving school in Wales, where Hughes met summer-hire students who were specializing in marine biology. She became a ferocious advocate of the sea around her. 'I love to dive in the UK. Sometimes the visibility is almost zero, but the life is fantastic. When I first met my partner, he was just back from Saudi Arabia, and he was talking about how great the diving was, and I said, "Rubbish! It's much better here!"'

Later we climbed to the computer room on the upper deck. Hughes sat down and called up a series of slides that showed the ocean currents. The cold water from the Faeroe Bank flowed into an enthralling maze of currents that wandered through the seas, looping under Africa and into the Indian Ocean. There, the ocean streams carved an arabesque before sweeping back westward past the Cape of Good Hope, and entering the Atlantic to flow north again. 'I find it amazing,' Hughes said.

The weather affects these currents, freshening them with rainfall and bending them with wind. In turn the currents affect the weather, heating the atmosphere and cooling it. Like the workings of a clock, this system has ticked away with comforting regularity; but it needn't. The climate can turn on a dime. Evidence from ice cores and the sediment layer shows that rapid climate change was normal in the earth's past, and that the present interglacial period has had unusually stable weather. This is not the rule, but the exception.

Even in our own stable period the climate has wobbled. In 1410 a London chronicler recorded that, 'Thys yere was the grete frost and ise and the most sharpest wenter that ever man sawe, and it duryd fourteen wekes so that men might in divers places goo and ryde over the Temse.' In the Little Ice Age of 1550–1850, Europe suffered five separate periods of suddenly much colder winter weather. Londoners skated on the Thames. In the harsh winters of 1855, 1861, 1869, 1879 and 1886, food shortages led to bread riots in the British capital. I thought of this in January 2003, when torrential rains that had been flooding the south-east of England turned to snow. Roads around the country seized with gridlock. At the worst of the snow the Automobile Association was struggling to cope with 2,000 accidents an hour. Some railway lines closed. Parts of the London Underground shut down. Stories immediately appeared in the press about a new ice age heading Britain's way.

In 2001 the British government launched a six-year study of rapid, and abrupt, climate change. The main focus of the study was the overturning circulation of the Atlantic. One of the first experiments in the project was conducted by Richard Wood at the Meteorological Office's Hadley Centre for Climate Prediction and Research. Wood is a climate scientist who runs a model of the Atlantic Ocean.

Climate models are either simple or complex. A simple model will manipulate only a few variables. A famous example created by Hank Stommel of the Woods Hole Oceanographic Institution, in Massachusetts, reduced the overturning circulation to its most basic constituents—fresh water and salt water. Stommel mathematically added fresh water, and kept adding it until something happened. He demonstrated that at a certain point the circulation jumps straight into a new state—failure. It does not really slow down; it just stops.

Models like Stommel's are meant to help scientists think about problems, not to make predictions. There are other models for that, called General Circulation Models, which crunch large packages of data and produce conjectures for climate change. At the Hadley Centre in Berkshire, Wood ran such a model.

'We dumped a whole lot of fresh water into the North Atlantic to see what would happen,' Wood said. 'We shut down the system— the overturning circulation. When you lose that heat [from the Gulf Stream] you get a strong cooling. The thing that surprised me was that it's not just over western Europe that you see the change, but the whole of the northern hemisphere. Basically, the Atlantic Ocean loses all that heat, and the atmosphere whizzes that effect around the world. So within a few years of the circulation turning off, the whole northern hemisphere was significantly cooling.'

For the British Isles, the modelled effect of the shutdown of the overturning circulation was a cooling of between three to five degrees Celsius. Such a drop would be the steepest plunge in mean temperature in the last 8,000 years, duplicating some of the temperatures of the last ice age. This would have a devastating effect on what scientists call Net Primary Production—the vegetation of the earth. North of the Amazon river the rainforest would die away. For western Europe much would change.

As I write, at the end of April, it is bluebell time in Kent: the hillsides of the Weald are aglow. At Sissinghurst thousands of visitors take the Easter air among the tulips and euphorbia, and the last of the daffodils blaze through the grass. Yet in the farmland of upstate

New York, of Vermont, Ontario and Quebec, at latitudes far south of England, the last of the winter snow is falling. The ocean helps to deal such cards, and can reshuffle the deck. In Wood's modelling of the shutdown, snow cover in north-western and central Europe would stay in place a month or two longer. Not only would the weather get colder, but drier too. The models have not predicted all the possible consequences, but it is not hard to posit crop failure, a disruption of the food supply, and a swift rise in the price of what we eat. If winter suddenly became colder and longer, people would need more energy to heat homes and industry. Some businesses would crumble and unemployment would rise. In the warmth of an April day in Kent, the paradox of a global warming that would produce, in some regions, colder weather, seems especially cruel; the hills of the Weald would wait longer for the bluebells, if they came at all.

Predictions about long-term weather are always tentative. Climate scientists do not all agree on what might happen, only that something will. Richard Wood rates the chances of the collapse of the overturning circulation as low-probability, but admits he does not know *how* low. His analysis did not include a guess at the likelihood of this happening. One of the difficulties in assessing the odds is that the threshold of collapse remains unknown. Imperfectly understood systems such as the North Atlantic Oscillation—a see-saw of high and low pressure that takes place over decades—form part of the calculation. But so does man. Only a halfwit would deny our role in global warming. A graph prepared by the Intergovernmental Panel on Climate Change shows the atmospheric levels of carbon dioxide, methane, and nitrous oxide staying the same from AD 1000 to 1800, whereupon they begin to rise, finally shooting upwards at the end of the millennium: 1998 was the hottest year ever recorded; 2002, the second hottest. Nine of the ten hottest days have occurred in the last ten years. The 1990s was easily the hottest decade in a century, and possibly in a thousand years.

The Greenland ice cap is now calving chunks of freshwater ice into the northern seas at an accelerated rate. It is one of the reasons that the top 1.5 kilometres of water in the seas around the Greenland Pump have freshened rapidly. This freshening robs the pump of its salty power, and it is a fresher, weaker current that courses through the Faeroe–Shetland Channel.

From Faeroe Bank the water sweeps westward over the top of the Iceland Basin. On the way, it entrains some of the resident water mass, taking it on a long journey south around the tip of the Reykjanes Ridge before flowing back north to the Irminger Sea. There it collects the cold-water overflow from the Denmark Strait, which is also freshening. This river of icy water curves around Greenland and descends the Greenland slope into the abyssal reaches of the Labrador Sea. The deep layers of the Labrador Sea have been freshening too. The blobs in the lava lamp are losing some of their ancient characteristics.

'Other observations confirm,' Turrell and five other oceanographers wrote in *Nature* last year, 'that the deep and abyssal freshening we describe has already passed equatorward along the North American seaboard in the Deep Western Boundary Current... With "new and stronger" evidence of anthropogenic warming, coupled climate models seem to be reaching some kind of consensus that a slowdown of North Atlantic Deep Water production and of the meridional overturning circulation will be one outcome.'

O n the morning of our eleventh day at sea we came out of the Atlantic on to the inshore stations of the western shelf. A red sun rose behind the Outer Hebrides, veiled by masses of purple cloud. The sea turned a hazy mauve. The lights of little villages pricked the still-dark shore. All along the coast the numbers of *Calanus finmarchicus* were in retreat—a sad census, the poignant sight of those few, tender bodies beneath the microscope.

Four days later the *Scotia* completed the last of a spider's web of sampling runs east of the Shetlands and set her course for Aberdeen. The scientific crew bustled about packing equipment and scrubbing down the labs. I helped Sarah Hughes lug a few crates of water samples up to the hangar deck. She got a mop and headed back down to swab the place out for whoever would use it next.

We came into Aberdeen on the night of December 21 and tied up below the town. Christmas music floated down to the quay. In the morning Hughes brought her daughters, aged five and three, on to the ship when she came to say goodbye to me. They were jumping with excitement at having their mother back, and as they went down the shaky gangway, taking the giant steps bravely, the younger one paused and looked back with a child's perfect, wolfish grin. I watched them go, Hughes and her partner and the children, piling into the car with all the bustle of a young family and driving off down the quay and out of sight. I knew I would miss her passion for the world around her, and her fiery insistence on what is happening to it.

Wishful thinking was the enemy. She told me once, 'What amazes me is this kind of thing: I give a talk to the Salmon Trust—landowners, fishermen—and they have hopes that they can make things go back to the way they were. They own salmon rivers. They have memories of their youth, when they could go out and catch big salmon. They remember what things were like when they were young, and they want them that way again. And I try to say, our climate is going to change, and change *quickly*, one way or another, and human influence has caused the change to happen faster. There were other speakers, and they were telling them how everything was going to be okay. I was last, and I said, everything's *not* going to be okay.' □

GRANTA

THE EVIDENCE
OF MAN
Edward Burtynsky

Text by Noah Richler

Edward Burtynsky

In 2001, I travelled with Edward Burtynsky to the beaches of Chittagong, in Bangladesh, where many of the world's old freighters go to die.

I'd seen Burtynsky's work in a Toronto gallery the year before, coveting one of his pictures there, of an abandoned stone quarry in Vermont, filled with water the colour of jade. I remember scrutinizing the details of it for several minutes, peering up close, before convincing myself that it was not a painting.

This was Burtynsky's second trip to Chittagong. On his first trip, briefer than he would have liked, he had photographed the Bangladeshi workers cutting up the ships, some as large as 60,000 tons, with little more than hammers, and acetylene torches— remarkable, Lilliputian, work. Now he had come back to document with more rigour the process of the ships' slow fragmentation: from complete, seaworthy vessels, beached a half mile out in the mud, to scrap small enough for boys and men to carry away to the waiting trucks which would transport it to Chittagong's 're-rolling mills', there to be melted and forged into new shapes for the house-building trade. All the fittings, from brass clocks to cornflakes packets, will be taken away and sold.

Carrying a tripod on his shoulder, with a couple of local assistants scurrying after him with gear, Burtynsky looked a solitary figure as he picked a careful path through the monumental sections of freighter standing dismembered on the beach. In the haze of early morning, his best light, he was searching for a suitable vantage point for his large format cameras—wanting, as he has done his whole working life, to record the often mesmerizing situation of man's industry in nature. He insists there is no moral aspect to his work, and would rather you not call it documentary. He is interested, he says, in the 'industrial sublime'.

'I find it extraordinary that something as mundane as a bridge or a chunk of ship on a beach can appear otherworldly as well,' Burtynsky told me. 'In my mind, that ambiguity underlines how our society has become disconnected from our industrial roots. We don't know where our food comes from anymore, where our cars are made, or where our jets get fixed, so a whole part of our experience appears abnormal.'

Edward Burtynsky's parents, Ukrainian immigrants to Canada, arrived after the Second World War in St Catherine's Ontario, where

Burtynsky's father found good paying work at the General Motors plant. An amateur photographer, he gave his son his first camera when he was eleven. Burtynsky would use it to photograph machinery when the factory had open days, and his father would take the family to see where he worked.

The Welland Canal was nearby. Burtynsky would cycle to its banks and barter cigarettes for souvenirs from Polish and Russian sailors who waved from the decks of the enormous 'lakers', ships that carried freight through the Saint Lawrence Seaway to the Great Lakes and inland ports in Canada and the United States. Their scale, he says, astonished him. Later, when he was studying at art college in Toronto, he'd come home to photograph the first—and now bypassed and abandoned—Welland Canal, its old locks and industrial detritus. He called his project 'The Evidence of Man.'

'It made me think about what happens when man has finished with something, then walks away. There's a kind of melancholic disintegration there, as nature begins its work of pulling that thing back into the ground. When I'm photographing something in the industrial landscape, I'm looking at whatever is that residual thing.'

Burtynsky went on to photograph quarries in Vermont, railway cuts in Western Canada, rivers of tailings from a Sudbury nickel factory, oil refineries, and packets of densified oil drums and tin cans in the steel-making city of Hamilton. Human activity is in these photographs but it is ghostly, and implied by what isn't there—the departed stone that has left cubist shapes in the quarries, the food that was once inside the thousands of compressed tin cans. He visited the marble quarries of Carrara in Italy and the oilfields of California and then he found his most ambitious project—China's Three Gorges Dam and the massive, unprecedented, relocation of whole cities, brick by brick, that its construction has required.

As he worked with his camera in Chittagong, a line of shipbreaking workers walked past us barefoot in the oily muck. Burtynsky pointed out that the beach was rife with toxic waste. He took his shot, packed his camera and then, in passing, he told me that his father had died of cancer, aged forty-six. He died, as a number of GM workers did, Burtynsky said, because he spent his days in a plant where he was exposed to cancer-causing polychlorinated byphenyls. 'Already I've lived longer than my father has,' he said. □

Railcuts #1, Canadian
National track,
Skihist Provincial Park,
British Columbia

Railcuts #4, Canadian
National track,
Thompson River,
British Columbia

Rock of Ages #15,
Active Granite Section,
E. L Smith Quarry,
Barre, Vermont

Mines #22,
Kennecott Copper Mine,
Bingham Valley,
Utah

Makrana Marble
Quarries #13,
Rajasthan,
India

Mines #13,
Inco Abandoned Mine
Shaft, Crean Hill Mine,
Sudbury, Ontario

Nickel Tailings #30, Sudbury, Ontario

Uranium tailings #12, Elliot Lake, Ontario

Densified
Tin Cans #2,
Hamilton,
Ontario

Densified
Scrap Metals #3a,
Hamilton,
Ontario

Telephones #21,
Hamilton,
Ontario

Oxford Tyre Pile #8,
Westley,
California

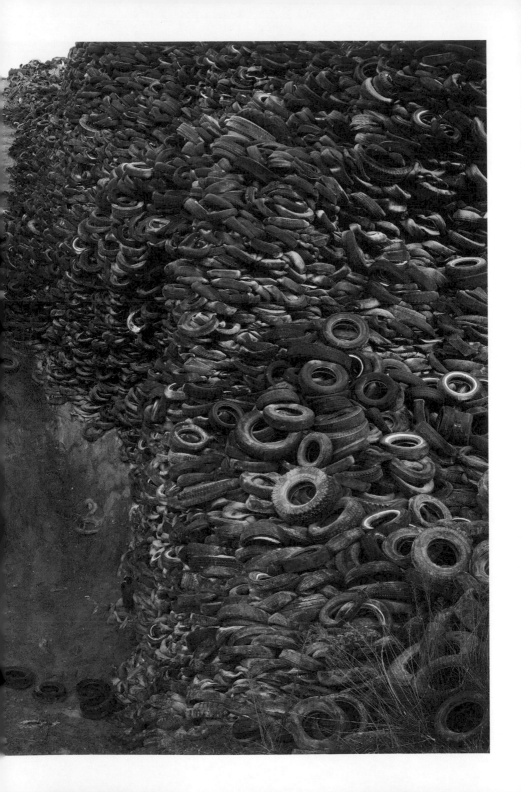

Shipbreaking #13,
Chittagong,
Bangladesh

Oil Fields #2,
Belridge,
California

Three Gorges Dam
Project, Wan Zhou #2,
Yangtze River, China,
November 2002

GRANTA

CAPTAIN SCOTT'S BISCUIT

Thomas Keneally

Terra Nova Bay, 1911

I first went to Antarctica in 1968, for somewhat under a fortnight. In those days one could visit Antarctica only as a member of an official group, and the American ambassador in Canberra, a noble soul who would later give his life to a disease caught while working for an Episcopalian aid agency in Ethiopia, invited me to go with him, as a member of his party. He was also taking his twelve-year-old son, whom he hoped would become the youngest person ever to stand at the South Pole itself. I am forever grateful to this man, the sober and genial Bill Crook, through whom I was able to experience Antarctica in so profound a way that it recurred in my dreams for decades to come. In particular, the huge Transantarctic Mountains, complicated peaks and glaciers which start behind Cape Adare on the northern limit of the Ross Sea and run south across the continent, returned to me in sleep. Scott's own beloved and much researched Royal Society Range, visible from the bases across McMurdo Sound, are just one part of this transcendent chain.

Another companion on the 1968 trip was a young US Air Force colonel named Alex Butterfield. We and Mr Crook and his son shared the giant landscapes and improbable, barely polluted vistas of Antarctica. Only at McMurdo Sound was there any garbage, including a litter of crashed aircraft piled up on the edge of the tide crack's jumbled ice. While Antarctica seems apolitical, and was and still is managed, apparently fraternally, according to principles framed by the 1959 Antarctic Treaty, political realities foreshortened our 1968 journey a little. Nixon was elected President, and Bill Crook, a Democrat, needed to resign his position in Canberra, while Alex Butterfield would go to Nixon's White House as deputy assistant to the President, and would have a not inestimable part in the Watergate scandal. When asked by the Senate Watergate Committee whether there were any recording devices in the White House, he said he had hoped he would not be asked that, but admitted there were tapes, and so, with a word, changed history and became a Republican Party pariah.

But none of this happened before the Crook group had experienced the bulk of Ross Island, that historic mass in McMurdo Sound which is cemented to the rest of Antarctica by the Ross Ice Shelf, an august shelf of ice the size of France. Nor before we had visited Scott's two huts—one of them on the edge of the McMurdo

Sound station—and Shackleton's haunted Cape Royds hut, and lived beneath the midnight sun, and been to the South Pole on a plane which landed and took off on skids. And at that featureless, 10,000-feet-high South Pole, the younger Crook stood, suffering from mild altitude sickness; a sturdy lad though, who did not flinch in the glare of the polar plateau. We lined up around the striped barber's pole which had been put in place during the International Geophysical Year (IGY), ten years before. In that decade, it had moved a little off ninety degrees south. The great ice sheet covering the Pole was always moving infinitesimally outwards down to the sea.

This trip augmented a tendency of mine to see Antarctica as another state of being. Nobody was a native of the place. Only in the past sixty or seventy years had a scatter of human myths become associated with it. But even in its massiveness it had made no tribe unto itself. It had provoked no native tongue, no rites, no art, no jingoism. Its landscapes existed without the permission of humanity. And everything I looked at, even the nullity of the pole, produced jolts of insomniac chemicals into my system. It was not landscape, it was not light. It was super-landscape, super-light, and it would not let you sleep.

In 1968, among all the science and bulldozers and energy of the McMurdo Sound station, no one seemed to be doing much for the huts of the 'heroic age'. On the northern point of the bay in which McMurdo Sound station stood, unattended, Scott's Hut Point hut, the *Discovery* hut. This hut had been used by Scott's 1901–04 party, and been pressed into use again by Shackleton in 1908, and then once more during Scott's journey to the Pole in 1910–12. During the First World War, Shackleton's tragic Ross Sea party had sheltered in it as well. Symbolizing all this Antarctic peril undertaken willingly, a cross on the small hill above the hut commemorated Seaman Vince, one of Scott's men, who perished of hypothermia in 1902.

Standing utterly unlocked in 1968, the hut was sunk in its old, ice-dried timbers in a bank of ice. There was accumulated ice inside sections of the hut as well, but also the remnants of Edwardian derring-do: boxes of Fry's cocoa, preserved fruit, condiments, tins of Huntley & Palmers biscuits, items of harness, old magazines and fragments of newspapers. There was no organization taking responsibility for Scott's huts at Hut Point and Cape Evans, or for Shackleton's at Cape Royds.

Those who took anything out of any of the huts could excuse themselves in the belief that they were merely saving a relic from gradual climatic destruction. Thus, glibly self-absolved, I approached an open tin of Huntley & Palmers hard-tack biscuit, the hard tack which soldiers from 1914 to 1918 ate in the trenches. I took two thirds of a biscuit as a souvenir. Antarctic explorers, including Scott and his doomed four, subsisted on a diet of this biscuit, often mixed with and softened by water and pemmican, that is, chunks of compacted, dried meat. These staples, hard tack and pemmican, proved an inadequate diet, and helped weaken the young Shackleton to the point that Scott sent him home from the 1901 expedition. Ultimately, the limitations of pemmican and hard tack would stop Shackleton ninety-seven miles from the Pole in 1909, and then destroy Scott himself in 1912.

The two thirds of a biscuit I took, hard to begin with when manufactured in the late nineteenth or early twentieth century, had been near ossified by Antarctica's perpetual freeze. So I brought it home with me as if it were more a fossil than a food, and displayed it, in a glass case.

It has only been as time went by that I, like other members of the general public, became educated by an increasing awareness of conservation. I began to feel Scott's biscuit should be returned. I saw the 1985 television series, *The Last Place on Earth*, and the scenes of Scott's big man, Petty Officer Taffy Evans, raving and howling in the wake of the sledge returning from the Pole, and dying in his tracks. For a second it was as if he was making a claim on my biscuit. But to whom to return the hard tack, and by what mechanism? I decided I would take it back to the hut myself, if ever I got to Antarctica again.

The resolve to return to Antarctica grew in me as I got older. Some friends went on a Russian ship from Ushaia in Argentina down to the Antarctic Peninsula. The Peninsula is the Antarctic continent's tadpole tail, and has beautiful glaciers and hence beautiful mountains, and much subantarctic wildlife. But it is not beyond the Antarctic Circle, and is on the wrong side of Antarctica for anything to do with Scott. I decided last year I would try to go anyway. Ships commonly used in these excursions are ice-breaking or hull-strengthened Russian vessels chartered by American, Australian and other adventure-travel companies. These companies came up readily on the Internet. I found that journeys from South America to the Peninsula and to South Georgia, the island on which Shackleton is buried, are largely booked up a year ahead, and it was only by accident that I discovered that journeys to the other side of Antarctica, to the area I felt I knew and from which I'd taken Scott's biscuit—the Ross Sea, McMurdo Sound, Ross Island, the great volcano Erebus, the Transantarctic Mountains and the Ross Ice Shelf which was the path to the Pole—were also planned.

I found there was a berth available on the last trip for the summer season, throughout February, on an ice-breaker named the *Kapitan Khlebnikov*.

I fell for the *Khlebnikov* the first time I saw a picture of it. It had an honest look, as if one would not need to dress for dinner—indeed the sort of ship on which there would be a good, rowdy bar operating during Antarctic midnights, as well as ample deck-space upon which to stand alone, rugged-up, in awe and exaltation. It weighed 12,000 tons and its bows were blunt and potent for crushing fields of ice. Its high castle, in which the cabins were placed, would guarantee that on the way to and beyond the Antarctic convergence, the zone of turbulence where Antarctic waters meet the waters of temperate oceans, we would experience a testing roll. Six Zodiacs were lashed down on the flight deck to take us to shore, and two helicopters. Its eighty crew members abounded with Arctic and Antarctic experience. This stubby, twenty-year-old ice-breaker promised to deal with the great radial skirts of ice which gird Antarctica.

So I was still in a childlike state of excitement as we drove through the tunnel in the mountain south of Christchurch, in New Zealand's South Island, and came down to Lyttelton, the exquisite, emerald, volcanic caldera which served Scott and Shackleton as their point of departure for the voyage south. Through a banal, corrugated iron fence at the bunkering wharf of Lyttelton we lugged our luggage with half smiles, like children entering a secret garden. Stepping over oil hoses, we climbed the stairs from the wharf to our ice-breaker. The air was filled with the shouts and talk of Russian seamen. A young ship's doctor, a Tasmanian, helped us get our gear to our two-bunk cabin. It was all wonderful. We exclaimed. The en suite bathroom seemed a miraculous luxury in such a romantic, journeyman lump of steel as the *Khlebnikov*.

The first night and day at sea were benign. We met our sixty or so fellow passengers—Americans, Australians, British, Germans, a Belgian or two, New Zealanders and a solitary Canadian. A blessed company, we thought, and so it proved to be. We exclaimed about the quality of the food—we had presumed that we would be eating tough-guy style to match the expedition; that it would be borscht and herring. The choice of three menus astonished us, and seemed in comforting tension with the colder and colder seas, the icier and icier air, the polar memoirs we were all immersed in, and the unarguable Antarctic conditions into which we were being taken.

The second night introduced us to the circumpolar current, a definite but irregular line in the ocean, visible from space as a huge pleat. The colder Antarctic waters here begin their dive beneath the warmer waters from the northern oceans, and the zone is full of the turbulence and violence of this meeting. Wind howled and the ship rolled to angles of more than thirty-five degrees. The passengers might have been temporarily sick but were generally delighted by the experience. Many of them had been here before. Their memory of things was validated by wind and rough seas. They were returning to the most intense of their memories. They drank merrily, but were slightly awed to meet the ship's officers, Captain Petr Golikov, the mates, the radio officer, the engineering officer, the two helicopter pilots. As the swell mounted, these were to be our guides to the underworld. In the morning, the expedition leader, Kate Adie, an American, greeted us by intercom with a resonating *'Dobroe Utro! Good morning!'* She and the captain, in consultation, would determine where the *Khlebnikov* would take us. To celebrate our southern ocean initiation, the ship's notice board sported the words of Samuel Taylor Coleridge: 'The fair breeze blew, the white foam flew, the furrow followed free, /We were the first that ever burst into that silent sea.' Well, maybe not the first, but at least it felt like it when we stood on the flying bridge seeking ice, and Antarctica's first scalding air numbed our faces.

Among our company was a Scot who was researching a book on the lesser-known Antarctic explorers, and five Australian scientists who were being accompanied to the Australian subantarctic island, Macquarie Island, to pursue research into the irregularities of the earth's magnetic field, geology, marine biology, seals, penguins, albatrosses, etc. The presence of the scientists gave us tourists a sense of being part of a noble cause. We were also to pick up a group of four men, three New Zealanders and an Englishman, stuck by ice at Cape Adare, our first point of contact with the Antarctic coast. The drama of genuine Antarctic need augmented our long days.

The earliest icebergs we spotted were irregular in shape—eroded, conical, or else rather like ruined fortresses. But then large tabular bergs, higher than the ship, and some hundreds of metres long, appeared and displayed their water-level blue caverns. The first whales we met were orcas, and orcas and minke whales would accompany us the rest of our journey, with humpbacks and an occasional southern right whale thrown in. The populations seemed enthusiastic and numerous, but further north the whaling fleet of Japan, which had not signed the International Whaling Commission's Charter, awaited their arrival.

The ship traversed and broke ice bars and then met solid banks of ice, and began to break it, growling, transferring seventy tons of ballast water back to the stern to raise the ship by the bows, then pumping it forward at great speed to bring the bows crashing down. I stood in the bows transfixed by the fracture of ice, the way it moved, its sundry, plastic varieties. And distantly, a mere ice blink, Cape Adare, the Transantarctic Mountains and the coast running westwards, began to show themselves. Cape Adare grew more and more massive throughout the day. We could see the tops of mountains fifty miles away, and all distance was foreshortened by the clarity of air, so that the chain of coast seemed not mere geology but the instantly legible manifesto of gods. Amid the mountains ran the broad all-altering hands of glaciers. Everything one had ever expected of the inhuman continent, all in a second's glance!

Adare, a black volcanic cape at the western entrance to the Ross Sea, was the site of the landing of the first European, Carsten Borchgrevink, in 1895. Borchgrevink, a Norwegian who had settled in Australia as a schoolteacher, in 1899 had built the first hut of the Heroic Era there on unsuitable Cape Adare, a venue for vicious gravity-fed winds. The four men we were to collect, an Englishman and three New Zealanders, were working on the restoration of the hut, and the *Khlebnikov* was to take them off when we called there.

We received instructions on how to visit the fragile hut—there are now protocols in place—and what our demeanour should be towards the some 4,000 Adélie penguins who lived on the strand beneath the high plug of granite—no sudden disturbing advances amongst the chicks of the rookery; photographs to be reflectively taken, not from a challenging human level, but from penguin level.

By mid-afternoon the captain had got the ship to work, slicing open areas in the ice, but we reached a point where there was nowhere for the ice we penetrated and cracked to go. We could see, beneath the huge black-and-white face of Adare, the fast ice with its necklace of brilliant but dominant icebergs. In the end, the helicopters went to get the men and their gear, and they were welcomed aboard, telling us how it had been camping in tents by Borchgrevink's hut in 200 km-per-hour gales. I mentioned that from my lay-perspective across the sea ice, it looked as if they were captives of the Erl King. 'That's how we bloody felt,' they told me.

The fourth member of the group was, improbably, an urbane British heritage architect who genially confessed that at the height of their discomfort on the Cape, he had made a slighting remark about his life's task having been to restore some of Britain's finest buildings, and his having no interest in restoring garden sheds in Antarctica. To the New Zealanders, however, these Ross Sea huts of the heroic era were the garden sheds of the gods.

Captain Golikov assured us he would do his best to get us into Cape Adare on our way back north again. We took off in helicopters in teams of eight and inspected the region—huge Mount Minto in Australian Antarctica, Mount Melbourne, the Rennick Glacier, and such a glut of ice, and the bergs golden in the high late-afternoon sun.

Satellite pictures had recently shown two enormous icebergs, slabs of the Ross Ice Shelf itself, which were preventing ice from escaping from the Ross Sea. Icebergs feature in the popular mind as the accused in the sinking of the *Titanic*, and thus a North Atlantic phenomenon. But ninety-three per cent of the world's icebergs are Antarctic, and genuinely titanic. The one named B15 guarded the approaches of the southern Ross Sea. (These bergs, by the way, are given code letters according to the section of the Ross Ice Shelf they break away from.) B15 was said to be the size of Jamaica. Then, at an inconvenient angle far out in the Ross Sea, C19 lay diagonally, like a 200-kilometre-long lock gate, completing the job of blocking in the ice of Antarctica's classic quarter. The captain took us looking for C19, yet it seemed that it found us, a perfect tabular wall of ice, fifty metres high and filling the horizon. This great vehicle had earlier, according to satellite pictures, collided with the penguin rookery at Cape Crozier, producing a seismic effect picked up in Hawaii, and a cataclysm for the penguins. Collisions with other hefty icebergs had also affected its drift. We could not see atop it, and its cliffs had not been indented by waves or by melt, so that it was possible to look at its flanks as representing the point it had broken from the Ross Ice Shelf, along one clean, enormous crack. The captain, to make up for our non-landing at Adare, decided that his helicopters would transport us up there, to the top.

Heavily dressed, we flew up over the coast of this republic-unto-itself, and on inland, if *inland* is the term, to an uncrevassed area marked out by the ship's staff with red flags. An ice bar and an igloo had been built there, on C19. Landed, we could not see the edges of the berg, nor sea ice, nor the ship, so that C19 had become a new version of the earth, limitless white tending away into a sky clear to the south and to threatening snow clouds at the north. It was a strange, vertiginous and unearthly experience. In the immaculate snow, I carved my grandchildren's names, in the hope that subsequent snowfalls and giant gales would sweep loose squally snow from them, and treat the indentations lightly for a while. It will takes decades for it to break up and melt.

The sea ice was only a year old, but the ice of this berg was from water that fell on Antarctica when our ancestors lived as nomads in Central Asia, some 10,000 to 15,000 years ago, and the air bubbles trapped within were fossil air, a guide to the atmosphere, lower in carbon dioxide, the air that early Sumerians, the first Chinese farmers, and the few thousand migratory ancestors of Europeans were fortunate to breathe. By 2050, they say, carbon dioxide will have reached twice the level, 550 parts per million, that existed before the Industrial Revolution. There is argument about the effect of this on earth—powerful scientific opinion predicting a rise in temperature, a severe global warming beyond our previous experience. Hence CO_2 readings of the bubbles in such great ice masses as C19 are considered indicators of danger, even though some scientists argue that our CO2-laced modern atmosphere has given increased benefit to plants. Laypeople, confused by conflicting scientific opinion—the scientists, like us, being too recent in their observations of the Antarctic continent—we celebrated this ice and air from before human cultural self-consciousness! We played, like stiffly dressed children, on an antiquity.

Whenever I could, I stood in the bows of the *Khlebnikov* feeling the impact in my spine as it growled its way in sunshine, shattering ice apart. We moved into a canyon in the huge Campbell Ice Tongue, just to have a look, and saw a world of heroic ice-fractures. This was not seamless and immaculate ice, like the ice of C19, but ice dramatically marked with the soil it had picked up years past, while grinding its way down from the Campbell Glacier. It was full of cracks and arches of pressure, and the soil streaks were vertical, not horizontal, such was the pressure under which this ice had travelled.

Terra Nova Bay, where the Italians have a base, lay nearby, between the Campbell and Drygalski Ice Tongues. Many of the ship's passengers, including my wife, would make their first footfall on the Antarctic Continent at the base, which is said to be a model of its kind. It is occupied only in the summer, with all its geodesic and other equipment maintained throughout the winter by computer from Italy. All waste is shipped out, which is also the rule with the *Khlebnikov*. When one of the passengers threw up while crossing sea ice in McMurdo, that waste too was shovelled up, to be returned ultimately to the outer world.

The *Khlebnikov* had made its way to within a few kilometres of shore at Cape Royds, the protected cove where Shackleton's 1908 *Nimrod* hut stood, when we saw—another ship! This unfamiliar vessel, parked in the sea ice, was a psychological challenge to all we felt. It revealed us to be tourists, like those others over there. Their ship was merely ice-strengthened, and we pitied them for being on it when we saw them take off for Cape Evans across the ice in open people-movers—the Antarctic version of a tourist bus. The sight opened the question, how much tourism can Antarctica stand? That is, how much could it take of us?

The Americans intend to attempt to put down a track—to call it a road is perhaps melodramatic—across the Ross Ice Shelf, up the

Thomas Keneally

Beardmore Glacier, and to the Pole. There are logistical reasons for it, all to do with the support of the base at the South Pole. Many argue that anything artificial would not survive for long on the fractured face of the Beardmore: the track wouldn't last. But even the idea of such a track sucks the myth out of the Pole, the myth on which every Westerner of my generation has been raised. And the existence of fast-ice airports, such as Williams Base at McMurdo, which could hold the weight of commercial planes, raises the possibility of fly-in tourism, by whose standards our approach by sea might one day look blessedly idyllic, primitive and adventurous. The idea of large-scale tourist operations in McMurdo Sound is absolutely possible and, to most even of the *Khlebnikov*'s passengers, horrifying in conservation terms. Will conservation win out over tourism? I seem to remember that it never has. Boeing has been the great democratizer of travel experience. And each of us would willingly exclude others, while excusing ourselves, the essential tourists, from any such edict. So the Ross Sea Novotel and McMurdo Sheraton could be built within this century. Children will gambol on the ice shelf where Scott exhaled his last, pained breath.

We walked to Shackleton's hut on a track laid across sea ice that seemed solid as earth. The hut itself lies in a depression in black rock, not far from an Adélie penguin rookery. It was the base for Shackleton's 1909 journey to within ninety-seven miles of the Pole. Its interior is, like all of them, full of intimate presences, but the vulnerability of the supplies and belongings that men left here is still obvious. Tinned peas stacked by the hut wall are rusting open and displaying their desiccated contents. A question for the preservationists: what should be done with this sort of artefact, and artefacts of all kinds scattered about the site? For example, by the pony stable still stands a wheel of the first automobile introduced in Antarctica, a Johnson. Where should it be placed, and how maintained? Scott's Cape Evans hut presents the Antarctic Heritage Trust with the same sort of problems. This is the one from which he left to go to his death, and is far more spacious than Shackleton's, and more openly 'atmospheric'. No other expedition produced so many known names—Dr Wilson, the two Evanses, Birdy Bowers, Ponting the photographer, Oates, Cherry-Garrard, author of the ultimate Antarctic text, *The Worst Journey in the World*, Petty Officer Crean, etc., etc. This hut too lies

140

in a depression north of its cape, but not really enough of one to provide much protection. Scott somehow fitted in many 'gentlemen explorers' who had separate quarters from the 'men'—seamen, craftsmen, pony handlers. All was very skilfully and intimately secreted within the hut. In the pony stables next door, metal sheets were hammered against the timber to stop the continual kicking of the ponies from disturbing the sleep of the expeditioners.

Scott's bed in his personal alcove, and his study-table with its notebooks and newspapers, are affecting to this day, to the point that some of our fellow passengers found our night-time visit the central experience of their journey. From the hill above, where there is a monument to Shackleton's dead, it was the sight of the hunched hut amid the massive indifference of the Sound's ice, and the streaks of volcanic black and white which delineated offshore islands, that resonated most profoundly for me.

The Dry Valleys of Antarctica have some bearing on the question of whether the ice cap is likely to melt. The melting of the cap would accelerate global warming and obliterate the coastal civilizations of the world, raising the water level an average of seventy metres, ultimately drowning London, coastal Western Europe, Manhattan, sections of Sydney, Shanghai, Hong Kong. It will not do so overnight. When it last happened, at the end of the last Ice Age, the meltdown took 200 years, and ice loss at the moment is one hundred times slower than that, and, as some scientists say, it may merely be a random fluctuation, not a harbinger of disaster.

The Dry Valleys, discovered by Scott, lie on the Antarctic mainland across McMurdo Sound. Professor Barry McKelvey, the Australian geologist on the *Khlebnikov*, has specialized in these cold desert valleys since he was a young geologist. One of them is named after him. They are ground from which the glaciers have retreated leaving moraine, an intimidatingly broad vacancy, and tiny, isolated small patches of mosses and lichen never more than a few millimetres high, which McKelvey referred to ironically as 'the forests of Antarctica'. Large mountains separate the valleys, and they are still impinged upon by muscular glaciers, the Canada, the Commonwealth, whose faces do not melt away into trickles of water but which stand sixty or seventy metres high. One knows, and can feel the ache, that something more than this is meant to be here. For one thing, you don't need to walk far here to find the mummified corpses of crab-eater and other seals, some of them 3,000 or more years dead. They have come up here compelled by some ancestral memory, and they have died here, after a twenty or thirty mile journey from the Ross Sea, all achieved on flippers and out of their element, over the harshest land.

Though the Dry Valleys offer clues to the question of the ice cap's history, according to Professor McKelvey the answer is still unclear. McKelvey has come to the conclusion that the ice sheet has never been stable—two million years ago it went into serious decline, and in retracting, dumped its debris even on top of present-day mountains. It has grown considerably again since then. McKelvey's studies have convinced him that the ice cap is like a living thing, expanding sometimes, retracting at others, but strong enough to sustain itself through previous periods of global warming. It is a comforting hypothesis which I hope is true, and material I've read since seems to give strength to it. In the last thirty-five years the temperature of Antarctica has been dropping by 0.7 degrees Celsius (1.8 degrees Fahrenheit) per decade, further mystifying those who are trying to predict what will happen to us in a warming world.

Because of all the ice in McMurdo, we were helicoptered rather than boated to the great American base, which resembles an exceptionally tidy mining camp (unless one enters the enormous Crary Science and Engineering Centre, in which case one would believe oneself on a campus of the University of California).

Here and at the more intimate New Zealand base, Scott Base, which lies nearby, researchers share their findings on all Antarctic issues. At both bases they are aware of a diminution in the hole in the ozone layer. Winter over the Antarctic creates the chemical conditions in which the return of sunlight is the catalyst for destroying ozone at six to thirty miles above the earth. The hole split in two in 2002, and was now, in 2003, merely a fraction of its size in 2001, when it was the size of Canada, the United States and Mexico. It seems that the attack on the manufacture of CFCs and halons— chlorine and bromine chemicals—through the Montreal Protocol might have contributed directly to the improvement. Some scientists believe however that it's too early to judge, that the chlorine and bromine take years to disappear anyhow, and that the size of the hole each year is influenced by air temperatures. The New Zealand woman directing research at Scott Base, however, seemed reasonably sanguine that the hole, which has created wide DNA damage in the eggs and larvae of Antarctic fish and other Antarctic creatures and is a threat ultimately to all DNA on earth, might disappear altogether by 2050.

We were shown genially around the base, but I felt that our being barred from Hut Point, the home of my purloined biscuit, because a store ship had docked and the road was too busy, was symptomatic of the tension between Antarctic tourism and Antarctic bases. So too, perhaps was an incident involving Captain Golikov. Some miles out in McMurdo lay a big tanker which would supply the base with its winter oil. Because of the extraordinary extent of the ice, the US Coast Guard ice-breakers could not make a path for it, and Golikov offered to do so, very confident that the design of the *Kapitan Khlebnikov* fitted it better for these conditions. He was rebuffed. Perhaps jingoism had something to do with it, as well as the fact that the *KK* had fallen from the high office of Arctic ice-breaker to become an Antarctic tourist ship.

And now the admission cannot be delayed. What about the biscuit? Having set myself up to return the biscuit, and having told a number of people about my purpose, and having been assured that I would almost certainly meet someone on the trip associated with the preservation of the huts of the so-called Heroic Era, on the day we left for New Zealand to meet the boat, I went without it.

It was inexplicable, even to me. Maybe it was that, a loose-lipped confessor, I'd told so many people about my intention that I thought the thing had actually been packed already. Whereas thermal underwear and waterproof pants demanded to be packed physically one by one, my brain may have fooled me into believing the biscuit was part of my baggage, since it had an emotional and moral weight which I'd already hefted.

But, once aboard, I had consoled myself rather easily, I have to say. Not only because I was sure that somewhere in Antarctica I would meet an authoritative person who had something to do with the maintenance and preservation of the historic huts. It would be better if they handled it anyhow, rather than if I, during a visit to Hut Point, simply tried to slip it into a hard-tack tin.

One of the New Zealanders we had collected from ice-bound

Thomas Keneally

Cape Adare, Nigel Watson, was the head of the operations of the Heritage Trust. I took him aside the evening he was rescued from Cape Adare and made my hard-tack confession. He told me that American naval personnel had taken much greater plunder from Hut Point, and one man had returned canned goods and books to him. I made the point that there had been no equivalent to him around in 1968. Of course, he said, I understand. But in case he let me off too lightly, and reduced me to the status of minor Polar pillager, I confessed to him the venality, vanity and greed which underpinned my crime. He bought me a drink to calm me down. It was agreed I would send him the biscuit for assessment. I had met the man. I felt that Antarctica could now be unambiguously enjoyed.

So consoled, I climbed Observation Hill with some friendly American Hercules pilots for guides. Members of Scott's expedition had placed on top of here a large wooden cross, facing out across the ice shelf on which they had found his body. Observation Hill is a relatively modest volcanic tor, a mere child of Mount Erebus, but the view is superb, and the last great one we had before the *Khlebnikov* turned north again.

From that point on, storms and ice prevented any further landings. The sea off Cape Adare had an extraordinary look—a conglomerated solid ice surface in which there were, nonetheless, deep swells, serving as a promise of how rough the weather would be northwards. No one sane would have tried landing. At Macquarie Island, our six young scientists were taken ashore at some peril to all parties, in seas which sometimes had the Russian sailors on the ship's stairs armpit-deep in water.

We had seen our last iceberg and, after a while, our last heroic wandering albatross. After Antarctica, nothing is the same, I decided; that was the real reason I went back, to refresh my wellspring of images: the size of the ice fields and mountains, their air of calm self-absorption (they are so free, still, of the usages of the human race) as they fill your sight like an independent and immaculate planet. As for the biscuit, it is now in the hands of the New Zealand Heritage Trust, Christchurch, New Zealand, who are assessing it for its return to the Antarctic. □

GRANTA

BONE LITTER
Marian Botsford Fraser

Playfulness north of the Arctic Circle

At the inn in Yellowknife, they could be just any little family: father, mother, small daughter, having breakfast. The restaurant is a brown plastic place, where ageing and hung-over white waitresses serve pancakes so big they flop over the plates' sides, and slop coffee with a shaky hand into thick cups. They shuffle on their crêpe-soled shoes, squeezing between tables, their butts sometimes almost in your breakfast. The family sits in a booth.

I'd spent two weeks paddling a canoe down the Coppermine river into the Arctic Ocean. The dissonance between then and now, there and here, is almost physically painful. Places like hotels and airports and bars are the messy, ugly interstices of the Arctic, where cultures collide and disturb one another. The shift from serenity, silence, clarity of light into these compressed, explosive outposts is poorly tolerated by whites and natives alike.

Outside these outposts, the imprint of thousands of years of aboriginal settlement is slight, a scattering of human and animal bones on shale and the thin tundra soil. A close reading of the Arctic is a reading of far-flung bones: caribou antlers, musk-ox skulls— mother and baby side by side. A perfect circle of ten bowhead-whale skulls covered in a foot-thick layer of peat. Bone fashioned into knife handles and harpoons. Graveyards ancient and modern. *Inukshuks* stand like guardians on the horizon, rocks piled into human shapes, marking a route or signalling a food cairn.

The debris of white people's intrusion is aggressive and offensive: a cache of rusting 150-year-old cans of food in a stone cairn on a hillside in the high Arctic, oil drums full of fuel tossed on beaches, plastic peanut-butter jars and liquor bottles. Even orange peel takes forever to decompose.

Our passage down the Coppermine river was observed only by wildlife: collared lemmings, moose, caribou, horned larks and gyrfalcons, a wolf pacing our canoes from a high ridge. One day, six Americans were dropped by a floatplane for a spot of fishing, but we were mostly alone, two canoes attended by swarms of blackflies, and angry terns, and flotillas of whistling swans.

On the final day after 200 miles of solitude, we were unsettled by the gradual sighting of fishing shacks, then low-slung houses, and finally the shabby beachfront of the Nunavut village of Kugluktuk. We slept on the beach beside the Arctic Ocean, and the Inuit children played past midnight in the sunshine because they could. I flew back down to Yellowknife before flying north again to the High Arctic. Yellowknife is the last outpost of the south and the first of the far north, or the other way around depending on your perspective. It is a rough frontier town of 18,000 people, the centre of government for the Northwest Territories, lying 600 miles north of the nearest city (Edmonton, Alberta), on the shore of Great Slave Lake. It is where people based further north, in villages or mining camps, come to re-provision, do their laundry and banking, and drink.

Breakfast at the inn in Yellowknife is my first restaurant meal after two weeks in the bush. The room is full, hot, smoky. People don't talk a lot; this is a fuelling stop.

The other patrons are mostly red-faced white people, a few Dene, fewer Inuit. Prospectors, a smattering of tourists and the family in the booth. The woman is a sweet-faced, tiny Inuk in pink slacks, a black sleeveless sweater, with glasses, carved whalebone jewellery, shiny black hair cut nicely around her face. Her cheekbones are a flat, sweeping curve. She is soft-spoken and vivacious, smiling at her little daughter who is bouncy, and laughing excitedly. The man is white, large-bellied, working his way grimly through fried eggs, hash browns and sausage and thick white slabs of toast, saying nothing.

The mother sips her coffee and smiles sweetly at the tired waitress. It is ten in the morning, a sunny, cold summer Saturday in Yellowknife.

Noon at Yellowknife Airport. In the middle of the terminal, the child is screaming loudly for her mother and won't be comforted by her father. They are an island of noise; people don't sit close to them. People walk up and down, up and down, all waiting for the same plane north.

The mother is drinking alone in the small bar. She is perched on a bar stool, like a child herself, her little legs braced on the legs of the stool. She is smoking and drinking straight gin or vodka, for all the world as if it were midnight in a nightclub. She is oblivious to time and the flight call, but the bartender is not.

The mother slips off her bar stool and weaves a route back to her family sitting on plastic chairs by the window, the hard summer Arctic light making silhouettes of them. The father has his arm around the child, who ignores him. The mother is somehow able to quiet the child, pulling her on to her lap. But her face is now a shifting thing, like ice breaking up, and she is not seeing the child or her husband or anything else. She has left herself.

The plane load is the usual mix of whites, mostly bearded men in parkas even in midsummer, with weather-beaten faces: miners, geologists, government workers. There is a scattering of white women with young children going to visit their menfolk, and a few Inuit families; the plane goes to Resolute and Cambridge Bay.

The woman begins the journey in quiet good humour. She is overtly cheery. She insists on cuddling the baby of the woman sitting behind her. She has attracted the attention of everyone but no one apparently pays her any attention. Her own child is wary, restlessly flipping a bright green rubber snake with a flicking red forked tongue and yellow eyes.

When the woman moves to the back of the plane, smiling a loose-hinged grin, there is a small softening of tension around the seat she has vacated. The man again puts his arm around the little girl and stares out the window into blinding white cloud.

The crew serve crusty lasagna, coleslaw, a harsh red wine. There is no movie; people settle into magazines or turn into their headsets and close their eyes. They are in the limbo between south and north, shedding one persona and suiting up with another. Some people are going home, but others are bracing themselves for isolation. They both fear and crave it.

A small boy is sitting in the row in front of the family. He and the little girl are playing hide-and-seek through the cracks between the seats. Their hands sometimes clasp over the seat top and then they laugh with delight. The little girl still clutches her snake. The father is now reading a newspaper.

The woman pushes her way back along the aisle from the back of the plane. Even before she can be seen, she can be felt. She reaches her own seat, then stands rolling her back against it, moving her head from side to side, eyes greedy for contact.

All you goddamn fucking white people
You red-headed people
I hate every goddamn white person
You think you're so goddamn good

Trying to go up north
Forget it.

I hate all you arse holes
Fuck you.
I'm a fucking native person
All you fucking white people
Going to Resolute Bay.

Her voice is harsh and nasal and loud. It clashes with the sweetness of her demeanour; she is tiny and almost prim to look at. Her speech has the flat, sing-song rhythm of a recitation, like the priest-led unison readings of a church service. A doxology, a benediction. A curse. Most people look into their laps. A flight attendant with swept-up blonde hair and a smile trembling on her red mouth swiftly approaches the woman who has now braced herself between two seats.

Leave me alone you fucking whore
You fucking red-headed people
I hate you

She arches backwards over her own seat, reaches in and pushes the shoulder of the man. The child is whispering to her snake and hugging the arm of her seat. The father tries to interest the child in a bottle. He awkwardly uses the newspaper to shield her from her mother and in a low, intense voice commands the mother to shut up. Shut. Up.

Take the kid before I beat
The fucking shit out of her
Daddy's little horror
Daddy's little horror

All you fucking whores stop listening
I'll pierce your ears
I hate you
I hate all you fucking white people

It's goddamn fucking white men made me this way
I hate every goddamn white person
Even married to one
I hate him
I hate you, just like all the others.

This last is spat out over the head of the child towards the man. His face is contorted. His eyes beg her to sit down.

She slides into her seat and is silent briefly. The child is snuffling. She pulls the child on to her lap, takes the bottle from the father's hand without looking at him directly. The child curls into her mother's breast with the bottle and her arm creeps up to her mother's neck and her fingers softly caress her mother's chin. The mother starts to croon loudly, brokenly, no words, a keening not a lullaby, rocking unevenly, her face close to her child's face, oh my baby my baby I love you so much, her body says.

There is no other sound except the burr of engines for some time. The little boy in the seat ahead has just his eyes up over the seat. His face is ashen.

The woman shoves the girl aside into her father's arms. The rubber snake tumbles into the aisle. The little boy reaches out and grabs it and passes it between the seats to the girl. The girl offers her bottle to the boy.

It's going to crash
It's going to crash
It's going to crash

All you fucking white people
Think you're so fucking good

Hey, little boy
What you want to say to me?

And you,
You
Leave me
Alone

Fuck off
Just look after yourself
And the fucking kid.

Changes in pressure and engine noise signal that the plane is about to land. The pilot's announcements are perfunctory, in English only, with sly reference to 'scheduled and unscheduled departures at Resolute Bay'. There is a collective wordless response to this, an exhalation of air, another change in pressure. The descent begins over water, large floes of ice skirting the shore.

The plane lands, turns, and comes to a stop. People start to talk again as they gather their things. No one looks at the woman but they glance at the child now holding her father's hand. A press of people conspires to form a barrier that prevents the woman from rising from her seat; she stares straight ahead into the seat back. The passengers move in a tight herd off the plane and into the small terminal building. People are greeted, met by colleagues and family. They await the luggage.

'Hey, get a load of this...'

People turn, fall silent and then line the windows to watch the family, the three of them on the tarmac with an officer from the Royal Canadian Mounted Police.

The man and the child are off to one side, spectators too. The woman and the policeman approach each other like wrestlers. She's fast and canny, suddenly active again. He is large and burly. He has a grim look on his face and he is swinging handcuffs.

He lunges suddenly, grabs her arms and tries to handcuff her. She kicks his shins and claws at his chest. She goes limp, slumping to the ground. She curls into a fetal position, roaring still. Her pink slacks are stained with grease and her sweater rides up under her breasts. One shoe tumbles off.

The man and the child stand perfectly still, silent.

The crowd inside the terminal howls with laughter as if they were watching a good street brawl or a bar scene in a Western. Mostly the men laugh and the women are silent.

The RCMP officer picks the woman up like a child, scoops up the shoe. He handcuffs her and carries her to a waiting van. She screams and bucks and scratches his face. The man and the child, wrapped in her father's jacket and still clutching her snake, re-board the plane. The man doesn't look back.

The crowd breaks up and returns to collecting luggage, chuckling.

'Good show, eh?'

'I hear she used to take on the whole village.'

'Hey, I saw an Inuk once with a hat that said: INSTANT ASSHOLE. JUST ADD ALCOHOL.'

'Yeah...for sure.'

Resolute, on Cornwallis Island, lies 1,000 miles south of the North Pole. It has two distinct faces. One is known simply as the base, a group of buildings that serve the airport and also house a lapsed military operation and weather station, government workers, and the Polar Continental Shelf Project, which provides support services for scientific teams researching Arctic climate, hydrography, geology and native cultures. The other face of Resolute is the small Inuit village, three miles away on a rough shale road, a village plopped down here in the late 1950s by the Canadian government as a means of reinforcing Canada's sovereignty in the Arctic archipelago, its inhabitants moved from Pond Inlet on Baffin Island and from northern Quebec, a thousand miles to the south and east. Their new homes were assembled from cheap corrugated iron and second-rate siding. In Inuktitut, Resolute is known as *Quausuittuq*, the place of no dawn. An enormous garbage dump sprawls close to the base. Food, lead, aluminium, steel engine parts and refrigerators have been dumped here. One year, more than forty hams made their way out of the Polar Continental Shelf kitchens into the dump and out again. Seabirds feed. Inuit from the village and knowledgeable old hands from the base forage discreetly.

Tonight is the annual Polar Bear Swim at Resolute. After dinner people from the base travel down to the shore in open trucks. They huddle around a huge bonfire in which a large box marked EXPLOSIVES burns with a fierce heat. The sky at nine in the evening is a light afternoon azure.

The people from the Inuit village do not attend the Polar Bear Swim. Four beluga whales have been killed that day; their white carcasses proudly line the beach, where they will be butchered and the prized *maktaaq* (blubber and skin eaten raw) parcelled out to all the families.

There are small patches of clear, pearl-coloured water between litterings of ice. A few young white men plunge off the ice floes into the glacial water and run back to the fire. There is covert drinking from bottles in brown paper bags, and then a truck carries people off to a party at one of the government workers' rec rooms.

'We've got wine and women!' the men shout over the pulse of cranked-up Led Zeppelin. A harvest moon thinner than tissue paper rolls low in the pale midnight sky.

South of Resolute, across the Barrow Straits and on the lower end of Somerset Island, there is an ancient site, a whaling camp, with its houses built from the bones of the bowhead whale. The camp shows signs of regular, seasonal occupation between AD 1100 and 1300. The Thule, the people who pre-dated the Inuit, lived and worked here.

The bowhead, in dramatically depleted numbers, still travel along this shoreline. On a still, clear morning when the glittering mirages of mountain ranges rise out of the sea, so too do the bowhead, feeding, diving, blowing, playing. It is so quiet that over a distance of half a mile you can hear the whales breathe.

On one hillock, there is a magnificent whalebone house. Although most of the structures along this stretch of coast would have been used only during the whaling season, this appears to be a winter house. The polished skull, mandibles and other large bones are firmly held in peat and sod, and the walls extend down into the permafrost. The entrance is formed by two complete whale skulls.

The bones have a dense whiteness, buffed by wind and snow and ice, bleached by a thousand years of midnight sun. This house was seen and noted by the British explorer James Clarke Ross when he sledged up this coastline in 1832.

During that same expedition, led by his uncle John Ross, and beset by ice over four winters, James Clarke Ross also sledged from the Boothia Peninsula, across the strait to King William Land, up to Cape Felix (where Sir John Franklin's expedition would be caught for nineteen months in ice twenty-five years later), and down to Victory Point, which he named, and where the last scraps of records concerning the Franklin expedition would be placed in a stone cairn in April 1848.

The British explorers hauled their own sledges along this coast, dragging coveted and useless supplies, setting up caches of tinned and salted meat, seeking those caches left by other expeditions. They did not know how to kill whales, and most did not care to eat the seal meat and whale-meat that would have sustained them and saved them from scurvy and cannibalism. The remnants of the Franklin expedition were found by the Inuit as skeletons on ice, men staggering to their deaths. Or in tents that told a macabre tale: neat piles of sawn bones, a kettle containing human remains, and complete skeletons wearing two or three suits of clothes.

For miles and miles here, there are whalebones, strewn along the shoreline, and large gravel pits where whale-meat and blubber would have been stored. There are sod houses and tent rings and whalebone houses, and a ceremonial house, where the whaling crews would have assembled to await the whales which were crowded into the shore by the ice, almost herded by the ice into a cul-de-sac where they would be hunted in small craft known as *umiak*, with harpoons. Then, 800 or 900 years ago, the pods of bowhead would have been sixty to one hundred strong, joyous, exuberant, languorously leaping out of the waves and then diving with their young as the Thule *umiak* shot out from shore, the men silent, or shouting and hollering with the blood of the hunt pounding in their temples.

The Thule would kill perhaps four yearlings in one season, and then bring them ashore for processing and storing. They would return to the same site year after year over 200 years. There are almost 1,000 caches in this area, close to the shoreline.

Then, in the fourteenth century, there was the great cooling down, the thickening and chilling of the ice that marked the end of this Thule whaling period, the end of this phase of habitation, and the beginning of the colder, Inuit age through which, several hundred years later, the Europeans would come seeking the Northwest Passage and the North Pole.

The Thule left the record of their culture in whalebone, in the household detritus excavated from the sod houses. Tiny carved tools, some with precious copper and flint blades. Seal and fox bones and hair; when this is dug out of the thawed permafrost, it smells strongly of meat. Strips of baleen like wet brown cardboard. Patches of grease where oil lamps sat.

The explorers left written messages to one another in stone cairns and buried their dead when they could in graves marked with small wooden crosses. They also wrote on the landscape, literally. Five hundred miles north-west from here, on the southern shore of

Melville Island, there is an enormous sandstone rock, an erratic
boulder twelve feet high and some twenty feet long. It is visible from
the air and from the sea. It marks Winter Harbour, where William
Parry was first caught in ice over the winter of 1819. His surgeon,
a Mr Fisher, carved a record of this wintering into one end of the
rock; there was time to do so. The lettering is large and careful.

HIS BRITANNIC MAJESTY
SHIPS HECLA & GRIPER
Commanded by
W. E. Parry & Lt. M. Liddon
Wintered in the adjacent
Harbour 1819–20
A. Fisher, sculp [here the rock curves sharply away and the word is
not finished]

The lettering is embellished with black and orange lichen. At the
base of the rock there are tiny, yellow-green poppies and soft,
floating tufts of musk-ox hair.

This rock became a posting box, a beacon for subsequent explorers,
just like the Inuit *inukshuks* built on promontories. As British,
American, Swedish, and Canadian ships steamed and sailed through
the Arctic waters over the next century, seeking the Northwest
Passage, looking for Franklin, looking for each other, looking for
Franklin's bones, they frequently beached at Winter Harbour.

In 1852, the explorer Francis Leopold McClintock (looking for
Robert McClure who was trapped for two years in the ice of Mercy
Bay 200 miles further west) came to Winter Harbour. Above the
spacious letters of Mr Fisher's 1820 record, these words are carved
in a cramped hand:

HMS
Resolute
Capt Kellett cb
and
TENDER INTREPID
Com MCCLINTOCK
7 Sept 1852

In 1909, at the end of a decade of journeys by Robert Peary, Frederick Cook, Roald Amundsen and Otto Svedrup, mostly seeking the North Pole, another ship came this way and another message was left, this one on a large metal plaque embedded in the landward side of the rock. It reads:

This memorial is created today
to commemorate
The taking possession for the
Dominion of Canada
of the whole
Arctic Archipelago
lying to the north of America
from long 60W to 141W
up to lat 90N
Winter Harbour Melville Island
CC Arctic July 1 1909
JE Beringer

This declaration of Canadian sovereignty is carved out 400 miles north of Resolute, where the remnants of the arbitrary relocation of the Inuit in the 1950s make their lives. (Under a settlement worth $10 million made by the Canadian government in 1996, some chose to return to their ancestral homes.)

On a small ridge overlooking the whaling site on the shore of Somerset Island, there are thirty or forty burial mounds, each about four or five feet long. The mounds are cairns, piles of rock over mossy graves. Some are in excellent condition. They have survived centuries of weather and the curiosity of men and lemmings.

On the end of one grave, a rock has fallen away leaving a neat opening. I kneel, peer inside, my eyes gradually adjusting to the gloom. There is a tiny skull on a pillow of bright green moss, and arm and leg bones neatly crossed, as if they had just been gently placed there in mourning.

The 900-year-old ancestor of the woman on the plane. ☐

'Spiky, eclectic and idiosyncratic by turns,
following no party line, but taken together a
convincing demonstration that some of the
best current English writing comes from
beyond the cultural ring-fence of the M25'
DJ Taylor

'Triumphant proof that the short story is
alive and kicking in the UK'
Peter Ho Davies

Going the
Distance

edited by **Alan Bear**

Tind
Stree
Press

£7.99 | ISBN: 0 9541303 5 9 | www.tindalstreet.co.uk | tel: 0121 773 81

GRANTA

DO FISH FEEL PAIN?
James Hamilton-Paterson

If you wouldn't do this to a **dog**,
why do it to a fish?

Campaign poster for PETA (People for the Ethical Treatment of Animals)

Do Fish Feel Pain?

Spearing fish is a savage business. It causes the fish gross physical damage and seldom kills them outright. Over several years I spent long months at a stretch living on an islet in the Philippines, learning how to spear fish in the local manner to feed myself. I had a lot to learn about the construction of spearguns and about the techniques of underwater hunting without scuba gear, whether diving alone or in company. But I also had to unlearn my own culture's ideas of the acceptable ways of treating game animals.

The locals were certainly short on sportsmanship. Their style was to hunt at night when many reef species are dozy, if not—like mullet—apparently fast asleep. In one hand we gripped a cheap torch ingeniously waterproofed with rubber or plastic and in the other an unwieldy wooden gun powered by rubber cut from inner tubes. With both hands thus occupied we held our breath and swam down into pitchy depths, maybe to thirty feet, in pursuit of the next day's food. The steel spear was eyed at its base like a needle. Spliced through this hole was a length of polythene fishing-line with a stop at the end. The technique was to spear the fish or cephalopod and sweep it on down to the end of the line so that it trailed behind as you reloaded the gun and went on searching. After two or three hours of this the torch batteries were flat and we dragged ourselves from the sea, coral-grazed and weary, with grains of luminescence running off our bodies and, with any luck, a few pounds of edible flesh on our lines.

I soon realized there is a big difference between a coarse fisherman sitting on a river bank, hauling up and killing his catch with a quick blow from a priest, and sharing a medium with one's prey. Below the surface, encumbered with gear and limited to snatched lungfuls of air, you are at a huge disadvantage in any hunt. Yet you can stare your quarry in the eye through a few feet of water, learn to read its slightest twitch or attitude (such particulars vary with the species), slowly acquire familiarity with the behaviour and appearance of all sorts of marine creatures. Down there you can hear the spear actually strike, *pok!*, hear the animal's whirring struggles, maybe its squawks or grunts, see the dark strands of blood, watch its mouth jerk open in a hopeless O. That was the moment of maximum adrenaline because you still had not caught your supper. Often the spear struck too close to the edge of your prey's body or the barb failed to set and the animal could tear itself loose to escape in the dark with the flick of a fin. Often, too, you were at the end of your breath and desperate for air, and perhaps the fish was large enough to swim away even towing the weight of the spear. To lose a spear was shaming and besides, they took a lot of making. For every reason, then, it was necessary to make a supreme effort and lunge forward as fast as possible to get a grip on both spear and fish. If in doubt you safely 'threaded' the animal with a further stitch by pushing the spear completely through and piercing it again in a more secure place: typically through both eyes or behind one operculum (gill cover) and out through the mouth. Often you had to surface, bursting with stale air, and dizzily perform this operation while buffeted by black waves in a tangle of line and barbed spear and struggling prey, the torch clenched beneath one arm and the wooden gun beneath the other. It was not an easy way to feed yourself.

But even in that triumphant moment of the hunt I remember not enjoying pushing a steel rod through a living creature's eyes. I could feel the slight scrunch of bone and it was gruesome to release it then and watch by torchlight as it swam furiously in all directions with the line through its head, trailing its sightless eyeballs. If the fish was big it was best to kill it straight away because its tuggings could seriously upset your aim, while a dying stingray could blunder into your legs with its agonizing thorn. For this humane deed we would carry a knife strapped to one ankle. But we indifferently allowed smaller fish and cephalopods to die of their wounds. It was noticeable that some species (cuttlefish, parrot fish) tended to die more quickly than others. Moray eels (a fearsome prey underwater at night) and porcupine fish (whose livers were delicious) could survive for hours, even out of water. In those rural backwaters where there are few refrigerators, wounded game is habitually kept alive as long as possible, whether birds, fruit bats or fish.

By day, when not asleep, mending gear or fetching water over from the mainland, I would drift for hours face down among the reefs watching the creatures that lived there. I do not believe that a nature photographer stalking the one great shot or a marine biologist hoping to make a career-boosting discovery watches with sharper attention than the hunter-gatherer needing to fill his stomach. Thus it is often claimed that hunters know their prey with a degree of intimacy that mixes fear, affection and respect to form a bond at least as great as that of zookeepers, big-cat tamers or the leathery ladies who live with apes in the wild. This may be a piece of special pleading based on sentimental hokum, I can't judge. But I do know that for months at a stretch the sea inhabited me as much as I it; that the castles, thoroughfares and alleys of the offshore reefs, together with their tiniest inhabitants, became as familiar and fond to me as a native city. Like any angler who grows intimate with the hoary old pike he despairs of ever catching, I was on greeting terms with a vast grouper that lived in a hollow outcrop twenty feet down. I was almost certain he could no longer get out; that he had probably swum in as a juvenile and grown fat on the fish that wandered in and out of the small holes through which I could glimpse his mottled hide. I came to feel a real affection for this creature: a hopeless piscine equivalent of Garfield who had indolently grown to fill his own prison. He would have been easy to shoot, impossible to retrieve. I could no more have speared him than I could my own foot, and I never told anyone of his existence because I knew the locals would have had no such qualms but would have dragged him out in bleeding lumps.

More fleeting but just as intense were the acquaintances I struck up with cuttlefish. We would lie within yards of one another for long moments and gaze into each other's eyes. Impossible not to see intelligence of a kind in those crumpled pupils, in the violet lightnings playing around their mantles, the passing clouds of changing colours in the chromatophores beneath their skin. That long moment, with the creatures warily poised for flight and the tentacles bunched downwards in what I came to think of as their 'horse's head' attitude, looked as much like thought as it did a knife-edged awareness.

I was entranced, but an entranced hunter nevertheless. Still, I could be caught unawares in moments of sleep or reflection by images of the violence I so regularly committed at night. I employed several strategies to suppress my unease. I told myself that fish brains were far too rudimentary for the creatures to experience pain in the way humans did, conscious of a desire for it to stop. They were cold-blooded, too. Inconceivable to imagine gripping a puppy in one hand and shoving a barbed spear in through one eye and out the other. I even managed to convince myself that by transfixing a fish's eyes I was swiftly killing it by destroying its brain, and that its violent swimming motions afterwards were like a beheaded chicken flapping its wings.

James Hamilton-Paterson

I told myself this even as I knew it to be untrue: that the brains of most fish species are not between their eyes, as I regularly discovered when sucking every last morsel from the skulls of my barbecued prey. I told myself the grunts of apparent anguish made by some fish on being speared were merely an alarm response to warn their kind; that any notion of distress was too anthropomorphic to apply to a cold-blooded and relatively brainless creature. And when some species opened their mouths in what looked like a rictus of agony it was surely just a way of expelling whatever they had just eaten (and sometimes a cloud of particles did come out), the better to hyperventilate.

But the most effective way of drowning my misgivings was by reference to local habit. The village youths and men who fed their families did so without the luxury of remorse. They needed as much food as they could catch as quickly as possible, and the efficient flurry of the enterprise was its own rationale. I wished to be accepted, to prove a reliable companion in the hunt, someone who didn't panic when his spear jammed immovably into coral fifteen feet down and the nylon line looped itself around one ankle in the darkness. I was exhibiting a syndrome comparable to that of soldiers on the battlefield who are shamed into bravery by the mere presence of their comrades, more scared of accusations of cowardice than of mortal injury. In this way I noticed peer pressure making me crueller in company than when I fished alone, an unwelcome reminder of something I had noticed thirty years earlier as a boy when hunting pigeons with a .410 and butterflies with a killing jar. In the presence of others my dying victims lost their individuality and became safely generic. I now wonder whether this same syndrome, much disguised and domesticated, is what underpins the way we shop for chicken or frozen fish-fingers without a thought to the deaths of individual animals. Our friends and neighbours do it; everybody does it. A worldwide economy encourages our habit. How can it be wrong? Those pale, shrink-wrapped bricks of deep-frozen stuff are a commodity. It seems bad taste to break the pact and say that it was once the flesh of living creatures who on our behalf have been put to death for it. At least (I tell myself) I have often bloodied my own hands to eat. I have personally stopped little fish-hearts; I have executed my own hens. I understand why from the point of view of one's conscience it feels better to have hunted and killed individual creatures to feed oneself than to have hired anonymous slaughterers and then callously pretend the 'product' had never truly lived. From the ethical point of view, though, it probably makes no difference; and it is ethical matters that we must consider.

'Do fish feel pain?' is a subsection of the more general question of whether any animal experiences pain as humans do. This in turn splits broadly into two lines of enquiry: the philosophical and the physiological. Both are narrowly watched by the evangelists of the animal-rights movement who cherry-pick research results to suit their cause. Science has largely concentrated on identifying the neural pathways, nociceptors (pain-sensitive receptors) and areas of the human brain involved in sensing pain, as well as listing the symptoms associated with it (crying out, increased heart rate, muscular tension, raised temperature, etc.). Inevitably, our assessment of the varying ability of non-human animals to experience pain is anthropocentric, judged as being more or less likely according to how nearly their nervous systems approximate to ours. The majority of pain research so far has been conducted on mammals such as monkeys, cats, pigs and rats; a good deal less on birds; and not much at all on lower vertebrates and invertebrates. Here, it is probably relevant that the US Animal Welfare Act deals exclusively with mammals and birds and ignores cold-blooded animals. To date, this approach has produced results that pretty much tally with the daily experience of veterinary workers and with what most of us instinctively feel. There is a consensus that while all vertebrates can probably feel pain, most invertebrates probably can't, with the likely exception of the cephalopod molluscs (squid, cuttlefish, octopus, nautilus).

This sounds neat enough, but not for long. Firstly, the notion of the normal human brain as exemplar of the fully developed cerebrum deemed necessary for a full awareness of pain can break down badly (as it also does for intelligence) in dramatic cases like that cited by the British neurologist John Lorber. One of his patients was a postgraduate student with an IQ of 126, a first-class honours degree in mathematics, a regular social life and virtually no brain. 'Instead of the normal 4.5-centimetre thickness of brain tissue between the ventricles and the cortical surface, there was just a thin layer of mantle measuring a millimetre or so. His cranium is filled mainly with cerebrospinal fluid.'

At present we can make little of this and similar cases in the literature, and must agree with the archaeologist Steven Mithen that 'we simply do not understand the significance of brain size for thought and behaviour.'

Secondly, the discoveries of the late Professor Patrick Wall about the causes of pain have rendered obsolete the idea most of us grew up with of a simplistic, linear model of signals travelling along nerve fibres from the site of the injury to a pain centre in the brain or, in Wall's own words, 'a sort of burglar alarm that goes off when you are injured'. Wall and a colleague developed the current prevailing model, the Gate Control theory of pain. This proposes that as messages of pain sent by the nociceptors enter the nervous system they pass through a series of 'gates' or controls in the spinal cord. These gates can increase or decrease the pain or else delay it altogether by using the body's own painkillers: the enkephalins and endorphins collectively known as endogenous opioids. In this model the brain is not just a passive receptor of pain impulses; it actively determines how many of the gates to open according to circumstances. Here, a battlefield example is once again relevant since in addition to throwing light on bravery it supplies the classic instance of the soldier who sustains serious injuries in combat but continues to fight on obliviously. Only later, when the immediate emergency is over, does his brain allow the neural gates to open and the full pain to be felt. It is a commonplace of our own experience that our reaction to pain is not a uniform sensation and also much determined by circumstances and culture. Whether we make a song and dance about a needle piercing our skin depends almost entirely on who is within earshot and whether we are darning a sock, donating blood, undergoing acupuncture or being tattooed. To be tattooed against one's will would be a mild anguish; to be tattooed as a fashion statement or as part of a tribal coming-of-age ceremony is reportedly a matter of pride, even a pleasure. I have seen people in the Philippines, Egypt and Italy make a good deal of fuss about minor injuries but endure what I assumed to be major pain with amazing stoicism. Of course, a common racist belief has always been that foreigners don't feel pain 'as we do', instinctively shifting them further down the phylogenetic spectrum towards the bovine.

This metaphor reminds us that our usual pain model appears to break down for animals, too, since cows will sometimes prance at insect bites yet have been observed grazing apparently peacefully with one leg mangled. It is not easy to make sense of this unless we propose either that grazing to a ruminant is what fighting is to a soldier, a programmed imperative that overrides everything, or else cows really are as dumb and insensible as they sometimes appear. The same applies to sharks that voraciously tear chunks off a comrade during a feeding frenzy and gulp them down despite having been themselves disembowelled. Even chimpanzees (currently and fatuously being championed for membership of the human race as though the genus *Homo* were as infinitely expandable as the European Union) will pick away at serious injuries with no evidence of concern.

In *Lives in the Balance: the ethics of using animals in biomedical research* edited by Jane A. Smith and Kenneth M. Boyd, the six physiological criteria currently used to judge whether an animal might be capable of registering pain are summed up in a table that cross-references them against various groups of animals. They are:

1. Nociceptors present—having a nervous system with sensors specifically for pain.
2. Central nervous system.
3. Nociceptors connected to central nervous system.
4. Endogenous opioids present—the animal has the capacity to make its own painkillers.
5. Responses can be modified by analgesics.
6. Response to damaging stimuli analogous to that of humans.

It is this table that supports received wisdom and proposes a hierarchy of pain consciousness that runs from humans through other mammals, birds, herps (herpetofauna, i.e. reptiles and amphibians), fish, cephalopods, insects, and on to earthworms.

Authoritative (and commonsensical) as this looks, there is still plenty of scope for uncertainties and exceptions. It seems reasonable to suppose that the capacity of an animal to produce endorphins has evolved to counteract pain. On the other hand endorphins in non-mammals might have an entirely different function. Or, given that they have now been detected in cephalopods, it may indicate that this branch of molluscs can feel pain after all and deserves to come higher up our scale. And while it appears plausible that if an animal reacts to damaging stimuli as we do, it may be sensing something analogous to our own experience, this cannot be taken for granted. Humans soon learn the association between heat and pain, often supplemented by some vivid memories. Yet a beheaded cockroach also turns out to be capable of 'learning', as shown in G. A. Horridge's classic experiment in which he suspended decapitated insects above baths of electrified saline that shocked any of their legs that drooped into it. After less than an hour's 'training' it was concluded from the position of the creatures' legs that their vental nerve cord mediates learning. This is, of course, a pretty broad way of construing 'learning', and few would argue that a headless animal was experiencing pain as opposed to being a biological specimen reacting to stimuli. Still, examples like this delicately erode the edges of what certainties we think we have.

Suddenly we are on that greyish borderland between science and philosophy, where everything depends on how one defines such things as 'pain', 'sentience', and 'awareness' in animals at a time when humans have themselves barely begun exploring the nature of their own consciousness. It is a hoary truism that we can never know what it is like to be someone else, not even a close relative, let alone a foreigner. When it comes to animals, no amount of anthropomorphism can bridge the ontological gulf. We will never have a dog's view of dogness nor, leaving aside the philosopher Thomas Nagel's imaginative leap in his essay 'What is it like to be a bat?', can we truly experience what it is like to be a bat. Exactly what suffering I have caused thousands of fish and dozens of hens can no more be known than the animals could unequivocally have expressed it. The only clear thing is that anyone interested in the philosophical aspects of animal rights must keep up with relevant and fast-changing scientific research. Rights are awarded, and awards require evidence.

This is true, for example, if the concept of 'replaceability' is ever to be made credible. 'Replaceability', in the language of animal-rights philosophers, means that the humane slaughter of certain animals such as chickens and fish is justified if it can be established that they are the kind that 'live in the present', having neither memory of their own immediate past nor apprehension of the future. The late Richard Hare, whose most famous student is the animal-rights philosopher Peter Singer, argued that animals living in the eternally sliding present would have no way of preferring to live a single long life as opposed to a series of shorter lives. Peter Singer summarizes this in *Practical Ethics* as 'a life that is biographical, and not merely biological' and considers that this applies to pigs and cows but not to fish and chickens. As the philosopher Gary Varner comments, 'The utilitarian justification is simple: humanely killing such an animal does not reduce the total happiness in the world as long as that animal is replaced with an equally happy one; but the human producers and consumers benefit from such a system. Q.E.D.' Singer's stance on the replaceability of the fish and chickens that, unlike irreplaceable cows and pigs, can't write their autobiographies, betrays a lively sense of the droll. Still, I have no idea how he squares this with his other view that the demarcation line between animals that can and can't feel pain ought to be drawn somewhere lower down between shrimps and oysters (although I gather he has since repented and decided no longer to eat bivalves).

Besides, Hare's category of Zen-like animals living eternally in the present with no memory of the past provokes much more interesting speculation about whether a drug that erases memory might also reduce a human being temporarily to the status of Mr Singer's abiographical animals when suffering pain. Certain anaesthetics do indeed have this capacity to erase memory, most notoriously gamma hydroxybutyrate or GHB, the 'date-rape' drug. Does pain that is experienced but instantly forgotten—an agony without an echo, as it were—fall short of pain as we normally understand it, whose duration is at least as significant as its intensity? If so, this is presumably the reasoning behind the practice of circumcising newborn boys without anaesthetic. We assure ourselves it is their bodies that cry, not their minds. This, of course, is also my own defence against the poor ghosts of those thousands of fish, those dozens of hens.

Whether or not animals feel pain, we can certainly express our humane instinct that some of our behaviour towards them is just plain wrong. In December three years ago I spent time in the fish hold of a Scottish trawler out in the North Atlantic. This was a huge steel chute holding a jumble of fish—some commercial, most useless by-catch to be jettisoned—all waiting their turn on the gutting line. I was particularly struck by the Portuguese dogfish known in the industry as 'Siki shark'. These are small shark, mostly about a metre long, with razor teeth and rough brown hides. Their beautiful yellow-green eyes shone like neon lamps in the fish hold's dark shambles. Many of the other fish were showing signs of acute depressurization. Their eyes bulged and their swim bladders protruded grotesquely from their mouths. The Siki shark, though, seemed more resistant to the shock of being wrenched up from a kilometre below, and several were still thrashing or twitching among the heaps of corpses. One lay on its back almost languidly among the bodies, lolling with the ship's roll. Suddenly, with a convulsive shudder, it gave birth. The baby was about sixteen centimetres long, black, its eyes little luminous beads of the same shade and fluorescent intensity as its dying mother's. Over the next three minutes it was joined by a further five siblings, blindly burrowing among the dead heaps of fish in a hopeless search for the sustaining sea.

Here, two worlds could not have been more distinct: that of living creatures (capable of suffering or not) and the commercial fishery that dispassionately processes them. We elect to ignore this year-round, clock-round industrial slaughter, just as we do the abattoirs whose bloodwork remains hidden behind anonymous walls and the European Union regulations we convince ourselves are humane. Without implying moral equivalence between Siki shark and human beings, there is surely an analogy here with the way we facilitate genocide among our own kind. Strictly in this sense, 'tonnes' and 'product' have something in common with epithets like 'gooks' or 'slopes' and with the ethos that bestows subhuman status on people wearing pink triangles or yellow stars on their prison rags. Such creatures don't die real deaths because they are never quite as alive as us. It is we who have real feelings, who have refined sensibilities, not they. It is people like us with advanced nervous systems, memories and autobiographical skills who alone can reflect the finest shades of torment and express *l'homme sensible*'s most exquisite plangencies.

This hominid view lies at the root of our current unease about animals and their rights and, indeed, about the environment generally. It involves gross inconsistency, even hypocrisy; and this coalesces most obviously around the issue of pets. 'My' grouper, 'my' cuttlefish were individuals, and we can become intimate with individuals even if occasionally we murder them. As a child I had a pet hen named Blackie whom I could never have eaten. Since then, of course, I have consumed a mountain of her kind. Like most people I have been very attached to individual cats and dogs; but over the years a good few members of both species have made their way agreeably through my digestive system in South-East Asia. This is clearly normal human behaviour, just as it is to espouse the idea of rainforests while torturing one's own suburban patch into a prettified garden which is death to bumblebees, butterflies and slugs.

There was a minor outcry in May 2003 when a Danish artist invited the public to put live goldfish through a food blender. The director of the exhibition was initially fined for cruelty to animals but a judge later ruled there was no cruelty involved because the fish were killed instantly and humanely. The artist described his exhibit as 'a protest against this cynicism, this brutality, that impregnates the world in which we live', while a vet confirmed that the fish would have died painlessly. Certainly the exhibit outed those visitors who were willing to press the blender switch (as several had). We think of Stanley Milgram's classic experiments thirty years ago that found a biddable sixty per cent of subjects willing to administer lethal electric shocks to total strangers simply at the urging of a man in a white coat who said he would take the responsibility. It is, of course, *our* finger on the button and not somebody else's.

Ethical inconsistencies are entirely normal for nearly everyone. Few people like the idea of cruelty, but most are unwilling to be so purist about it. It is hard, for example, to see the current campaign against blood sports leading to a ban on angling in Britain, given that it is apparently the nation's favourite outdoor pastime. And if there were a ban, the absurdity of its not being extended to commercial fishing would be glaring.

Thoughtful people complain that media debates on issues of cruelty to animals are normally conducted in terms of raw emotion, particularly by pressure groups like PETA (People for the Ethical Treatment of Animals). The intellectual level of PETA's discourse may be judged from its failed attempt some years ago to take the New York town of Fishkill to court to change its name, presumably ignorant of the fact that the old Dutch word *kill* (which forms part of sundry names in the area, including Catskill) means a stream or creek. More recently PETA has campaigned against hook-and-line fishing with a poster of a dog hooked through its jowl and the slogan 'If you wouldn't do this to a dog, why do it to a fish?' Or a lugworm a Jain might retort. Where does one stop? Again in May 2003, much was made of the discovery by Lynne Sneddon's scientific team at the Roslin Institute that a trout's nervous system can transmit a pain signal to its brain. This was no great surprise, given most fishes' remarkable sensory equipment (whose limits are still uncertain). But it gets us no further towards knowing whether there is a trout-*an-sich* here experiencing pain, rather than the representation of an animal whose body is registering nerve impulses. Fish are often found with old hooks still embedded in their jaws and anglers say that salmon will sometimes work hooks out by rubbing their mouths along the river bed—the same reaction Sneddon observed in the trout whose lips she had thoughtfully injected with bee venom. There is no way of being certain that this might not provoke an agreeable or even exciting sensation in fish, just as the small chillies that most humans find agonizingly hot are pecked off the plants by birds with every sign of pleasure.

Definitions of suffering are always loaded and opaque. A sententious and repellent catchphrase of the times is 'I feel your pain.' (Hard to imagine anyone saying 'I feel your orgasm' with equal solemnity.) Evidently we find ourselves most admirable in our proclaimed sensitivity to others' suffering rather than to their pleasure. Much of our vocabulary of sympathy and empathy and pity (from the Latin pius) reflects this. But it is still worth remembering that we are always speaking relatively, from the viewpoint of the self-important West, and that we are but a small minority of the earth's peoples. Britons and Americans may choose to think that 'no one' wears genuine furs any longer, but they are certainly not speaking for Italians, many of whom have gone on wearing animal pelts because they look better, feel better and are in most ways superior to man-made substitutes. Similarly, the only thing that will stop people fishing is a lack of fish.

Our mistake in this debate is to think that these issues can be resolved by science and ethics and the passing of nice clear laws. There will always be an unbridgeable conceptual gap between our unique species and the rest. Our decisions will mostly have to remain matters of individual conscience because there can also be no clear solutions to the inconsistencies presented by our unstable notions of exactly what constitutes pain or cruelty. The golden rule of 'Do unto others...' (or in the words of George W. Bush, 'to like your neighbour just like you like to be liked yourself') fails in the case of animals we elect to hunt or eat, just as environmentalism's 'Precautionary Principle' of doing nothing that cannot be scientifically proven not to cause harm collapses under its own welter of negatives. Nevertheless, these things trouble us; and it is good that they should. It is a sign of our humanity that they cause us unease. An old definition of civilization used to cite the distance people put between themselves and their excrement. A post-sewerage definition might be the extent to which we delegate our cruelty. It seems that the more we push it out of sight behind abattoir walls and disguise it with jaunty deep-freeze packaging and logos of grinning fish, the more it disturbs us precisely because we have not individually willed what has become, on our behalf, industrialized indifference and a crime against the sea. We are all innocent; but by the same inexorable token we are all guilty of our innocence.

The cultural historian Mark Cousins recently observed to me that he would scold a child for being cruel to a brick. What he meant was that the object of a person's cruelty is often less significant than the impulse itself, and unchecked expressions of minor cruelty can mature into very much worse. A similar perception can be found in classical literature and it underlies the eighteenth-century books designed to teach children not to be cruel to birds or tear the wings off flies. In certain people the golden rule seems instinctive; others must be taught. As Susan Sontag tartly remarks in *Regarding the Pain of Others*, 'Some people will do anything to keep themselves from being moved.' The only drawback to these arguments is that people are manifestly moved by different things at different times and in different cultures. One society's cruelty is another's normal spear-fishing practice.

So I shall live with my own past blood deeds, though not tormentedly. It is not exactly unease they cause me but something more like the subliminal trembling that a ship's engine sets up throughout its fabric, evidence of a constant turning-over. I am not tempted to overvalue my scrupulousness, still less to inflate it into either ethic or campaign. We can none of us afford to be too grandiose in a universe of casually expendable beings.   □

Sources: Science magazine, the New Scientist, the Financial Times, and In Nature's Interests? and 'Harey Animals' (a discussion draft), both by Gary E. Varner.

Cheltenham Festival of
Literature

In association with OTTAKAR'S

10 - 19 October 2003

Book fever takes over Cheltenham in October as the world's finest minds travel on a journey into their imaginations.

Over four hundred novelists and biographers, poets and storytellers, philosophers and explorers, artists and filmmakers descend on the town for ten days of ideas and entertainment.

Authors appearing include:

Martin Amis	Edmund White
Sarah Waters	Clive James
Steven Berkoff	Gillian Slovo
Michael Frayn	Ranulph Fiennes
Phillip Pullman	U A Fanthorpe
Esther Freud	Fred D'Aguiar
Tibor Fischer	Patricia Duncker
Michael Ignatieff	Jack Mapanje
Tracy Chevalier	Dan Rhodes
George Monbiot	Allison Pearson
John Boorman	Jacqueline Wilson
Adrian Mitchell	Eoin Colfer

For a free brochure in August
E festivalbrochure@cheltenham.gov.uk or **T 01242 237377**

Bookings T 01242 227979 · www.cheltenhamfestivals.co.uk

GRANTA

HOT NEWS
Mark Lynas

Mark Lynas has spent the past three years travelling throughout the world to witness the effects of global warming. Overleaf, some brief bulletins from the frontiers of climate change: Alaska, Australia, China, Tuvalu, the United States and Peru.

Mark Lynas

The professor's whisky

Fairbanks, Alaska—Gamblers as well as scientists take a close interest in Alaskan temperature records. Each winter the people of Nenana, a small town just south-east of Fairbanks, place bets on the exact day, hour and minute that the spring ice 'break-up' will begin on the the town's river. The tradition began when railroad engineers put down a wager of $800 in 1917; by 2000, the sum at stake had grown to $335,000, attracting punters from all over Alaska and assuring round-the-clock vigilance of the river from Nenana citizens. Records of the results provide a valuable insight into how the weather in Alaska has warmed over the past century. The average date of the spring thaw is eight days earlier than it was in the 1920s—Alaska has a week less winter. Alaskan scientists have little doubt that they are witnessing a rapid acceleration of global warming in the earth's high latitudes. Most of the state's interior, including Fairbanks, was used to seeing winter temperatures drop forty or even fifty degrees Celsius below zero. Recently, even twenty below has become rare. Professor Gunter Weller, a climatologist with the University of Alaska, remembered a New Year's Eve party in 1968, at the end of his first year in the state. 'I put a shot of very good scotch in an ice-cube tray and left it outside, it was frozen within half an hour. You wouldn't see that now, no way.' On average, he said, Alaskan winter temperatures have shot up by six degrees Celsius in the past thirty years; a warming which has also been recorded in many parts of the Canadian and Siberian Arctic.

The effects of the thawing permafrost are striking, even when seen from a taxi in urban Fairbanks. Roads have new undulations and sometimes wide cracks; crash barriers are contorted and buckled; houses tilt. Alaska spends $35 million on repairing permafrost damage every year.

A cynic or an Old Testament-inspired theologian might say that Alaska has only itself to blame. Its oil wells produce nearly a million barrels of crude a day, which, when refined, helps feed America's 200 million automobiles, the exhausts of which…but the rest of the story is familiar. The Eskimo residents of Kaktovik, a small town on the shores of the Arctic Ocean, personify this conflict between cause and effect. On the one hand, they regret thinning sea ice, new patterns of weather, and fewer animals to hunt. On the other, they enthusiastically support the oil industry for the jobs and money it provides. In Kaktovik, when I asked people about the contradiction in their attitudes, they shrugged. One woman sighed, 'All I can say is God bless us all.'

The white death

Great Barrier Reef, Australia—The cliché is true. Coral reefs are the 'rainforests of the ocean'. They are the most biologically diverse of all marine ecosystems—tropical reefs hold nine million different kinds of plants and animals, including a quarter of all known sea fish. When I walked along the beach at Heron Island, at the southern tip of the Great Barrier Reef, turtle hatchlings were emerging from the white sand and enormous shoals of pilchards turned the shallows dark brown. Heron Island seemed to be as thrillingly alive as the books suggested. Its coral told a different story.

Large sections had turned bone-white, losing the gentle greens and browns that are the marks of a healthy reef. I went snorkelling with Professor Ove Hoegh-Guldberg, one of the world's most distinguished marine biologists, who pointed out which corals had died, and which might yet manage to survive. Out of the water, he explained that coral dies when sea water temperatures pass the tolerance levels of the coral polyps, which then eject the algae that normally live deep within their bodies and provide food. For a few days the corals can cope, but if the water stays too warm for too long then they die in massive numbers.

Professor Hoegh-Guldberg has long ago abandoned the nuanced language of science; he feels the crisis is too urgent. In his view, the dead and dying coral is probably 'the most serious human impact on an ecosystem ever, certainly for at least the last 2,000 years'. The year 1998 has been the most disastrous so far—the great bleaching and death of tropical reefs from the Caribbean to the Maldives, with ninety per cent mortality rates in some areas. He estimated that a sixth of tropical corals had been destroyed. 'We've never seen an ecosystem lose sixteen per cent of its key organism in a single year before. If we lost that percentage of the rainforests in a single year, people would be screaming.' Some of the corals which died on the Barrier Reef were 700 years old: evidence that what is happening is unprecedented within at least several centuries.

Writing in the journal *Marine & Freshwater Research*, Professor Hoegh-Guldberg has estimated that, as global temperatures continue to rise, coral deaths on the scale of 1998 will become an annual event within twenty or thirty years. That day on Heron Island, he said, 'You'll see coral reefs disappear, an explosion of toxic algae, and a change in the whole marine food chain in these regions. It's not going to be pretty.'

A river ran through it

Gansu Province, China—'We have a saying,' Dr Zhang was telling me, as we stood on a dried-up river bed near the city of Wuwei, 'that in this region nine out of ten years bring drought.' He looked around at the pebbles and sand in the shadow of a now superfluous bridge. 'These days it's ten out of ten years.'

All six rivers around Wuwei have stopped flowing. Even China's grandest rivers are not what they were: the Yellow River, the second biggest after the Yangtze, now fails to reach the sea for more than half the year. Not far from Wuwei, two deserts are spreading towards each other. Dr Zhang, an official with the regional water bureau, pointed them out as we drove east, over the route of the old Silk Road, to the ancient oasis town of Minqin. The left-hand side of the road was already mostly sand. On the right, beyond a narrow strip of greenery, the dunes of the second desert were shimmering through the heat haze. Once they joined up, Minqin—once one of the most productive agricultural areas in China—would be cut off.

According to government figures, more than 2,500 square kilometres of land in China turns into desert every year, providing grit for the increasingly strong dust storms which roar down off the Inner Mongolian plains every spring, into Beijing and the south. Chinese dust-storms can be killers; one 'black wind' in May 1993 left eighty-five people dead, and the corrosive action of the wind was strong enough to strip the tops off tarred roads.

Dr Zhang and I were discussing all this in an academic kind of way when he suddenly wound up the car window. A dust storm, the fifth so far this year according to Dr Zhang, was about to hit. We could see peasants hurrying from the field towards their houses, coats wrapped around their heads. Workers from a road crew took shelter behind a wall, their shirts around their faces. Then the world around us took on an eerie red glow as the wind swirled China's topsoil high into the air.

Going down with Tuvalu

Tuvalu, South Pacific—I had been in Tuvalu for only two days when the first puddle of water appeared at the side of the small airstrip. More puddles soon joined it. The sea had welled up suddenly through thousands of tiny holes in this tropical atoll's bedrock of coral. People gathered to watch the water flow down paths, around palm trees, and into back gardens. Within an hour it was knee-deep in some places. One of Tuvalu's increasingly regular submergences had begun.

A similar thing occurs most winters in Venice, but Venice has a budget of £1.6 billion to spend on a system of protective floodgates. Tuvalu is one of the world's smallest and most obscure nations, 10,000 people, scattered across nine tiny coral atolls. Sea level rise here is a crisis of national survival: very little of Tuvalu is much more than twenty inches above the Pacific and its coral bedrock is so porous that no amount of coastal protection can save it. According to Professor Patrick Nunn, an ocean geoscientist at the University of the South Pacific, in Fiji, atoll nations such as Tuvalu will become uninhabitable within two or three decades, and may disappear altogether by the end of the century. Pleas by a succession of Tuvalu's prime ministers (and those of other atoll nations such as Kiribati and the Maldives) for dramatic cuts in greenhouse-gas emissions have been ignored by most other states. Tuvaluans will have to move.

The first batch of evacuees—seventy-five of them—is scheduled to move this year to New Zealand, 2,000 miles to the south. Many of the older people say they will refuse to move. Toaripi Lauti, the first Prime Minister of Tuvalu as an independent country (it was a British colony until 1978), said, 'I want my children to be safe. I tell them: you leave so that Tuvaluans will still be living somewhere. But I want to stay on this island. I will go down with Tuvalu.'

Government officials are angry at the international community's lack of response, and particularly angry with the Bush administration in Washington. Paani Laupepa, a senior official in the Environment Ministry, said, 'America's refusal to sign the Kyoto Protocol will affect the entire security and freedom of future generations of

Tuvaluans.' Tuvalu has recently started legal action to try to win compensation from the countries emitting most greenhouse gases. 'But how do you put a price on a whole nation being relocated?' Laupepa said. 'How do you value a culture that is being wiped out?'

Gustav and Mitch

North Carolina Outer Banks, USA—The storm, named Gustav, hit us just as the National Hurricane Center in Miami predicted it would. 'Tropical storm-force winds…high surf and dangerous rip currents are expected along the US east coast from New York southward to the northern Florida coast tonight.'

Sheets of sand, sea spray and rain battered our vehicles. We couldn't see further than a few feet. Advised the day before of Gustav's approach to the Outer Banks, I'd flown all the way from Oxford to see it, and to join a group called the Hurricane Intercept Research Team. Mark Sudduth, the team's leader, was very excited. 'Look at this radar!' he shouted, pointing to his laptop screen and an impressive orange swirl of torrential rain—Gustav's middle, which in the event turned seaward before it reached hurricane strength, or us.

Has global warming produced more storms like Gustav? The answer, at least in America, seems to be no. According to James Elsner, a tropical meteorologist at Florida State University, the number of storms hitting the eastern coast of the United States has fluctuated from decade to decade, but a trend is difficult to identify. Hugh Willoughby, the former director of the US government's Hurricane Research Division in Miami, agreed. 'Property damage has gone up like crazy,' he said. 'But those statistics are driven entirely by economic factors—there's just more stuff sitting around on the beach waiting to be blown or washed away.'

But are the storms stronger and wilder than before? The answer may well be yes. The tropical Atlantic moved into an 'active phase' in 1995, and since then an unusual number of very large storms have hit the United States, most famously and destructively Hurricane Mitch in 1998. Hugh Willoughby said that global warming could certainly be a contributory factor, and the theory is supported by computer modelling carried out at the Geophysical Fluid Dynamics Laboratory in New Jersey, which predicts stronger storms in a warmer world: higher sea temperatures provide more energy to raise rainfall intensity and windspeeds. Hugh Willoughby predicted another 'very active' season for 2004.

My father's glacier

Huaraz, Peru—I kept my father's photographs to hand as I climbed up the same valley he had climbed almost twenty years earlier, on a geological field trip in 1980. I wanted to use them to compare and contrast, to see how the landscape of the Peruvian Andes had changed; especially the glaciers.

Peru's glaciers have a vital role in the country's hydrology, keeping the coastal rivers running right through the Andean dry season. Lima—which, after Cairo, is the world's largest desert city—depends entirely on the water which comes down from the Cordilleras. The problem is that the glaciers are melting at an accelerating rate: glacial retreat is now happening three times faster than before 1980. In the last thirty years, 811 million cubic metres (about three times the volume of water in Lake Windermere) has been lost from the reservoirs of natural ice above Lima.

So I knew there would be change, that the glaciers in my father's pictures would almost certainly be smaller. It was the scale of it that was shocking. The biggest glacier in his pictures had retreated by half a mile; a dramatic ice fall in the foreground was now a few pathetic patches of snow. Another glacier off the main valley—my father's photograph showed ice fanning into a small dark lake flecked with ice floes—had almost vanished completely. The entry to the lake was now bare rock, and the lake iself swollen with extra meltwater. It looked completely different.

Later, in England, my father looked at the photographs I'd taken on my trip. We came to one of the lake—the lake now minus the glacier. He said that it had been such a beauiful glacier—he'd never forgotten it. 'It was the whole *character* of the place.' □

PRISONERS OF CONSCIENCE APPEAL FUND

Providing relief for non-violent victims of religious, ethnic and political oppression

The Prisoners of Conscience Appeal Fund has, since 1962, made relief grants to thousands of persecuted individuals both in the UK and abroad. Very often these grants are the first financial help that our beneficiaries receive after enduring gross human rights abuses, and they can been life-changing.

In addition to our normal grants, we have now begun a special project to help post-graduate students. Mr O, an actively campaigning teacher and environmental scientist from Kenya, is one such recipient. After organising peaceful mass protests against the government over land and pollution issues, he was detained several times in the space of five years, during which he was subjected to severe torture in inhuman and degrading conditions. Despite his organisation having been denounced by the government, Mr O and his group continued operating secretly, advocating the rights of his people. Eventually he escaped to the UK and subsequently gained a master's degree in environmental management. He then wished to gain a PGCE in order to teach geography in the UK but, as he was still classified as an asylum seeker, was ineligible for normal funding. We made a grant of £5,000 to cover a large portion of his fees and costs so that he was able to undertake the course and thus make a valuable contribution to life in the UK.

The need for our work has sadly not diminished over the years. Please help us to continue; we rely entirely on charitable donations.

Prisoners of Conscience Appeal Fund
Granta Appeal, FREEPOST NW5 944
London SW9 9BR
Tel: 020 7738 7511   Fax: 020 7733 7592
info@prisonersofconscience.org   www.prisonersofconscience.org

Registered Charity No. 213766

GRANTA

THE FIRST PUNCH
Jon McGregor

The first punch is a shock. We're taking a short cut across where the old steelworks used to be, that huge old strip of land between the river and the canal with the motorway flying somewhere way overhead and down here it's almost quiet. Silver birch trees and rowan bushes bursting up through the concrete foundations. Thistles with bright purple flower heads, stray yellow rapeseed flown in from the fields outside town, those white flowers with the petals like trumpets that wind their way across the ground and up round anything they can get their feelers on to. Butterflies and dragonflies and the evening-song of birds that have lived here for centuries. He says, you wouldn't have thought this was a foundry just five years ago would you. Everywhere there are scattered lumps of machinery, lost cogs and gearwheels, stacks of plate, coils of wire. He says, the way these trees come back you wouldn't believe it. He was one of the last workers to be laid off here, and he can still point out where the steel was smelted and poured and formed; the outlines of the old sheds and foundry-halls spread out across the whole site like a giant blueprint, ankle-high walls rearing up to hold a tall window frame, a door hanging off its hinges. But mostly there are trees and bushes and birdlife, and it's a good place to walk on a long summer's evening with the sky stretching hazy blue over our heads, a couple of pints swimming through us and one or other of us talking quietly now and again.

So when the first punch comes, it's a shock. Straight into my stomach and my body folds around it, the breath knocked out of me and I stagger backwards with my feet scraping and scrabbling on the stony ground. Perhaps it doesn't make sense that I'm surprised, because why else would we be out here, talking about these things, all this talk of I love my wife and if anyone ever tried I know what I'd do, but as I drag the air back into my winded lungs I'm surprised and I don't understand.

I look up at him, laughing, as though it might be a joke or I can somehow turn it into one, and I say what what are you doing what's this? He brings the heel of his open hand crashing into the side of my head like a lump-hammer. I almost fall to the ground, and there's a high-pitched ringing noise in my ears and I can't think and I don't know how to respond. I lift my arms up around my head, turning away, and he pulls my wrists to my side as he slams his forehead into the bridge of my nose.

I'm on the ground, and he is standing over me. Everything is muffled. I'm aware of the sound of running water somewhere. He stoops over me, and punches each side of my head alternately, each punch knocking my head across to meet the next. My arms reach up again to shield myself, but he just punches on through them. He is breathing heavily, watching me, concentrating.

When he stops, there is pain. A hot roar of pain flooding through me. I turn my head to one side and vomit on to the ground. He stands away slightly, getting his breath back.

And this is not right. I should be running away, or defending myself, or calling for help, but I am doing none of these things. I am lying on the dirty ground, watching him, waiting for his next move.

He says what did you think you were doing?

He says how did you even imagine you were going to get away with it?

He calls me a cunt, and he kicks me in the side, his boot fitting neatly between my hip bone and the base of my ribcage.

The first time she ever touched me, she touched me on the back of the head, her fingers trailing down through my hair to the nape of my neck, up again, down again, suddenly pulling away as though scorched against a hotplate. She said sorry sorry and for some reason I said sorry too and we didn't say anything else about it. But the way it felt; her long fingers pressing lightly and firmly, the slight scratch of her fingernails. I could feel the lines they had traced across my scalp, tingling.

It had come from nowhere, a lull in the conversation, her hand drifting there with her eyes fixed firmly on mine and I didn't pull away or say anything to stop her, and afterwards I wanted her to do it again and I wanted to leave and I wanted her not to have done it.

We were sitting in the park. We'd finished our lunches and were about to go back to work, back to our different offices in the same building and I can't even think now how it was we'd first come across each other and started talking the way we did. I was thinking about the cases I'd be dealing with that afternoon and suddenly there were her fingers trailing down the back of my neck and she was touching me.

The First Punch

I don't know how we got to that. I've never been clear how anyone ever gets to that.

A few moments later she said excuse me but you just looked a bit sad. I said did I? and she said kind of wistful and I said oh I was just thinking about work and she laughed. That laugh.

She was younger than me, about ten years younger I think but I never really noticed. It never seemed important, meeting for lunch and drinks after work and sometimes being on the same bus. It was only ever about conversation. Our ages, or the rings we both wore, were nothing to do with any of it. We were good at talking to each other was all it was. I could tell her about work, and Eleanor, and fatherhood, and I wouldn't feel like she wanted me to stop. She could tell me about her job, and her husband, and his job, and all the things she liked and didn't like about her life, and I wouldn't feel like there was anything I needed to say. Sometimes our conversation was funny, sometimes it was patient and sad, but always it just came easily and kept on going. And I thought I believed that the sheer startling fact of her physical beauty was no part of the way I enjoyed her company. But the way it felt, that day in the park when she just ran her fingers down through the hair on the back of my head, that was something; and her voice saying because she thought I looked like I was feeling sad, that was something more again.

It had been a long time since anyone had done that.

I wanted to say thank you but instead I said sorry. She laughed, and she said you look good when you're thinking, pretty. I was embarrassed for a moment. Pretty seemed like a strange word to use of a forty-year-old man with lines around his eyes.

But all that happened next was I looked at my watch and stood up to go back to work. She said have a good afternoon, I walked away, and when I turned back to look she wasn't looking at me. She was reading something, running her fingers up and down the back of her head, through her dark tangle of hair. I went back to work, and I tried not to think about it, and the next time I saw her was that afternoon at her house. His house.

He comes towards me, and my body tenses, my forearms crossing over my face. He crouches beside me, and pulls my arms away, pinning them to my chest with one hand. I look at him. His eyes are

187

wide and clear, he is sweating a little, there are strands of hair sticking to his forehead. He takes off his jacket, rolls it up, and puts it under my head for a pillow. He doesn't say a word. I look at him, my vision still clouded, my mouth gaping soundlessly. He smiles.

I say, but but what but I didn't do anything.

He smiles again. He says you loved it didn't you?

I look at him, and I don't know what to say. I say, I didn't, what? no, no I didn't.

He winces, turns away, turns back. You fucking liar he says, don't fucking lie to me.

The memory of her. Standing there in that dress. Her bare shoulders and the way she looked at me with those eyes. The movement of the dress when she turned in the doorway, the way it swung around the backs of her legs. That was all it took; her looking at me like that, those eyes, the way the dress swung around the backs of her long bare legs as she turned in the doorway there.

He rushes in towards me and stamps his foot down on to my chest and again all the breath is forced out of me, again there is staggering sickening pain. He does this three times, and the third time, barely realising what I am doing, I roll over and start to crawl away, scraping my hands on the brambles, heading towards the sound of rushing water. I can hear shouted voices somewhere, and laughter. I am crawling for perhaps thirty seconds when I hear quick footsteps behind me and feel a sudden snapping impact to the back of my head. I stop crawling.

He rolls me over, on to my back, and places the pillow beneath my head again, looking down at me with a look on his face as if he wants me to speak. I am shivering. My breathing is ragged and torn. I can hear the shouted voices from somewhere over by the river, I can see the cars rushing across the flyover way up in the sky.

He says don't fucking lie to me David.

He says I don't need people lying to me, I won't have it, I need to be able to trust people, it's not too much to ask is it?

I look at him. He takes out a packet of cigarettes, putting the pack to his mouth and biting one out like a splinter from a hand. He puts the packet back and lights the cigarette.

He says she's my wife yeah? I know what she looks like, I know what happens when she's wearing that dress, I know what it does to the way she looks yeah? I bought her that dress so that she'd look like that, he says. I don't know what I'm supposed to say, I watch him and I keep breathing and I listen to the sound of the voices somewhere getting quieter now.

He says and you're telling me you were in the house with her, in the middle of the afternoon, and she's wearing that dress, and you didn't even want to?

He calls me a liar again, he comes closer and he looks at me and he smokes his cigarette.

The second time she ever touched me was that afternoon in her house. I can't quite remember why I was there, she'd asked me to pop round and help move a sofa or a table or something but when I got there she didn't mention it. It was a hot day, she had her hair all tied up on top of her head and wisps of it were falling out, she kept tucking them behind her ear, fanning herself with a piece of paper and saying whoo I'm hot aren't you? And every time she said it she giggled, nervously or embarrassedly or excitedly I couldn't tell. She had a laugh that made my ears flush red. He was out at work, she told me that, more than once.

She poured us both a cold drink, orange juice with lemonade, and she dropped ice cubes into the glasses. She dared me to suck a whole ice cube and I dared her back, and we stood there in her kitchen with our mouths puckered around a block of ice each, grimacing at each other, her eyes watering and sparkling, and when she spat hers out and laughed and leaned towards me that was the second time she touched me. Her two hands flat to my chest, gently, briefly.

It had been a long time since anyone had done that.

It was a blue dress she was wearing, pale blue as though it had been washed too often, and it hung from her bare round shoulders on straps as thin as parcel string. It was cut into a sort of v at the back, and when she turned and reached up to a shelf, leaning back slightly, I could see almost down to her waist before I looked away.

We sat in the front room with our cold drinks. She sat beside me, not close enough to touch but turned towards me with her legs folded beneath her and one arm laid out along the back of the sofa. And she talked a lot, quickly, she laughed and the way she laughed made me feel uncomfortable and good at the same time. And when she didn't talk she took a long slow sip of her drink, looking over me at the top of her glass, a long slow look which I wanted to look away from but couldn't.

She asked me how were things with Eleanor, and I said the same, that she wasn't spending so long in bed but that she still wouldn't leave the house and she still looked puffy-eyed when I came in from work. I told her the doctor had been talking about a different medication and that I wasn't sure that was really the answer. This was almost a routine conversation by now. She said it's good you know, what you do for her, I respect that, and I said no, really, I mean she's my wife what else would I do?

She was wearing a long bead necklace, she was twisting it between two fingers and when she let it go it fell against bare skin.

She said I'm glad you're here it's good to have you here and I said well it's good to be here and I was being mock polite but really I meant it. It was good to be there, on her sofa, with a cold drink, her sitting with me, in that dress, tucking wisps of dark hair behind her ear and talking and laughing. She said is it? suddenly, demandingly, is it good to be here, are you glad you're here? And I said yes, yes it is, yes I am, and I was confused and she was quiet.

I finished my drink. I went to the toilet. I washed my face and my hands, and when I came out of the bathroom at the top of the stairs that was when it happened.

She was standing in the open doorway of the room next to the bathroom, leaning against the door frame slightly, she'd taken her shoes off and she had one ankle curled round behind the other.

The blue dress hung down to her knees, but with one leg lifted like that it rode up a little, about a third of the way up her thigh.

I looked at her.

That was all. I just looked at her.

She lifted a hand to adjust the knot of hair at the back of her head, and smiled.

And that could have been enough, that moment, standing there looking at her, and her smile, for me, that hot day with the windows open and the sleepy sounds of summer drifting through the house, a lawnmower somewhere, children shouting.

She said how do I look? and it seemed like she really wanted to know, standing there beautiful and desirable every inch of her, like she wasn't sure, her elegant bare feet and the smooth straight rise of her legs, the way her dress pulled against the curve of her hips and the press of her breasts, her shoulders, her neck, her eyes. Her eyes looked strange for a moment, when I looked, anxious almost. I said you look good and she said do I? really? as if she wasn't sure, as if she thought I might be humouring her somehow, as if there was no one who told her each day how good she looked. I said, very quietly, yes you do, you look very good. She smiled again, looking away for a moment, looking over her shoulder into the room. I still hadn't moved. When she turned back her eyes looked different and she wasn't smiling. She said, quietly, looking straight at me, do you want me? I did. I wanted her. Hugely and deeply I wanted her. I said, I whispered, yes. She said, her voice quiet and unsteady, oh good, and she turned quickly in the doorway, stepping into the room, out of sight. I didn't even breathe.

That movement, the turn of her hips, the swing and lift of her dress, the backs of her legs.

I don't know how long she waited. I didn't move. I couldn't. She reappeared, and when she spoke this time her eyes spilled clearly over into tears, her voice cracking. She said don't be shy I'm waiting for you. She said don't you want me you said you wanted me. I said I do. She said well come on then, and she opened her mouth slightly, and there were tears down both her cheeks, shining. I wanted her incredibly. I hesitated. I turned and walked down the stairs, out into the afternoon sunshine.

My hands are folded together on my chest, I am having trouble breathing and the pain is everywhere now. He looks at me. His cigarette is halfway to the filter. He coughs a little, turning to spit on the ground. He says excuse me, sorry.

He walks towards me and crouches down. He says, listen, you and Eleanor, that's your problem.

He says I don't care if she's not giving you any. I don't give a shit if she makes you sleep in the spare room or if she never even wants to undress in front of you again. I'm not bothered. It's got nothing to do with me. But you're not having mine, all right? He says it very quietly, smiling, as though he's trying not to laugh, and he stands up.

I didn't tell him anything about Eleanor. He shouldn't know all that. I've only ever talked to one person about these things.

He taps the end of his cigarette, and flakes of ash flutter to the ground. He says I'm sorry about all this mate, but it had to be done. He says you got to be able to trust people David, else what's the point?

He says I'm not having you or no one fucking about with that, all right?

He flicks his cigarette away and looks at me for a few moments, as if he's waiting for me to say something in return. There is nothing I can say.

He turns and walks away from me, heading towards the bridge over the river where the footpath leads to the steps up the side of the hill, through the woods and out into the streets to the house where he lives with his wife.

I watch until he disappears amongst the trees and the bushes. I stand up, slowly and painfully. The sun is low in the sky, everything is bright and clear and peaceful and I feel sick. Dizzy. Confused.

I start to make my way home. It feels like a long way. As soon as I start walking I have to stop for a moment, my breath caught tight in my bruised lungs.

The cars rush across the flyover. Birds crowd together overhead, sweeping across the sky. Dandelions and thistles and blackberry bushes force their way up through the broken concrete.

I walk towards the bridge, towards the steps up the side of the hill and the house where I live with my pale and tearful wife. I will ask her how she is. I will fetch her what she needs from the kitchen. I will take her to the bathroom. She trusts me to do this for her. It's important. You have to be able to trust people. □

GRANTA

LOOT
Christopher de Bellaigue

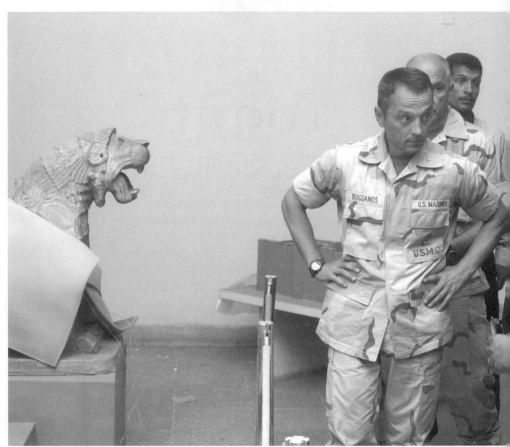

Colonel Matthew Bogdanos in the Iraq National Museum, May 2003

When I first went to the Iraq National Museum, I tried to get in through a gate that in its design had been inspired by Nineveh, the ancient capital of Assyria. The gate had a big hole in it, above the door, where it had been pierced by an American tank shell. The door was locked—it turned out to belong to the children's museum— so I walked further down the street, as far as the entrance to a garden that served both museums. There, instead of a ticket-seller and someone to tear off a stub, I found a twenty-year-old private from Mississippi. To begin with, he was reluctant to let me in; I had no press pass. When I showed him my passport, he softened. 'Seeing as you're a Brit, and you helped us in the war, I'll be nice.' I thought of my French father, and said, 'And what if I were French?' He replied, 'I'd tell you to get the fuck out of here.' We laughed, and I went in.

Baghdad in May was a broken city, with un-citizens and vacant plinths where once there had been a government. Approaching along a highway from Basra, I passed mile-long convoys of lorries and transporters. These promises of aid and coercion gave me a guilty sense of security; with this, the Americans would surely be able to fill any vacuum, even one that Saddam had left behind. But when they got to the capital, the lorries and transporters—and their military protectors, bored men and women swinging their legs out of the sides of their Humvees—retreated behind the walls of appropriated palaces. They rarely ventured out, and then only for short periods. They seemed unwilling, or perhaps unable, to rule.

I was drawn to Baghdad by news of the looting that had taken place in the museum during the second week of April, as the Americans were taking the city. Shortly after, a distraught museum official, Nabhal Amin, reportedly put the figure of lost and destroyed items at 170,000. Many Western newspapers accused the Americans of indifference to the catastrophe. More recently, it had been determined that, although some irreplaceable pieces were lost, much less was missing than the media had originally suggested. The Americans had sent an assistant district attorney and marine reservist called Matthew Bogdanos to conduct an inquiry into events, and to recover as many of the lost items as he could.

On the road to Baghdad, I'd read a primer on Iraq's tribes and history that Gertrude Bell wrote for British officers during the First World War. (It is exemplary for its succinctness and lightly worn scholarship, as well as for the certainty of its judgements.) Bell was an influential member of the colonial establishment that established a British mandate after the war, the exponent of a sly imperialism that was to place an imported Sunni king, Feisal of Mecca, on the newly invented throne of a newly invented state which had many Shi'a citizens, perhaps even a majority of them. No one, nowadays, is surprised that the scheme failed, and that it led to a series of dictatorships, of which Saddam's was the most dreadful. But Bell seems to have believed that imperialism could be both master and servant of the nascent state. Having fallen out with the colonial administration, she founded the Iraq National Museum and drafted an antiquities law that obliged Leonard Woolley, the British excavator of Ur, to divide his findings between his two employers—the British Museum and the University Museum in Philadelphia—and also the new museum in Baghdad. Iraq's distant past may have convinced her that its disparate peoples constituted a nation, with a unified cultural history. She certainly realized the importance of physical heritage to nationhood. Now, in 2003, it appeared that the Americans didn't have this sensitivity. You sensed this criticism behind the sneers of their detractors; it was why they'd permitted the looting. And so I wanted to meet Colonel Bogdanos, and find out what kind of occupier he was.

I crossed the museum's garden and went in through what looked like the main door, into a hall beneath a low cupola where there was a small crowd of people, most of them foreigners. I recognized two from the TV and newspaper analysis of events at the museum. One of them, a handsome man with white hair, was leaning heavily on a stick—that was Professor McGuire Gibson of Chicago University's department of archaeology. Gibson was talking to a short shapeless man with a precarious smile—Donny George, the museum's research director.

Over the preceding few weeks, George had come to personify Iraqi culture. (More so than Selma Nawali Mutawali, the museum director, who kept away from the media, or even Jabbar Ibrahim Khalil, the director-general of the antiquities board.) He spoke good English. He'd given interviews. He'd flown to London to brief officials from the British Museum on what had been lost, and how. On the question of numbers, he was more circumspect than Amin; there was no way of knowing how many items had been lost, it seemed, until a time-consuming audit had been carried out. But when it came to blame, he clearly conveyed the impression that the Americans should have done more. 'Mr George,' according to the London *Guardian*, 'described how he went to the US Marines' headquarters to beg commanders to send troops to the museum three days after the looting began.' 'They did nothing for three more days...I don't know why,' Neil MacGregor, the director of the British Museum, was quoted as saying. 'It's very extraordinary...that with American troops in Baghdad, American troops almost at the gates of the museum, this was allowed to happen.'

I knew, or thought I knew, this much:

At 11 a.m. on Tuesday April 8, Iraqi fighters entered the museum grounds, firing on US forces that were outside the grounds. Jabbar, George and the only remaining museum guard fled. A fourth employee, Muhsin Abbas, was reluctant to leave his house in the compound. During the ensuing fighting, one or more Iraqis fired rocket-propelled grenades from the roof of the children's museum; the firing was stopped by the tank shell that holed the Assyrian gate. By Thursday, and perhaps before, fighting in the compound had subsided, to the extent that looters and vandals were able to enter through the back gate which had seen the heaviest fighting. On Thursday, Abbas entreated an American tank commander, positioned at an intersection a few hundred yards away, to move his tank to the museum gates; the commander refused, and the looting continued until Friday. On Saturday, George, who had taken refuge in his aunt's house, heard radio reports of the looting. The following morning, having exacted a promise of immediate American protection for the museum, he and Jabbar returned to their posts. The help didn't come. On Tuesday, George used a journalist's satellite phone to contact colleagues at the British Museum. Tony Blair's office was informed that the Iraq National Museum was still unprotected. The following day, Wednesday April 16, the Americans arrived.

As I observed the foreigners at the museum, who turned out mostly to be archaeologists, two American soldiers crossed towards the group. There was a tall, genial-looking fellow with blonde hair; he followed a smaller, compact man wearing a T-shirt who rolled his shoulders as he walked. The short one was in charge; without glancing at anyone, he approached George and they talked for a minute. The American had a sharp nose and little pale eyes. When he'd finished, he walked back through the group of people again, looking straight ahead. I saw his name, in capitals on the seat of his combat fatigues: BOGDANOS.

There's an empty space on the second floor of the Iraq National Museum where there used to be a limestone head of a goddess, dating from around 3100 BC. The head is called the Warka Head after the place (which is now called Warka, but which the ancients knew as Uruk) in southern Iraq where it was found. Photographs show her lips pursed and horizontal over a shy chin, no cheekbones to speak of, and a sensational arrangement of eyes and eyebrows: two enormous almond-shaped vacancies surmounted by a continuous, undulating and very deep indentation. The rhythm of this, her eyebrow, flows into her nose. Now she's gone.

In her heyday—when she was being propitiated, bribed and flattered—the civilization of Sumer, the lush region in which Uruk lay, was spreading its influence into Iran and up the Euphrates valley to Syria and Anatolia. (Sumer corresponds to southern Mesopotamia, which is a Greek word meaning between two rivers— in this case, the Tigris and Euphrates.) By the time of the Warka Head, much of Sumer had been under irrigation for more than 2,000 years. Crop surpluses financed the purchase from neighbouring regions of timber, precious stones and copper for tools and weapons. The Sumerians gave their gods houses, not unlike their own, that we know as temples; when reconstructed and enlarged, these came to resemble a mountain of ascending platforms and were the prototype of the temple tower, or ziggurat.

During the museum tour, I stuck close to McGuire Gibson. He clumped quickly around, discharging information and wisdom. At the bottom of a flight of steps that led up to the first-floor galleries, he pointed out a window made of glass bricks that the looters had smashed in order to get in. It suggested that the thieves—I mean the professionals who took the good stuff, not the freebooters who stole light bulbs and trashed filing cabinets—knew the museum plan. As we went up the stairs, Gibson observed that every step was badly chipped. 'The thieves were probably bringing down the Basitki Statue,' he said. 'It weighs more than three hundred pounds. They must have bounced it down the stairs.' I asked what the Basitki Statue was. 'It's a naked man, but we only have the bottom half. They found it in the north, while they were building a road. It's a marvellous example of Akkadian metallurgy, almost totally copper—which is much harder to pour than bronze.' I asked the date. 'Around 2300 BC.'

That was the era of Sargon, the founder of the Akkadian Empire that spread outwards from central Mesopotamia and eclipsed Sumerian city-states like Uruk. It extended its influence northwards—up the Tigris into Assyria (which lay in what is now northern Iraq), and up the Euphrates into Syria. Unlike the Sumerian tongue, whose origins are obscure, Akkadian is from the Semitic family of languages, whose modern members include Arabic and Hebrew. Akkadian went on to become the lingua franca of Mesopotamia and was used as a diplomatic language throughout the Middle East.

Up on the first floor, Gibson stopped by a steel strut supporting a big black stone. 'At least they didn't take the basalt stele,' he said. The stele has two depictions in low relief of a Sumerian king killing a lion. In one, he's shooting the beast. In the other, he's spearing it. The king wears a patterned skirt and has bunched hair and enormous eyes. I'd seen him, or kings like him, in other contexts: doing battle or holding an animal that was about to be sacrificed. Gibson told me why he thought the basalt stele was important. 'These are the first indications we have of what kings do. If you think about it, it hasn't changed very much. Look at Queen Elizabeth. She hunts, goes to church and reviews the guard.'

Here were the origins of the human struggle to be civilized; and, a later mark of that continuing struggle, how civilized it had been to dig up the evidence and put it on show, making self-congratulation—look at what we were, look at what we are—so convenient. But now the link to both those ordered pasts, the ancient and the recent, had been cut.

The corridor leading to the galleries was lined with offices that had been ransacked; their papers were strewn over the floor. Most of the display cabinets were empty, and some of them smashed. The contents of most of the cabinets had been put in vaults. (About one hundred pieces, the heaviest and most fragile ones, had been left in the gallery when the war began; forty-two of them had been stolen.) About thirty of them had been smashed. No one knew when life—in the museum, in the city at large—would start again, or what it would be like when it did.

Christopher de Bellaigue

In fact, the severance had happened long before the war. In 1991, reverberations from America's aerial attack on the nearby telecommunications ministry had shattered some pieces, leading to efforts to pack others into the vaults. Many of the museum's most valuable items—the royal treasure of Ur, for example, and the gold jewellery of Nimrud—were deposited in the vaults of the Central Bank of Iraq. According to Gibson, George and other staff members had decided to leave these pieces in the bank, to reduce the likelihood of theft. 'They knew that war could restart at any time. They were even afraid that people from the government would come and take them.' After 1991, sanctions meant that the museum's air-conditioning units couldn't be repaired. Chemicals for restoration were impossible to buy. The museum was closed for a decade; it reopened only in 2001.

Gibson spoke of the invention, in ancient Mesopotamia, of the world's first writing system. The Sumerians started by scoring line drawings on damp clay. Later, they impressed straight lines with a stylus. The impression of the stylus formed a wedge, which gave the script its name, cuneiform, from the Latin *cuneus*, wedge. The result was a sort of picture writing, written in boxes from right to left. The desire for mass reproduction was met by the invention of the hollow cylinder seal, made of stone (originally wood, Gibson reckons) and incised with writing or images; it left an impression when rolled out on clay. (The thieves who entered the Iraq National Museum knew where the museum's collection of cylinder seals were, and stole thousands of them.)

Our tour ended in the Assyrian gallery which was the most normal-looking in the museum; none of its enormous bas-reliefs, many of them from Khorsabad, could possibly have been moved. The staff had put sandbags on the floor, to cushion the sculptures if they were dislodged during the bombing. (None was.) Looking at the bas-reliefs, it struck me that the coldness of Assyrian sculpture equals its magnificence.

Before now, I'd had no reason to doubt the belief that there is little, save the shared experience of Ottoman and then British imperialism, to bind Iraqis together. Shi'a and Sunni Muslims in the south and middle, Kurds in the north; what was their common thread? (Not Islam; that could be an agent of division.) But Bell and the others who built up the museum had detected a thread. So, in our era, had people like Gibson. He got mildly irritated when I disparaged Iraq's claims to nationhood: 'That's propaganda by people who want to split the country.' The thread ran through Sumeria, Akkad, Babylonia, Assyria. It wasn't ethnic; it wound around deities and language, ways of governing and warring.

A few weeks later, I read an English translation of the epic of Gilgamesh, king of Uruk. Gilgamesh spends most of the story behaving perfectly yobbishly, before finally (and undeservedly) stumbling on wisdom. The epic probably started as a series of lays sung by Sumerian minstrels. Later, the Babylonians enlarged and standardized it, and translated it into Akkadian. But the reason I was able to read it with relatively few lacunae is the important place the epic occupied in the great libraries of the Assyrian kings. There had been a common literature, it seemed, from the Persian Gulf almost to Turkey, common ideas of kingship and sagacity. Until a few weeks ago, there had been Saddam; his bootprint was on every face.

Leaving the entrance under the cupola, I saw smoke rise over the city. It came from high-tension wire that people had dug out of the ground; they were burning the wire to retrieve copper. I crossed to the building where the American guards were billeted, and asked for Bogdanos.

What I knew of him was that he had soldiered in Central Asia and distinguished himself in counter-narcotics on the Mexican border; that he'd boxed for the New York City Police Department Widows and Orphans Fund and been decorated for counter-terrorism in Afghanistan. More pertinently, in this new context, he had an MA in classical studies. His biographical details didn't mention his unsuccessful prosecution of Puff Daddy, but that's a blip in a career that I imagine, one day, will be gilded with public office.

He came out of the guardhouse: brisk, unfriendly. This, he said, is a recovery operation, not a criminal investigation. 'The first job is to determine what is missing and for that you determine what you had and then what you have and do the math.' To date, he said, nearly 1,000 pieces had been recovered, mostly from repentant locals. But, he added, 'we've been hampered by the lack of a comprehensive inventory produced by the museum.'

The following day, unveiling his 'preliminary findings' via a live feed to the Pentagon press corps, Bogdanos said that staff members had produced 'partial inventories' for the gold and jewellery that they claimed to have moved to the central bank. The staff had vowed, furthermore, not to divulge the whereabouts of a secret storeroom 'until a new government in Iraq is established and US forces leave the country'. A few days before, a reporter had asked Bogdanos whether he was accusing the Iraqis of obstruction. He replied, 'I offer only facts, not opinions. You can draw your own conclusions.'

To me, he said, 'There are several different dynamics at work here. Make sure you quote me right! I don't like painting broad brush. I don't take a binary view. Moral judgement gets in the way. I may have my opinion about the former regime and about members of the museum staff who were Ba'ath Party members, but I keep those opinions to myself.'

I asked Bogdanos what the museum meant to Iraqis. His answer was autobiographical. 'I've been humbled...yeah, that's the word...by the reaction. People, complete strangers, have been coming up to me and saying thank you. I go walking in the community, into the marketplace—I go to a little coffee shop. They call me the colonel from the museum. No matter how much I insist they won't let me pay.'

Imagine Bogdanos going for his morning coffee, exchanging pleasantries with the regulars, striking a rapport. Think again. This is Baghdad, a city that's jumpy as hell, where American soldiers aren't permitted to remove their flak jackets and helmets in public, let alone hang out with the locals in coffee shops. No American goes out to coffee shops in Baghdad.

It seemed strange that it had taken the Americans from April 8 until April 16 to secure the museum. The staff, I pointed out, said that the battle for the museum had been largely fought on the 8th. Why, when he was entreated on Thursday, had the American tank commander regretted that he didn't have the 'authority' to guard the main repository for the greatest of ancient civilizations? Why had a civil affairs officer assured George that protection would be dispatched immediately, only for it to take three days to arrive? Didn't this constitute, at the very least, an astounding breakdown in communication?

Bogdanos looked angry. 'I don't understand this minority reporting.'

He paused. 'Look, I've spent my entire adult life studying antiquities, and all the antiquities in the world—all of them—don't equal a single human life. Iraqi, British, American—it makes no difference.

'So, you want to know why the staff left on the eighth and the US got here on the sixteenth?' I nodded. 'THIS WAS A COMBAT ZONE.' Not quite a shout. 'Have you ever fired in anger?' Bogdanos had guessed the answer, but waited for me to shake my head. 'No one who has shot in anger would ask that question. The kids who got here—the heroes—did so as fast as was humanly possible.'

He was hitting his stride. 'It's clear beyond peradventure that the Iraqis violated international law by firing from the museum.' He was referring to the rocket-propelled grenades that were fired from the room of the children's museum; unused grenades had also been found on the roof of the museum library. 'I could get outraged,' he said, 'but that doesn't get me anywhere. Now let me ask you a question.' He leant forward. 'Can you explain why one of the storage magazines had been opened without being forced, and why it had a firing position inside? How did that door get open?'

'Someone let them in there?'

'It's a reasonable hypothesis.'

According to Bogdanos's preliminary findings, 'the first and second-level storage rooms were looted, but show no signs of forced entry on their shared exterior steel door. The keys to this door were last seen in a director's safe and are now missing... Turning to the basement-level magazine, the evidence here strongly suggests that this magazine was compromised not by random looters, but by thieves with an intimate knowledge of the museum and its storage procedures. For it is here they attempted to steal the most traffickable and easily transportable items stored in the most remote corner of the museum. The front door of this basement magazine was intact, but its bricked rear doorway was broken and entered. This magazine has four rooms, three of which were virtually untouched. Indeed, even the fourth room appears untouched except for a single corner where almost thirty small boxes originally containing cylinder seals, amulets, and jewellery had been emptied, while hundreds of surrounding larger, but empty, boxes were untouched. The thieves here had keys that were previously hidden elsewhere in the museum.'

Towards the end of our conversation he said, 'Let me ask you another question: Who did the looting?' He answered himself: 'The Iraqis, yeah.'

Clearly, there was abundant evidence that the looters had been tipped off—about the location of important keys, and of suitable items to steal. There was not, so far as I could make out, evidence to suggest who had done the tipping off: former or current staff members, senior or junior? The fighter in the first-floor storage magazine seems to have entered the museum along with the looters, after the battle had been largely won and the other Iraqi fighters had fled. But could one sniper have resisted a concerted American effort to secure the museum and its grounds? The Americans clearly hadn't shrunk from firing back at him; his nest was pockmarked with their bullet holes. In front of the museum, there was little evidence of fighting—except for the Assyrian gate, which had been holed on the 8th. At the back, however, there was much more evidence of an armed struggle.

Strangely, Bogdanos's report had the effect of discrediting some of his verbal insinuations. The report found 'no evidence that any fighters entered the museum compound before the staff left on the eighth'. That hardly suggested collusion with the fighters. It acknowledged that the staff judged the museum safe for return on April 12. That was four days before the Americans showed up, 'as fast as humanly possible'.

The next day, I met a tank sergeant called David Richard. He'd been one of the first Americans into the compound, on the 16th. (George later told me that Richard had been the commander whom Abbas had asked to move his tank to the museum gates.) According to Richard, fighting in the vicinity of the museum compound had been 'the most prolonged constant combat that I experienced in the war'. He suspected that a police station at the back of the compound, formerly manned by regular policemen and museum guards, had been used by Iraqi fighters as a command post for defence operations. But he contradicted Bogdanos's assertion that the Americans had secured the museum as soon as they could. Even when the area around the compound was completely in American hands, Richard went on another mission, to secure a small airfield. When he went back to the museum, on the 16th, he was met by at least fifty reporters.

Bogdanos's findings ended: 'We are proud to have begun the journey and honoured to have served.' Shortly after, he left Iraq. His stay had coincided with a dramatic downward revision of loss estimates—under 10,000 pieces had been stolen and destroyed, it seemed, rather than the 170,000 that had been reported. More than 900 artefacts had been returned. But Bogdanos never addressed the questions that needed answers if the Americans' conduct was to be judged: precisely when did fighting in the compound end? If the compound was safe enough for dozens of looters and, later, dozens of journalists, how come it was lethal for the marines? He asked different questions—about the Iraqis. What was the extent of staff collusion with pro-Saddam fighters? How did the looters get into Mutawali's safe? Is it worth losing sleep over dyed-in-the-wool Ba'athists? Editors and reporters duly lost interest in the old questions, and started asking the new ones. That was Bogdanos's achievement.

None of the staff denied that inside knowledge had been a factor in the looting: but whose inside knowledge? At the start of hostilities, 300 people had been working on the site. Part of the problem for any reporter—certainly for me—was that, George apart, the museum staff was reluctant to talk. Jabbar never gave me an interview. He looked uncomfortable if we passed in the corridor. Mutawali slammed doors in my face. But the museum had never been an open place; few government offices in the Middle East are. Its ledgers and inventories were always less penetrable than those of most Western museums. Even that may not have been entirely the Iraqis' fault. According to Neil MacGregor, the standard of management suffered when 'sanctions started to bite'.

Alongside some sensible preparations for the war, there had been appalling sloppiness. In June, it became known that a BBC television presenter, Dan Cruickshank, had discovered the reconstituted lyre of Ur, one of the museum's most famous pieces, among a heap of other things in a chaotic room. But what did this prove? Negligence, fear of foreign reporters—these aren't the same as thievery and plots.

A few days later, I stood on top of the huge ziggurat at Ur, in southern Iraq. It was early evening, and Moayed, my translator, was jumpy. Ur is about ten kilometres from Nasiriyah, where we were staying, and he was worried that the road would be dangerous after nightfall. I'd got used to Moayed's fretting. On the whole, he was a stimulating companion. He had a good stock of malapropisms—my favourite was his substitution of 'terrorism' for 'tourism'. I liked his poetic conviction that everything would turn out for the worst. This was exemplified by a warning that he gave to our driver, not to honk at a tractor that had blocked the road: 'He'll get out his Kalashnikov and shoot us.'

The British had failed to prevent the destruction by looters of the steel factory near Basra where Moayed had worked as a supervisor. (Three thousand people lost their livelihoods.) I'd met him among the scores of engineers, doctors and teachers that clamoured every morning for a job outside the main UN hotel in Basra. (The UN eventually announced eighty vacancies; more than 5,000 people applied.) He didn't like working with reporters. It took him far from his wife and five children, and made him even more depressed about how the country was faring. One day, he told me of a man who is asked how he can stand sour. The man replies: 'Because there is sourer.'

In 1991, when Iraq's defeat in the Gulf War led to an uprising across the south, a fairly senior Ba'athist official, a relation, sought sanctuary in Moayed's home. Moayed agreed that the man should stay, even though, had the rebels come to hear, they would have killed Moayed as well as his guest. After the rebellion's suppression, the official made sure that Moayed was rewarded with a titular honour denoting loyalty to the regime. Moayed felt no such loyalty, but the honour was useful as protection. Moayed told me this story with neither pride nor shame. He expected me to understand that this was the sort of compromise you had to make.

There were two military men on the ziggurat. One was Viktor Hancock, a handsome black soldier from Las Vegas. His joy was photography; Operation Iraqi Freedom had inspired him to shoot more than 220 rolls of film. Today was his eleventh visit to the ziggurat. 'Beats the Luxor,' he said with a smile, referring to Vegas and not the Upper Nile.

Our guide around the site was an affable air force major with an interest in archaeology, Jon Anderson. He indicated the airbase that the Iraqis had built in Ur's shadow. Since the Americans had taken the base on March 22, Anderson reported, there had been almost no vandalism—a marine who tried to make off with a Third Dynasty brick had been 'disciplined'. During the 1991 Gulf War, American troops sprayed bullets at the southern side of the ziggurat, and used their bayonets to dig up pottery pieces that have yet to be returned. From Anderson's vantage, the new liberation was a blessed event. 'It's been an honour to be part of the effort.'

About 200 yards to the east lay the graves that Leonard Woolley started excavating in 1926; almost nineteen hundred were found, dating from about 2600 BC (well before the rise of the Akkadians) to about 2000 BC (after their eclipse). The most celebrated of these were the 'Royal Graves', so called because of the opulence of the grave goods inside, and the great number of sacrificed retainers. We descended the ziggurat and walked towards a wide pit that once contained more than seventy bodies—they'd apparently been drugged and laid out in rows. Anderson pointed out a feature that he liked: drains, holed with third century BC fingers, from which waste water percolated into dry soil.

Anderson led me past an embankment left by Woolley's men, and down a surprising flight of steps. We descended a second flight, into a cool chamber with a pointy brick vault that seemed on the verge of collapse. In this chamber, and others like it, Woolley made some of the most celebrated finds in archaeology. There were gold vessels and statuettes; diadems of Indian carnelian and Afghan lapis lazuli; and headdresses, surmounted by sheet silver and inlaid stones, that were excavated on the skeletons of their wearers. There, too, was the lyre of Ur—or rather, the remains of it. It would join the compendium of national symbols. (If you smoke Sumer cigarettes, you'll know it; it adorns the pack.)

The next morning, we went to the house of a woman in Nasiriyah called Iqbal, who worked for the antiquities department. We'd arranged to go with Iqbal to Umma, an important Third Dynasty city-state. It was one of at least six archaeological sites that were being looted across Dhiqar, the province of which Nasiriyah is the capital. Some had been invaded by armed gangs, 200-strong; guards assigned to the sites had fled. The gangs worked speedily and without regard for the archaeologists who'd preceded them. Meticulously revealed topographies—the outline of a city wall, for example, or the foundations of a temple—had been casually obliterated.

Hearing about the looting and its strange wantonness, I was reminded of a conversation that I'd had with an American official in Baghdad. The official had been flabbergasted by the destructive energy that the Iraqis were directing at telephone exchanges and hospitals, homes and universities. 'I've never encountered anything like this,' he said. 'It's like the whole country has turned itself inside out. It's very un-Muslim. Wholesale thievery, as far as I remember, is not part of the Qur'an.' Many Americans had believed that Saddam would leave behind model citizens. How long, I wondered, before they came to regard the Iraqis as savages, undeserving of liberation?

Exemplary savagery, many Iraqis maintained, would stop the looting, but the Americans didn't want blood on their hands. In Nasiriyah, we'd heard a colleague of Iqbal's, a man named Hamdani, accuse the occupiers of indifference to the looting. Hamdani had urged the Americans to post guards at important sites, and to mount helicopter patrols. Since Nasiriyah's fall, he said, he'd been palmed off from one civil affairs officer to another. 'I've spent fifty days of humiliation searching for security for the sites, and all I get is words.'

After two hours, we reached Umma where we saw about a hundred people on the tell, many of them with spades. Dealers were on hand, local people told us, to buy jewellery and cuneiform seals. A few days before, two American helicopters had landed at the site, and taken off twenty minutes later. Later, I discovered that McGuire Gibson had been in one of the helicopters. He described a 'devastated landscape...an Early Dynastic cemetery was being plundered and other buildings were being riddled with new holes.'

Could it be stopped? Officially, it already had been. Pietro Cordone, the Italian diplomat whom the Americans had appointed to superintend Iraqi culture, told me in Baghdad that 'about ninety-nine per cent of the sites have military guards.' Their combined vigilance, he said, had 'put an end to the stealing of artefacts'. I asked him about de-Ba'athification in the department of antiquities. He said, 'We are working on that now.'

In a restaurant in Nasiriyah, Moayed and I had a conversation about what it meant to be an Iraqi. The restaurant owner, a former Olympic basketball player, was at our table. We were joined by a man whose profession was not revealed to me—only that he'd graduated in geography from a local college. The geography graduate ascribed the birth of national conscience to the discovery of oil. That sounded rather mercenary, I said. Not at all, replied the basketball player; he vividly recalled being seized by an urge to kiss the Iraqi flag during a tournament in Manila. What about ancient culture, I wondered. Had they been affected by news of looting at the ancient sites?

After an animated tripartite discussion, I got a reply to a different question: who was responsible for the looting? Moayed told me that there were two theories. The first was that the Israelis were pulling the strings; they wanted to destroy all traces of civilizations that had not recognized Jewry. The second theory was that the looting and theft were being perpetrated by the Kuwaitis, who were determined to wipe out evidence of civilizations that had encompassed both Iraq and Kuwait—and thus to discredit Iraq's covetous adventurism

These were wacky theories, by any standards. I glanced at Moayed, expecting to see signs of morose amusement. I saw none; later, he told me that, in his opinion, both theories were credible. From Baghdad to Ur, the looting had been invested with political, not sociological significance. The theories were serving, or reflecting, agendas of which I'd been only dimly aware.

On June 8, the BBC broadcast a programme about the Iraq National Museum by Dan Cruickshank—the man who'd spotted the lyre of Ur. The programme took Bogdanos's view of events: the colonel got star treatment, the museum staff looked villainous. Cruickshank concluded that the looting had been an inside job; the museum, furthermore, was a 'Ba'athist stronghold...the treasures here are far too important to the Iraqi people—to us all—to risk leaving the museum in the hands of any staff tainted by a murky or mysterious past.'

A couple of days after that broadcast, David Aaronovitch in the *Guardian* praised Cruickshank for showing that the story of American negligence was 'bollocks'. On June 13, Charles Krauthammer of the *Washington Post* identified George as the source of a 'lie' designed to 'highlight the dark side of the liberation'—the propagator of the spurious claim that 170,000 pieces had been destroyed or stolen. Both writers, who were strong supporters of the war, castigated those who had tried to make the looting a symbol of America's philistinism and arrogance.

In these versions of events, there were only heroes and villains. People seemed unwilling to think in shades of grey about what had happened. During George's visit to London, the *Guardian*'s Fiachra

Gibbons had written that his 'bravery after the first Gulf war has earned him something of a reputation as an Indiana Jones figure'. Now, in the same paper, Aaronovitch was describing him as an 'apparatchik of a fascist regime and a propagandist for his own past'. During the BBC programme, Cruickshank said that Jabbar's appointment as the head of the department of antiquities had been 'political...endorsed by Saddam's regime.' This startlingly obvious piece of information made me think of Moayed and his position in the steel factory. I recalled a conversation that I'd had with Moayed about his participation, while he was in the army, in punitive missions into the marshes. These missions had been renowned for their brutality. I'd asked Moayed how many rebels he'd found and killed. He replied: none. I asked him how many reed houses he'd firebombed. He replied: none.

What if that was a lie? What if Moayed had killed and firebombed? The alternative would have been to lose his freedom or his life, and to endanger his family. After watching Cruickshank, I felt embarrassed at having asked Moayed these questions. I was the camp follower of an invading army. At some level, working for me must have been a humiliation. My questions showed that I'd never had to choose between a principle and my life, or the lives of people I loved.

That was one of the problems with Cruickshank's programme. The other was that his blithe judgements weren't backed by facts. His revelation that many of the stolen items had been 'taken from the museum before the bombing, before the looting, by members of the Ba'ath Party' relied not on scientific evidence, but on intuition: the staff's 'strange behaviour, not being straightforward, not answering questions'. One bit of evidence for his contention that George and the others had conspired to turn the compound into a centre of resistance was risibly unconvincing: a map of Baghdad on the wall of the police station at the back of the compound. How abnormal is it to find a map on a police station wall?

During the course of my own enquiries, I spoke to archaeologists and curators who knew the staff and had visited the museum shortly after the looting: Gibson; McGregor; John Curtis (the Keeper of the Near East at the British Museum), Henry Wright of the University of Michigan; John Russell of the Massachusetts College of Art. All refuted suggestions that senior members of staff had a hand in the looting. They believed that the battle for the museum had ended on the 10th, six days before the Americans turned up. They praised the staff for severely restricting access to storerooms and vaults—a necessary security precaution, at a time of great uncertainty and danger. According to Gibson, there was 'absolutely no evidence' that items were stolen before the war.

I remember George in May. He was grey and exhausted from duelling with Bogdanos. The department was ailing; old animosities were coming to the surface. Cordone was planning his de-Ba'athification, though no one knew how far he would go. George took me into an empty office that had been tidied up after the looting, and answered some of the allegations.

Mutawali's safe, he said, had been opened with the help of about twenty skeleton keys, which had been found. He said that a bunker in front of the museum, which the Americans said had been built for defensive reasons, had been dug by staff as a bomb shelter. I asked George about his commitment to defend the museum. He said he'd been told by the regime to hand out AK-47s to staff members before the war—but that he and Jabbar had given orders not to shoot at Americans. (In the end, everyone fled.)

I asked George about compromise.

He said, 'You've opened an old wound.'

George's membership of the small Assyrian Christian minority meant, he said, that he'd been treated like a second-class citizen: 'They used to call me a British-raised boy.' He remembered a conversation in which colleagues asked him whether he would join the other Christians who were leaving the country in droves, and he'd thought to himself, 'I'm not going and leaving the antiquities of my forefathers in the hands of people like you.'

Christian or not, George had been privileged with prestige and foreign trips. In Cruickshank's words, he and the others were 'servants' of a regime that was 'brutal and corrupt'. Perhaps they themselves were guilty of excess and cruelty. More likely, they succumbed to the same moral and intellectual corrosion that afflicted Moayed and many millions of his compatriots. Had we been in the their position, my guess is that we would have done the same: Bogdanos; Krauthammer; me; you.   □

GRANTA

WITH THE INVADERS
James Meek

April 5: a marine steps in between Omar and his father's body, see page 229

O ne Thursday in early July, just before midnight, I was on a London bus taking me home through rainy darkness. I was listening to a song by Gillian Welch, 'Revelator', which I'd often played in Kuwait and Iraq during the recent war. I suppose it was the song which made me remember something I had seen on my journey out of Iraq in April, when, it appeared, the fighting was over.

We were an odd convoy leaving Baghdad that morning. There was Ghaith, my new-found Iraqi assistant, and myself in the driver Haider's worn taxi, a Cadillac of 1980s vintage, followed by two frightened young mechanics in a tow-truck of about the same age. Hitched to the truck was the nearly new Mitsubishi Pajero which I had rented in Kuwait before the invasion, promising not to take it into Iraq. The Pajero, which had been broken into, ransacked and immobilized by looters in Baghdad in the days immediately after the fall of Saddam, still carried the livery which the photographer Paul O'Driscoll had adorned it with before we crossed the border: mud, gaffer tape covering the lights and chrome fittings, and orange patches and chevrons to signify to US and British forces that we were not hostile. I'd parted company with the colleagues I'd travelled from Kuwait to Baghdad with—Paul, who worked with me for the *Guardian*, had returned home via Jordan, while the *New York Times* team of Dexter Filkins, James Hill and their interpreter, Mandi Fahmy, were still working in the city.

Towing the car over 400 miles from Baghdad to Kuwait was tiresome. The tow-truck had four punctures. Twice the mechanics were threatened by armed men, once by US troops, once by vigilantes with Kalashnikovs; on both occasions the mechanics were assumed to have stolen the Pajero. But in the early hours of the journey we sped south under grey skies along a smooth, quiet motorway.

At one point, we passed a man and a boy walking along the side of the road close to some wheat fields. The man, dressed in a charcoal *dishdash*, strode forward without looking to the right or left. The wind making his tunic flutter was only a light breeze, yet his gait was suffused with weariness, as if he was moving against a gale. His face was heavy with anxiety and suffering. He held up his head proudly, but just to do so seemed to be an act of giant strength. The boy, about nine, was his opposite. He was jumping and skipping around the man in eccentric circles, laughing and talking, trying to

James Meek

attract the man's attention, losing interest, running on, running back.

When people go as correspondents to follow armies at war, as Paul and I did when we followed US and British troops into Iraq in March, they are supposed to keep only the sombre adult, grimly fixated on the horror, and leave the frisky child behind. But the two will not be parted. Without childlike curiosity, without a love of the momentary, the trivial, the surprising, the scary, the bright and the loud, what would be the point of going on? And without an awareness of the bloody burden of all the wars men make, how could the child ever come to understand the dark nature of the journey? I kept a diary.

March 21, road junction north of Safwan, Iraq
We've fallen down a whole flight of steps in the economic league, just by travelling across a line on the map, out of Kuwait and into Iraq. The first people we see are looters, picking their way through the rubble on the edge of town—ruined by this war, or the last one, we never found out—and looters are everywhere, coolly plundering equipment from every state institution going. We drive through the litter-strewn main street and women in black and boys in ragged grease-stained pullovers and tunics look at us with stares that say: 'Who are you looking at? What are you going to do for me?' They aren't unfriendly. Nor are they particularly inquisitive. Some of the guys smile and wave.

We drive on through, past the pictures of smiling Saddam and Saddam in Bedouin sheikh garb that the marines haven't got around to taking down, and try to find a quiet spot to park the cars and take stock without attracting a crowd.

We're faced with an emotional scene in the courtyard of the first house we go into, a tumbledown mud brick place opposite a great dry field covered in scraps of black plastic fluttering in the wind. An old couple who lost their son to Saddam's goons two years ago welcome us into the yard and spread rugs on the ground for us to sit on. It is a mad scene, hysterical, dozens of children crowding in, thin bright-eyed men standing looking into the group with their hands behind their backs and darting in to interrupt with their comments and stories, and Mandi, our interpreter, not knowing where to look and what to translate. The old man sobs and we are close to tears too. He says we have come too late, and for his son, of course, we have.

216

March 22, Rumaila oilfields

It becomes apparent that Basra is not going to be taken quickly, either by the British or the Americans, so we are uncertain what to do or where to go. Initially we strike out east from Safwan towards Um Qasr. We pass British tanks and troop carriers from the 7th Armoured Division. We drive between their gun barrels and the so far invisible enemy. It is an uncomfortable feeling. We head north up the motorway towards Basra. The Iraqis have made no attempt to destroy their transport infrastructure by blowing up bridges or mining roads. Occasionally the Iraqi army leaves signs of its presence, a blown-up tank which didn't have a crew in it when it was hit, a stinking scorched ditch which the Iraqis had filled with crude oil and set on fire in the mistaken belief it would confuse US imaging systems, a pile of grubby blankets and stale bread rolls under a bridge where soldiers hid. But these are little installations of failed, half-hearted defence in an otherwise empty, undefended landscape controlled by the US and the British.

We talk to various soldiers, mainly American, and I build up a story I think might work, about a farcical tank battle some marines had been involved in two nights earlier. The tank crews were restricted in the kind of ammunition they used in the oilfields for fear of damaging oil installations. They were not restricted in the number of Iraqi soldiers they could kill.

Just before evening we find a camping place with a group of British military policemen from 16th Air Assault. They can't do enough for us. They give us water and food and cover our cars with a piece of hessian so that we won't leak light. I'm so tired, I can hardly make out the words I'm writing. In the oilfields, despite the marines' tender care, some of the wells are burning. After dark, the military police on duty are silhouetted against the orange glow as it brightens and fades. Their bulbous helmets make them look like aliens.

At about 9 p.m. the MPs call for Mandi to translate. An Iraqi family at the checkpoint is trying to tell them something. I follow her and start talking to the MPs. One of them comes back from the group at the car and says: 'I almost shot a kid.' He'd told the people to get out of the car, and they had, and then he'd seen a movement out of the corner of his eye, and almost pulled the trigger; it was a child.

Today reports start to come in of journalists being killed, reports which turn out to be true. I call my wife and my parents to let them know I'm okay. I let the military police make personal calls on the *Guardian* satellite phone. Most of them call their mothers.

March 23, west of Nasiriyah, waiting to cross the Euphrates
Basra has not fallen; fighting continues. It is the tomato season in these parts and we talk to farmers with their trucks heaped with crimson fruit from plantations round Zubair. They are still going to try to make it to Baghdad. They are brave men. It is their livelihood.

Everywhere there is evidence that Iraqi soldiers never went on campaign without a change of civilian clothes: the gaunt young men in cheap shoes and a bottle of grey, scavenged water walking home after tearing off their boots and uniforms and running away from the war. When they talk to us about how many hundreds of kilometres they have to walk to get home it is without indignation or surprise. That is the way things are. I wonder how many of them will die of hunger or thirst or disease by the roadside, trying to make it back.

We swing west on the road that leads to Nasiriyah and eventually Baghdad. There are six lanes and the marines are using all six in the same direction, thousands of military vehicles pouring forward at high speed. At one point we drive up on to a bridge over the motorway for a better view. Paul and James take pictures but the point is in the motion. Very few civilians will ever see anything like this: a modern-day blitzkrieg, a motorized horde taking over a road which, though it runs through the desert, otherwise looks like any European motorway, and using it to rush into battle at commuter speed.

March 24, US Marine supply base near the Euphrates
Our fourth day in Iraq and two preconceptions look shaky. One is that we would be entering Iraqi towns; the other that we would be living and working away from US and British troops, with Iraqi civilians, in 'liberated' areas. Basra still has not fallen and fighting continues in Nasiriyah on the Euphrates east of here. We cannot reach either place. The marines have no interest in urban areas. They want to avoid them. This means these towns are under Ba'ath Party control, however tenuously, and are not safe for us. Left in open, mainly desert country, unpoliced, much of it considered a free-fire zone by US air power, and without access to working petrol stations,

shops or markets, let alone hotels, we have no choice but to seek the protection and assistance of the marines. To our everlasting gratitude, they provide it. All we can offer in exchange, which is not a small thing, is use of our satphones. On that basis Paul manages to blag 120 litres of petrol from a marine refuelling dump.

I want to see the legendary Euphrates, so in the morning I leave where our cars are parked, where the tarmac of the finished section of the Basra–Baghdad motorway expires, and walk forward through the fine dust of the unmade section, past queues of drab olive amphibious tracked vehicles—Amtraks—trucks, tanks and Humvees stretching for miles. The dust is continually thrown up and ground finer by convoys moving forward, but for the time being I have given up any thought of being clean.

The Euphrates is a disappointment: a narrow channel barely forty yards wide with a few palm trees along its banks. The marines newly dug in around a bridge express their scorn for the reality of the fabulous river. I walk a little distance away from the bridge—like this section of the motorway, it is not fully built, and can take only one tank at a time, or a convoy going in one direction—and crouch down by the bank. With my back to the bridge, I can imagine the marines are not here. The river does not seem so small, and it moves powerfully enough. This is at the western edge of the Marsh Arabs' old lands. In front of me is a thicket of delicate green reeds rising from the puckered surface of the water and bending in the wind. A high-prowed canoe shifts like a vane on its moorings and, on the far bank, there is a reed hut with an arched roof. It is peaceful for a moment, before a pair of marine Cobra helicopters the colour of cigarette ash chug low overhead.

We spend the day here, talking to marines and Iraqis. Already there is bad blood between them. Irregular Saddam loyalists have been taking the occasional potshot at the marines—a pea to an elephant—and the marines have been arresting locals, confiscating their domestic Kalashnikovs, searching their houses. A pathetic cluster of Iraqi captives in civilian clothes sits cross-legged in a circle of razor wire under the bridge. At another stretch of razor wire, the boundary between the marines' domain and the way to Nasiriyah, Mandi tries to mediate between the mutually uncomprehending marines behind their machine guns and scores of Iraqis who are

James Meek

trying to get through. One Iraqi family brings a woman with cancer, under the impression that the Americans will help her. They can't, and she is taken back. An Iraqi who works in the hospital in Nasiriyah says US aircraft have killed ten civilians and wounded 200 in an air raid on the town.

In a house a few hundred yards away, Iraqis give us strong sweet tea, a heavenly drink to us at this time. We sit in a big quiet bare room with rugs on the floor, lit by the doorway and a small triangular window in the whitewashed mud wall. One of our hosts says that it was the nature of his country which called forth Saddam, not Saddam who made the country. 'If in Iraq there's a leader who's fair, he'll be killed the next day,' he says. 'Iraqis have hot blood. If he's not tough, he dies the next day.'

March 25, the Basra–Baghdad motorway, just north of the Euphrates
We're parked in what the marines call a herringbone pattern on an unmade stretch of the highway. Herringboning is a tactic to prevent an attacking aircraft being able to destroy an entire column in a single run. It is a good idea, except that Iraq doesn't have an air force any more.

We've been on the road since 7 a.m. Woke up at about five, listened to the BBC for a while. The World Service's coverage has been disappointing. I haven't heard a single interview with an Iraqi civilian or a Western soldier on the ground since the invasion began five days ago. Even though the embedded correspondents have no idea what's going on beyond the units they're embedded with, the BBC deals with them as if they do, and presents their deep, narrow perspective as if it is deep and broad, in the worst traditions of twenty-four-hour rolling television news. There's no sign that anyone from the BBC is operating outside the embed system in southern Iraq, although some of them surely must be.

Our days are like this. We wake at about five or six. I make hot water on a little camping stove we bought in Kuwait, and give some to our neighbours from the *New York Times*, so we can all have coffee. We're down to our last twelve or so litres of water; Paul and I are using about three litres a day between us, mainly for drinking, but also for cleaning our teeth, washing our hands and shaving. Shaving in cold water is a long exercise in painful scraping, especially if you've let a growth set in. We haven't had showers since we left Abdaly on Friday morning. It's now Tuesday. The worst is the hair, which is carrying so much dust that it's solidified into the kind of stiff, abrasive, matted pad of wire wool you scrub pans with. I can't drag the comb through it any more. We eat breakfast from what food we manage to pick up along the way plus what we brought from Kuwait—tins of processed cheese, biscuits, chocolate.

We spend the day interviewing and driving, and scrounging from the troops. At night, the marines ask us not to show white light, even from a torch or a laptop screen, because, they say, it gives snipers something to aim at and it blinds the marines' night-vision equipment. The evening meal is US military MREs, Meals Ready to Eat: fat brown plastic packets containing stodgy shrink-wrapped cakes and biscuits and processed cheese. The centrepiece of the MRE is a green plastic envelope with a hot dish inside, one of twenty-four possibilities, which you slip inside another envelope containing a thin sachet of chemicals. You pour a little water into the envelope, fold the top over, lay it on its side, and the chemicals start to react and fizz, producing heat. It heats us the pottage in about fifteen minutes. It's not great food, but our condition is such that we look forward to it.

Later. A sandstorm. Everything stops. The car rocks on its springs. For what seems like hours there is a crinkling sound as millions of sand grains strike the rear of the vehicle. We try to open the door a little but every time the wind forces it wide open and dust rushes in. The edges of the road disappear on either side and the vehicles in front and behind become invisible. I feel afraid for the first time since coming here, an echo of an old, irrational fear which has nothing to do with the fear of being hurt or killed. It is a fear of going too far and not being able to find the way home again.

March 26, south-east of Diwaniyah
We've arrived at this forward supply base in the desert which in a short time grows from a few trucks and Humvees to a park of acres of fuel trucks, ammo trucks, trailers, bulldozers, generators and tents.

On the other side of the road, behind a sand wall, in a long deep ditch and along a catwalk, lie the bodies of dozens of Iraqis, most of them untouched by bullets or shrapnel; a blast must have killed them. They died after what, despite some marines' attempts to claim otherwise, was a feeble, ineffectual ambush. The marines crushed them effortlessly. With the sandstorm and the rain their faces and bodies have been covered with a fine coat of mud, making them look less like dead people and more like clay models, or like the dead Romans at Pompeii. In the article I write today I say they look peaceful, but this is because I don't have time to think of a better word. Eternal would be a better word. They look as if they have been there forever and have just been uncovered by the wind, the same wind that will shortly cover them up again. I walk along the catwalk, clocking the stuff they have left. Little parties of marines are there, souvenir-hunting, but all the good stuff, such as guns and badges, has already been taken by the infantry, who were on the scene earlier. What are left are helmets and filthy blankets and canteens. I think about taking a canteen, they look fine and almost new, but decide it would be too bad karma.

We're guests here of Colonel John Pomfret, the US battalion commander who smokes cigars in the evening and says things like 'I love the smell of diesel in the morning,' and 'I think we're all serving the same constituency,' and 'I believe in honour and nobility.' His mother was a refugee from the Kuomintang domains of China. I have a feeling this war is going to take a long time.

March 27, south-east of Diwaniyah
It's 8.30 p.m. I'm sitting in a tent with the other journalists, in our gas masks and NBC suits (nuclear, biological and chemical), in the second gas alert of the night. Everyone is trying to keep calm. Finding vials of mustard gas treatment on the dead Iraqi troops in the ditch across the road made the idea of them using chemical weapons seem more real. Looking at the map the other night I saw we were about ninety miles from Babylon. I remembered the nursery rhyme:

> How many miles to Babylon?
> Four score and ten
> Will I get there by candlelight?
> Yes, and back again.

Back again would be good.

March 28, south-east of Diwaniyah
The marines announce they are confiscating all Thuriya satphones on the grounds that the Iraqis can track them and take a grid location they can use for targeting. It's bad, though not the total disaster it appears. Paul files using another satphone system which I can use, though it's hard to get through. We still have the Thuriya hidden in the glove compartment of the car, turned off.

We're thinking of switching battalions to a unit closer to combat, namely the 5th. We speak to the commander, Colonel Dunford, and he seems to be happy to have us travelling with him. I'm beginning to think that, rather than regarding accompanying journalists as a nuisance, the marine field commanders see them as trophies. Until prostitutes get 4 x 4s and war accreditation, we are the nearest to camp followers the battalions are going to get.

The US advance seems to have ground to a halt. Colonel Pomfret says as much today. 'What we are going to be in is an operational pause, to rearm, refuel and rest. It doesn't mean we are stopping.' Or rather, it does. The ambushes on US convoys have freaked the marines out. Dunford doesn't mention it but his driver tells me he got shot at yesterday.

Over by one of the Hueys parked at the 5th I see a girl I assume is a journalist. I say girl not woman because she seems like the torchbearer of all-Californian (she *is* from California) girlhood, with straight shiny blonde hair sticking out under the brim of her bush hat, a glowing red-brown tan, snub nose and bright blue eyes, and an expression that says 'Hey! What's going on?' before she does, which she does. I assume she's a journalist, yeah, leaning there insouciant and apparently idle against the 'copter doorway, but she is a crew chief. Sarah Wilson is her name. She stands behind one of the two big machine guns in the doors of the Huey. A few days ago she'd been behind the gun while the bird was clattering over Nasiriyah, pumping .5 calibre bullets into a house, a house thought to be full of Iraqi resisters. A tank had called for help and she was on to them, 'Like, which house? Fire your gun at it or something so we can tell.' So the tank fires and the helicopter crew sees the house, and they try to fire their rockets, but the rockets haven't been loaded properly so they don't fire, so they bring their guns to bear, and the bullets hit the building, and the forward air controller tells them: 'Good hits.' Sarah's glad to have been busy, the first marine crew chief to have been in combat, because she didn't think she'd end up doing anything.

March 29, south-east of Diwaniyah
This is a down period now, after those first days of driving forward through Iraq, always forward every day; now we've stopped and it's frustrating. More for us than for the marines. They seem glad of the chance to do their laundry. Sports news, non-war news, is beginning to creep on to the BBC. Pomfret tells Dex he's grateful that his report in the *New York Times* about his 'operational pause' remark, which was raised at a Pentagon press conference and impatiently denied by the spokesman, didn't name him. My report named him, but neither he nor the Pentagon seems to know that.

I've been trying to work out what this mighty force of marines is lacking; what their billions haven't bought. The answer is language. It is not just that there's never more than one Arabic speaker per battalion, not just that they haven't put more money and effort into making more of their troops multilingual by conventional means, but that they haven't even tried to apply their ingenuity, their technological and organizational genius, their gift for systematizing life, to language-learning. They're afraid of enabling elements of another culture to enter the minds of their men and women, and the cost is high, to them and their opponents. They can't meet each other except by fire. An Arabic speaker in each platoon: they could slip into the cities in small groups and talk to people. They could ask questions first, and shoot later. But to get there their American minds would have to travel a little way into the mind of Arabia, and that is a journey that seems particularly terrifying to the institution of the US military.

March 30, Camp Pomfret, south-east of Diwaniyah
I go with James and Dex to watch Major Stainbrook and Major Cooper, the civil affairs duo, trying to help some farmers start the pump to put water into their irrigation system. There's Cooper, first language Irish Gaelic, second English, trying to communicate with the aid of a device called the Phrasealator. It isn't much better than nothing. The end result is that the pump starts working and water gushes out of a foot-wide pipe. It is a joy to see it move, white and cold and alive, through the channel of parched, cracked earth towards the barley fields.

March 31, Babil Province
We move forward at last, heading for the River Tigris. We are entering the Iraqi heartland. At dusk we come across a group of marines who have found a civilian trailer parked under a tree with two surface-to-surface missiles in the back, abandoned by the Iraqis. If they are leaving equipment like this behind, surely it signifies the final collapse.

April 1, Babil Province
In the morning we leave Colonel Pomfret's benevolent cavalcade and switch to the hard-riding 5th Regiment, whose headquarters battalion camped overnight at an unfinished petrol station by the motorway a few miles down the road, past the trailer with the missiles. We stop off there for a while; a group of intelligence experts has arrived to examine the weapons. They pull down the side of the trailer and we can see the name of the missiles is written on the side. In big blue Arabic letters it says: 'Al Samoud'. None of the intelligence experts knows this, because none of them can read Arabic, not even the letters. Mandi and Hussein, a Kuwaiti journalist embedded with Colonel Pomfret, enhance their intelligence for them.

A terrified Iraqi farmer, whose farmhouse is right next to the missiles, creeps back to the home he has fled in order to get some things. There is a stand-off between him and a group of patrolling marines because he is afraid, with good reason, that they might shoot him if he does the wrong thing, and he cannot understand what they are saying to him, and the marines don't speak a word of Arabic. He stands cowering and quaking and flinching in the middle of the yard, not knowing whether to lie down, put his hands up, go back, go forward, or prepare for death. Mandi steps in to translate. The marines tell him they're happy for him to go back and live on his farm, but the farmer doesn't believe them, or doesn't trust them. In all fairness, he is right; these marines may want him to move back in, and want to help him, but later other US troops will come who do not know him and his family, and who knows what could happen in the confusion of the night when heavily armed men are all around and two peoples do not speak each other's language.

There are two grey marine Chinooks parked at the petrol station. They are supposedly there in case they are needed for casualty evacuation but they are also used to transport Oliver North in and out of the marines' area of operations. The colonel is embedded with this helicopter unit for Fox News. He spends much of the day at the petrol station, as we do. He sits around telling young marines blood-curdling tales of Saddam the torturer— '...and he said, "I want him to last nine days" [before he dies of torture].' North urinates ostentatiously in full view of everyone in the centre of the petrol station forecourt, holding an aircraft navigation map to conceal his prick, while carrying on a shouted conversation with a group of marines a few yards away. The marines love him. He does a live two-way to New York with one of the medics who went to the village. I go over to say hello and he asks me whether I work for the *New York Times*. I tell him no, I'm from the *Guardian*.

'Who owns it?' he asks.

'The liberal conspiracy,' I say. No I don't. I tell him it owns itself. He's furious with the *New York Times* for quoting Pomfret's 'operational pause' remark. Later it transpires that some officers didn't want the journalists travelling with them after Dex quoted a regimental sniper describing how he had killed a civilian woman. 'The bitch wouldn't get out of the way,' was what the sniper said. The objectors were overruled.

In late afternoon, when it is already getting dark, the part of the battalion we are to travel with prepares to move. There is a drivers' briefing. The drivers are told what they should do in case of direct fire and in case of indirect fire. Later, when we're in the car, Paul says: 'What's the difference between direct and indirect fire?'

'I suppose direct fire is when they're shooting at you and indirect fire is when they aren't shooting at you but hit you anyway.'

April 2, near Numaniyah, on the River Tigris
Back from a trip with Major Broton to the Saddam Canal bridge, shot up by marines who went forward ahead of us last night. Broton went to help a man whose friend was killed by the marines because he didn't put his hands up. The corpse is lying in a shallow hole. The dead man's friend keeps thanking Broton, who comes up with a couple of old black plastic bin bags to cover the two ends of the body and helps manhandle it into the back of a small car. He writes a *laissez-passer* for the friend on a page torn from my notebook.

The company crosses the bridge and moves towards the Tigris. We pass through villages where the residents seem surprised to see us; not by the military presence, since we can't be the first to have passed through, but by the sheer quantity and purposefulness of the convoys. They wave at us if we wave at them first. Most of the roads here are built on embankments running alongside deep irrigation channels, through corn fields alive with larks and plovers. Despite its state-of-the-art navigation systems, the company gets lost for a while. As soon as we stop, baby goats dive under the Humvees for shade and the marines lovingly coax them out.

We find our designated night stop, a fallow field, and while the marines are setting up we go to the river, a couple of miles further on, to watch a pontoon bridge being built. An F18 comes down low overhead and performs a barrel roll, scaring the Iraqis watching from the far bank, who think they're going to be bombed.

Apart from the F18, it is quiet. This bridge-building has nothing in common with film portrayals of Second World War bridges being built with shells splashing in the water around. A tank captain at a checkpoint nearby, Ted Card, complains that he and his men are bored by the Iraqis' failure to resist.

April 3, north of Aziziyah
We drive across the Tigris and on the main highway from Kut to Baghdad join another episode of blitzkrieg as the marines race each other along the tarmac at high speed. We stop short of Aziziyah while Cobras and tanks clear the road through the town, ruthlessly blasting anything that remotely resembles resistance, while avoiding any responsibility for aid and order in the town itself. For hours we watch the helicopters passing through the smoke and hear the thud of automatic fire and the crack of artillery. There are two gas alerts. Eventually, after many requests, we get an escort forward into the town and are able to talk to civilians, who tell contradictory tales of who has been hit and hurt by the US attacks, who is in hospital; some say Iraqi fighters, some say civilians, some say both. The Americans, says one man, Abdel Karim, sent bombs like silver rain.

Our company drives past and we slip in with them and drive forward in the twilight. We pass shops gutted in the fighting and see figures dancing on the roof of a burning building, trying to put the fire out with buckets. Dozens of vehicles are on fire, but it is not the scene of the aftermath of the titanic clash between the marines and the Republican Guard we had been led to expect. It is beginning to look as if the guard is evaporating. A tank burns in a palm grove, the trees, lit by the flames, reflected in the still water of a pool. We stop for more than an hour close to where something vile is smouldering, a smell so pungent and toxic-seeming that I put my gas mask on. The frogs are not affected. They cheep lustily.

April 4, near Baghdad
Paul goes forward wearing a baby-blue flak jacket and an old US helmet from the Gulf War which is too small and makes him writhe and curse as he drives. I'm not much better, in an old Israeli-made flak jacket with worn Velcro and a helmet which is to my body as the cap is to a mushroom. 'Hey look!' screamed a marine the other day as I drove past. 'There's a guy with a fucking kayak on his head!'

There can be no doubt now. For those on the streets, at least, the welcome for the Americans, the smiles and the waves, are genuine. For the first time today I see someone attack an image of Saddam Hussein; a young guy, alone, hurling stones at a portrait of the dictator, not for anyone's cameras or for the US military's benefit but for his own release.

The marines' lack of linguistic skills continue to make them enemies. We see them destroy a harmless car with heavy machine gun fire because the occupants got out of it and, with no idea what the Americans screaming at them wanted them to do, ran away, leaving their vehicle. There has been a lot of fighting here today. Another first was seeing a burnt-out US tank, an M1 Abrams.

April 5, south of Baghdad
So many of the embedded reporters we see are paunchy old guys with hunter's moustaches and big camper's coffee mugs, whose families and friends are doomed to be bored with this war for decades to come. It seems to me I saw a big fellow sitting in a camping chair wearing a pair of waders the other day, but this is not possible. My wiser self has to keep pointing out to my vain self that I don't want to be one of those men. My wiser self also knows that wisdom is not the end and the answer to all things and that ultimately wisdom can

only uncover the dual nature of existence, the irreconcilability of states which is reality but which we strive, with our narratives, to hide.

Yesterday the marines sent Omar on his way with his shirt and trousers covered in the blood of his family. His mother and father, his uncle, two sisters and one brother were shot dead at the crossroads checkpoint. The marines said their coach hadn't stopped and had accelerated when warning shots were fired. I guess in the darkness when people are shouting at you in a foreign language and shooting at you it's hard to know whether to stop or whether they've just missed and you only have a few seconds to escape. What do civilians know about warning shots in the dark? So there was Omar, crying and lost, all covered in blood, and his baby brother behind him with his face shot up. Omar was looking at us, and the marines standing around exhausted by shame and fear and fatigue, and feeling even worse now because the reporters were writing it down.

What do you say to Omar? How do you look him in the eye? What comfort can there be? These marines weren't going to be punished or investigated. Dex wrote it up for the *New York Times* and I wrote it up for the *Observer*, and both papers ran it, but so far as I know it went no further. The marines killed eight civilians at this checkpoint, three of them children. What do you say to Omar? The fact is that his family have been murdered for no reason that was good for him. A supporter of the war would say that there will be greater happiness for all surviving Iraqis as a result. But they couldn't say that to Omar, because it is meaningless to him. That is the duality that we can never find our way around. In speech we are all purists; there is the good, the bad, the must-be-done and the cannot-be-allowed. In our hearts, we are accountants. I wrote about all those who died last night, the Iraqi general lying in the dirt behind the white Japanese family car, Omar's family, the marines, being petty cash in Donald Rumsfeld and George Bush's grand accounting. But the truth is we are all accountants, and the balance is not only in how good or bad this is for me, my friends, my family, my folk. It is: 'How close do I have to get?'

The reason old men can make wars is that they don't have to get close to it. Those who take responsibility don't have to look into Omar's eyes in the morning when he's drenched in his parents' blood, and those who have to look into his eyes don't have to take responsibility for it. It's a sweet scheme. I wonder what George Bush had for dinner last night. His fork must have been clinking on the china just about the time when his marines were killing Omar's family. It must be nice for the President to realize he doesn't have to say sorry to all the people who've lost the people they loved in this war. He doesn't have to say sorry to anyone.

April 7, Baghdad
The 5th is not going to cross the river into Baghdad today. The roads turn out not to be what they looked like on reconnaissance and satellite pictures. We leave them and drive south, looking for another regiment, the 7th, which we have heard is going into the city. We find one of their battalions poised to cross the River Diyala, queued up on the highway south of a bridge at midday. The troops are pumped up with aggression. Most of the lower-ranking marines have painted their faces with black and green camouflage paint, but they have made it war paint, reaching into their memories of trick-or-treating and horror films to make themselves look frightening. There are homages to *The Last of the Mohicans*, to *A Clockwork Orange*, to *Apocalypse Now*. More than one marine has contrived to make a direct tribute to Death by painting on his flesh an image of the skull within.

Hundreds of looters walk past, pushing generators and motorbikes stolen from a warehouse. The marines watch, concerned only that the looters are not a threat to them. They aren't bothered about the crime; their only response is to applaud the looters sarcastically. Hours pass and the adrenalin and testosterone begin to lose their potency. Dex is on tiptoes with frustration at being so close to Baghdad but not actually in it.

The colonel relents on his original refusal to allow us to drive forward and we cross the bridge over the Diyala under escort from Major Milburn, an English-born marine. The Iraqis tried to blow it up and had placed mines on either side but the marine engineers managed to clear the mines and bridge the gap with a folding bridge of their own.

We find ourselves on the Baghdad side of the bridge, just after marine tanks were machine-gunning something a few hundred yards away, and suddenly the marines are gone and it is getting dark. Paul wants to go back across the bridge, Dex and I want to go on to the battalion's overnight halt. But we reckon we can't stay by ourselves where we are. Paul is particularly anxious not to go on because there is an anti-personnel mine on the road which hasn't been cleared and we might not be able to see it in the half-light. As it turns out the choice is made for us. The battalion begins pouring across the bridge, blocking it, so we can't go back to the other side of the river, and all we can do is tuck in with the convoy and hope they stop for the night after a short distance.

We pull in between a couple of Amtraks and set off through the deserted industrial landscape with the glow of burning oil to our right. Paul is driving the *Guardian* car, Dex the *New York Times* car in front. No lights, so we have to make our way by the outlines of the vehicles in what ambient light there is. There is just enough to see the mine and drive around it. We press on and everything seems to be fine. Then we see something burning, up ahead, and hear a popping and a banging. It is an ammunition truck on fire, and the ammo on board is exploding. We can hear the bullets whizzing and pinging in all directions. We stop about fifty yards short. The armoured vehicles we are with just squeeze past the truck as fast as they can, but we aren't armoured, we can't go back, and we can't stay where we are. But if we try to scoot past the truck, we risk being blasted. We see Dex gesticulating to one of the Amtraks going past and then moving off. We see what he is trying to do—drive past the truck at the same time as the Amtrak, using the armoured vehicle as a shield. The two vehicles lurch forward, the Amtrak almost squashing the 4 x 4 until the driver realizes what Dex is doing, the *New York Times* car half off the road. They make it. Then it is our turn. We go past the truck with our Amtrak, same deal, the two vehicles squeezing past the truck. You can feel the heat from the flames in the truck. Just when we are parallel with it, the three vehicles together, our car half off the road, I see a bunch of concrete fence posts up ahead, blocking our way on the right. I warn Paul and we have to stop for a few seconds, though it seems longer, to let the Amtrak go by before we can go on. So we make it through and on to a side road, where we halt and crawl forward, halt and crawl. Helicopters are overhead and machine gun fire on the other side of a rise to our right. The sergeant in charge of one of the Amtraks, the one who realized at the last moment what we were doing to get past the truck, comes up to find out who we are and what we are doing.

James Meek

He is very friendly but in the course of the conversation it emerges that his unit isn't heading for a night encampment at all, it is going into combat, and we are going with it, in the middle of the night, without night vision equipment, radios or armour. The Iraqi military barracks up ahead are going to be bombed, then the marines are going to clear what is left building by building, then they are going to hit an airfield in diamond formation, tanks on the outside, soft-skinned vehicles in the middle. The sergeant offers us pistols. We need to be further back. They get on the radio and arrange for us to drive back down the column to where the colonel is, seventeen Amtraks down.

We drive slowly, counting the bulks of the Amtraks, slightly darker than the night, and find the colonel. He is furious. 'What happened to not crossing the fucking bridge?' he says. 'You're not fucking riding into combat with my boys.' He wants us to go back, but he is afraid we'll get whacked by the hair trigger his people are on for suicide bombers, seeing these two strange civilian vehicles in the night. So he has to give us an escort, which he is really pissed off about too. As he is being angry, though, he cools down and realizes that he did give us permission to cross and that there wasn't much else we could have done.

April 8, Baghdad
Wake up this morning to the smell of death. It could have been from the dead Iraqis a hundred yards up the road but more likely from the long-dead dog just a few yards away from where we stopped last night with a few light armoured vehicles, LAVs, parked around. The wind must have changed, because last night the air smelt good, and there weren't any insects. Now it stinks and the flies have incorporated us into their sphere of putrefaction around the dog. It's 7.10 a.m. We're by the bridge over the Diyala we crossed yesterday. Sitting by the roadside on James's camp bed, it's beginning to spit with rain, I can see Constablesque trees blowing in the dusty wind, a dark grey speeding cloud behind them from where some kind of oil installation got hit, or the Iraqis set it on fire. Mandi's helping mediate the passage of refugees across the bridge. Refugees, no, just people trying to go about their business without getting shot. A lot of bombing in the distance, a continuous thunder, but I feel safe here.

We've reached built-up areas already, clusters of yellow box houses. The houses closest to the marines have been searched by them and their inhabitants told to keep away. Marines have taken up firing positions behind piles of bricks and in foxholes, guns pointed towards the houses. We walk in over the dirt, past the raggedly laid bricks of the houses with their frayed black and green Shi'a flags flying. On the street we meet men who have just been arrested and tortured by Saddam's people, before the Americans came and the torturers fled. One has a fresh cigarette burn on his chest. While we are talking we stop cars to ask them for petrol. We find one guy who lets us siphon almost twenty litres out of his tank. He refuses to take any money. Another guy, a taxi driver, takes $10 for the same amount. Someone brings us strong sweet tea in little glasses on a tray. It is good.

April 9, Baghdad
We hook up with one of the marines' psychological operations (psyops) vehicles—a Humvee with loudspeakers on top—and head out, a convoy of four vehicles. Quickly we are in the city, in a built-up area with big city roads. We come to a junction where there are already some marines and there is a crowd, and traffic, and shuttered shops, and a red double-decker bus. Iraqis are looting a duty free warehouse nearby, pushing boxes of Dimple whisky out of there in shopping trolleys. Before we have much of a chance to talk to anyone the convoy is off again. I am driving and Paul makes me stop for a second while he jumps out and persuades one of the looters to give him a bottle.

The convoy's destination is the UNMOVIC (United Nations Monitoring, Verification and Inspection Commission) headquarters. The marines arrived after the looters. Everything inside the building is stolen or smashed. The marines are helping themselves to boxes of rations the UN left so we take some too, a change from MREs. Some of the marines come over and ask for whisky and I pour them measures according to their cups. We climb up to the roof of the building where two marine snipers lie watching the multi-storey buildings opposite. An aircraft drops a single bomb on a building a few blocks away, raising a tall cloud of cinders. Colonel Toolan, of the 1st, is on the roof looking thoughtful. The war is turning into something that isn't a war. It is beginning to look as if there is no enemy, and no real fighting to be done.

We go downstairs to find journalists from a different world, with clean flak jackets and pressed shirts, journalists who have recently showered, Brits from the Palestine Hotel, where only the previous evening Saddam Hussein's government had ruled, with all its apparatus of fear and corruption ticking and grinding in bloody greedy circles. These guys, from ITN, tell us that in the morning their old Information Ministry minders fled and that they'd simply gone with their drivers the couple of miles from the centre to UNMOVIC. The road is open. The regime has collapsed. All the fears of block-by-block street fighting, like Grozny, indeed all the hopes by Saddam Hussein of block-by-block street fighting, like Stalingrad, are gone. Very few fought. This has been a kind of rebellion against Saddam, a rebellion of not-fighting. They went to fight for Iraq, and they ran away for freedom. While we are speaking to the ITN guys we come under sniper fire and the marines shoot back, but it doesn't take away the sense that the shooting war is substantially finished.

We drive on a little further with Colonel Toolan and watch him with some of his tank commanders unfold a map of the city on the bonnet of a Humvee and discuss deployments for the rest of the day. They talk about whether they have enough tanks, but enough tanks for what? They no longer need any tanks, except for effect. Their opponents have thrown away their boots and uniforms, ripped off their badges, hidden their weapons, stuffed the cash in their holdalls, revved up the getaway cars, gone sadly home to their families, gone into shock and denial, turned to God. The mob is looting. The city is burning. It is time to say goodbye to the US Marines, who have been so kind, who have fed, watered, fuelled, sheltered and protected us and guided us to our destination. It is too bad they are trained, equipped and organized in such a way that they killed so many civilians, men, women and children, along the road. Their night-vision goggles can turn night into day but they have nothing to see other cultures as clearly. They can see Iraq only in so far as it deviates from the norm, and the norm, the only possible norm, is America. □

GRANTA

TWENTY-EIGHT DAYS IN BAGHDAD
Nuha al-Radi

Nuha al-Radi's mother in the orchard, May 2003

At the beginning of the American–British invasion of Iraq, in March 2003, Nuha al-Radi was living in Beirut. She was born in Baghdad but grew up mostly in India and went on to study ceramics in London. Thereafter she spent her time between Lebanon and Iraq trying to avoid coups and wars. She began to write a diary during the first bombing of Baghdad in the first Gulf War. It appeared in Granta 42, her first published work. The extracts that follow are from her new diary, of a month-long stay with her family in Iraq after seven years away.

April 30—Beirut Airport. Our fate doesn't seem to have improved since the fall of Saddam. Trying to get back to Iraq is a major undertaking. Everyone is afraid of being invaded by the US, so Syria has closed its borders to Iraqis and Jordan only allows a transit if there is a convoy waiting to take you straight from Amman airport to the Iraqi border. Through friends, I have got myself an invitation with an ABC television convoy. I am nervous as a tick. Will I make it? Cess dropped me off, so I said, 'What do you think is going to be the outcome?' 'Many divisions,' he said. 'Kurdistan split in two, the Shi'a split in two, a big fight for who is to keep Baghdad, which might get divided like Berlin.' What a depressing scenario. Yahya says it all depends on the economy, if the US brightens up all will be okay, but the US is in a bad way economically and to cover it up, they will attack somewhere else.

Amman—First hurdle over. I got through the airport, and the convoy leaves at 4 a.m. Amman airport was peppered with forlorn Iraqis sitting on various chairs awaiting their fate. I am horrified to hear that the US has taken over and is in residence in Baghdad College. That makes them my neighbours.

It's 3 a.m. and the convoy is getting ready. New huge white GMCs with a cargo of cameramen and equipment. It's a real industry, this going to Baghdad. I have already seen two convoys packed and gone.

May 1. Day 1—There is no Iraqi authority on our side of the border, only US Marines in all their gear—goggles, earmuffs, helmets, bulletproof vests. They can hardly walk. When our car reached them, one looked at our passports and yelled out to another marine in a nearby tank, 'One Eyeraki, and two Jordanians.' We were on our way. On the road every now and then a solitary burnt-out tank and three burnt buses, miles apart. Mariam, one of the producers at ABC, said they'd been full of Arab volunteers for the war. They never had a chance.

I hardly recognize Baghdad after seven years away. The city is covered in dust. Bombed and burnt buildings, huge plumes of smoke hovering. Barricades and US tanks all over the place. The only shiny things are the hundreds of new mosques—huge, bulbous growths, finished with ornate decorations. What was Saddam trying to prove? There are also hideous new flashy houses, built with the strangest architecture. Lots of huge columns and pseudo-everything in style.

We reach the Sheraton where Mariam and the ABC crew are staying. People everywhere. Kids selling bananas in singles. Journalists galore. Outside the hotel areas it's like a deserted town. Plants overgrowing their fences and coming out of the sidewalks. They are not expecting me at home. I surprise Ma and Needles, who have survived the war and are tired, but still in fighting spirits. Tomorrow I will go and check the house in the orchard.

Day 2—My poor garden, part overgrown, part desert. Trees, the beautiful palms, are still there, though three died this year. I saw a magpie, a black-and-white kingfisher and a crow. The birds seem okay, they must have adjusted to the bombing.

Constant firing from across the river. They say the army is practising, but what do they need to practise for, they've just fought a war? Ma and Needles live by the Tigris. Across the other side of the river used to be a military security complex and club. It is now occupied by the US Marines, who rush about all day in their tanks kicking up dust.

Day 3—Cleaning house and working in the orchard. Palm trees are the umbrellas for the citrus trees growing underneath. All orchards are planted this way in Iraq, otherwise the orange trees would not survive the long, hot summers. The crop of oranges this year will be zero. At the beginning of the war there was a huge sandstorm that lasted many days and took all the blossoms away. The dates fared a little better, with a little help from Ma. The male palms bloomed during the war and it was not easy for the climbers to pollinate the trees. At the end of the war, when the US occupied Baghdad College just beside us, the climbers were too frightened to climb. So Ma stomped off to the marines and asked to see the boss. When he showed up, she explained that it was the time for the palms to be pollinated and that in Iraq people climb the trees, as opposed to the US where they have ladders, and that the climbers were afraid that they would be mistaken for sharpshooters and be shot at. So he asked Ma whether they carried guns. 'How can they carry guns when climbing?' 'Okay, then they can do it,' he said. Ma said, 'We don't want you.' 'Yes, ma'am,' he said. 'We know.'

Still, no one seems to be in power. It's a coup with no leaders. They should have taken lessons from us—we have had many. First thing is to take over a radio or TV station with a tank or two, and then announce the takeover and declare a curfew, then read out: rule number one, number two, etc.

The television is not working—a fuzzy snowstorm. The only station it gets is an Iranian satellite station in Arabic, broadcast from Beirut. Ma and my aunt, Needles are hooked up to the generator at the Kubaisis next door, and they help out when there is no electricity, which is most of the time. It's good to have such neighbours.

My cousin Corset tells us a wonderful a story today: a mullah in the mosque near the orchard, the day after the fall of Baghdad, makes his Friday sermon. 'May God preserve and protect Saddam and keep him forever, etc.' and 'Down with the USA,' the usual speech. Of course he was immediately removed and asked what he thought he was doing. So he said, 'Well, I had already written this speech and didn't have time to change it.' He was on automatic pilot. Anyway, he is out of a job now and roaming the streets of Suleikh; we just saw him.

Day 4—The new US mayor of Baghdad, Barbara Bodine, doesn't meet with her employees. When they ask her what they should do, she says, 'Just keep things going.' But how can they, when nothing is moving? They sit in their various offices until noon and then leave. Bodine, meanwhile, meets with Americans in other offices, and nothing is passed down from these meetings.

Hala, Saddam's youngest daughter, wrote a letter to a satellite TV station to say that Iraqis are a very ungrateful lot. Her father built them houses and gave them shoes and they have no right to treat him this way. Poor misguided girl, she's in for a shock. Someone answered her saying, 'We saw your palaces with gold taps, and we are embarrassed to say what we found in your cupboards…' Corset says, 'Maybe sex toys?'

The poor orchard is so dry, we have just bought a diesel generator and a water pump to get some water out of the river. It's new, green, Indian, with spare parts, but it leaked immediately so they have gone in search of other spare parts. A lovely start. Every shutter in the house has clusters of bees and horrible hornets. 'They are not honey bees,' says Um Hussein, my guardian of the orchard. She says they also build their hives in the long grasses of the orchard and she walks into them sometimes and they swarm all over her. It's a good thing she's covered up from head to toe.

Two ministries, trade and communications, have been brought back with their old ministers in an effort to get them working again. I must say that as occupiers the US are a most inefficient lot.

Day 5—I am still at Ma and Needles' because I have no water or electricity at home. I hope everything will be working by tomorrow. Even the orchard might get water. I have geese with eleven babies wandering about. Every day we hear stories of mass graves being found. Tanks rush about spewing pollution. Petrol queues are miles long, so mostly one buys black market. No cooking gas at all, so some people have started cutting down trees for fuel.

The Italian Ambassador took a big US military chief to see the damage in Amal's house done by the recent bombing. He said, 'Sorry, ma'am, we didn't do it.' So who did? She was embarrassed to say anything because of her friend the ambassador.

Day 6—The new diesel pump has now been working for a day and a half and by tomorrow the water might reach us. In the old days, all agricultural land had to have a river frontage to help the irrigation, so properties came in long strips. Ma and Needles are on the riverside while our houses are a distance away. The Ottomans, to encourage settlements, gave land to their officers. My great-great-great-grandfather, Suleiman Faik Beig, was *katkhuda*, or deputy ruler, of Baghdad while it was still part of the Ottoman Empire and was given our orchard. He was also a writer and historian. He died in

1896 at the age of ninety-five having produced eight sons. Daughters, if there were any, are not mentioned. My great-grandmother put the orchard rights in my grandfather's name as she knew her daughter, my mother's mother, known as Granzy, was a bit wild and something of a gambler and could have gambled it away, as she did much of her property. And so, thanks to my great-grandmother's foresight, our orchard survives.

We now have eighty parties vying for a place in the new government to be formed. Iraq, we hear, is going to be divided into four parts. We are having a west added; we already have a north, middle and south. Garbage in heaps and flies everywhere.

Day 7—Still no government, no wages, the banks are closed—a lot have been broken into, looted and burnt. Three days after the war started Ma went with Amal to check her shop, where she also has lectures and cultural activities. Ma saw the bank next door's door open, so she said, 'Oh look, the bank's open...' It was being looted.

I now have water and electricity at home, only to discover all of my three loos are either busted or leaking. So it's buckets in each one, as replacing them is out of the question now.

Today a tape is circulating with a Saddam message in a croaky voice. Is it him or is it not? It's the bin Laden story all over again: no Saddam, no bin Laden.

The Kubaisis next door keep getting searched—three times so far: tanks, the lot. Their house is a huge new flashy palace with columns and balconies, the inside a dizzying design of black-and-white marble and lots of plastic plants. Um Mustapha, the lady of the house, got such a shock at the first search that her face swelled up with hives and has stayed that way. They even wanted to see the architect's drawings, just in case Saddam might be lurking within. The US army is taking over all the big government houses.

In the evening, a knock on the door. It is Adnan Pachachi, head of the Independent Democrats, and just behind him, Atta. Atta spent twelve years in jail and has written his memoirs but couldn't publish them under Saddam. 'I've already sent it to press,' he told us. We all went out to the garden. No electricity, but it was still light outside. A new beginning. People tell Adnan, 'What do you want with this headache?' (It's an Iraqi expression.) He says, 'I've lived a good life, worked for my country, and if I am called to do this last thing, and I can, it's good.' We all wish him luck. US tanks and marines are at the door wanting to know what's happening because of the big cars and security guys. Big Brother is watching you.

A French chef was asked to prepare food for 350 Iraqis and Americans when they met for a two-day conclave. Everything was prepared in Kuwait and sent by refrigerated truck to Baghdad with an armed escort. Couldn't they bring a few generators for the hospitals in the same way? Everybody agrees that the lack of electricity is intentional.

Day 8—I have been here a week now and we're still cleaning the house. Sol, Michael and Mac arrive tomorrow, to check on the museum robbery. Water got to the orchard today; the geese were thrilled. I'm kind of detached now and don't get so disturbed when I see the tanks with the marines in all their gear roaming around. Everyone insists they must have a cooling substance in their helmets, otherwise they could go stark raving mad in this heat.

More stories of mass graves being found. Horrific.

A US Marine has been shot and killed on some bridge in Baghdad. No Iraqi is allowed out of Iraq now, with or without a residence permit abroad.

Day 9—Rumsfeld says everything is improving day by day. I suggest he come live here for a couple of days and then say that. Still intermittent water and electricity, no cooking gas, no petrol, queues miles long, no salaries, no government, no security. So what has improved? The only thing the US got working was the oil industry, just as the oil ministry was also the only ministry they protected against looting and arson. They've found the engineers they needed. The war has been over a month today.

I just heard on the radio that families are putting up black rags to announce the demise of their relatives who are featured in the deck of cards—the US's fifty most wanted of Saddam's men. It's a tradition that started during the Iran war, when public mourning was forbidden by Saddam as too many soldiers were dying. A length of black cloth with the victim's name and age, etc. would be strung up outside the house announcing the death. In the countryside a few of the wanted men had their families put up these signs, but they didn't get away with it. Most of them are still on the loose.

Rumsfeld says they now have a presence in every town in Iraq and he is very pleased. Actually, what happens when a tank arrives is that there's always a congregation of kids and people. One is never certain if the people are being friendly or taunting the marines. I'd guess both. I just saw some very angry marines guarding the Adhamia mosque. The marines were yelling and shooing away the people. That's how accidents happen.

Day 10—First night at home. I lie down on my bed. Above, half a melon of a moon, and two stars on either side, my beautiful palm trees silhouetted against the night sky. In the background, if it's not the nearby mosque's imam ranting loudly, it's war sounds— explosions and shots, dogs in the distance.

I had lunch yesterday at the Italian Embassy. They have rented my uncle's house, opposite Ma and Needles. Who should be there but Barbara Bodine. Amal told her that in the 1991 war and in this one both her house and her shop had been damaged. She said, 'Well, we will try and avoid you the next time.' Wonderful diplomacy. Amal was very tearful and wanted to beat her up, but we were guests, so we behaved. I spent a lot of time talking to a Larry from the reconstruction group. I have nicknamed it UHU (after the glue) but I think it's ORHA (the Office of Reconstruction and Humanitarian Aid). I think UHU is better as that's what they are trying to do— stick the country together again.

Day 11—Sahira said she heard Saddam had spent five days in Adhamia recently. That's very close to us. My hopes go up and down like a yo-yo depending on who I am talking to. People are full of extremes and suppositions and theories. No one knows anything.

Lots of rape cases reported—hooligans, gangs, soldiers, all sorts. Women have stopped driving alone. If Iraq is going to be the showcase for the democracy that's going to hit the muddled east, miracles have to happen. The US is worried about security, not for the poor Iraqis, but for themselves.

Day 12—We went with Michael to the Palestine Hotel. All the seats in the lobby were occupied by chaps, just like the security goons in Saddam days. Missing are the dark glasses they used to wear. I said, 'Who do you think these goons are?' Michael said, 'The old security guys have just recycled themselves and become drivers or guides for the reporters. They kept their seats.'

Sol said on their way into Baghdad they'd passed a bus with all its seats taken out and tied on to the roof. Inside were rows and rows of satellite dishes; 'tis the rage now. They were forbidden in Saddam days. There are two things that show a change—freedom of speech and satellite dishes.

Day 13—Tonight there is a big halo around the moon. Rumsfeld has declared that their presence in Iraq is an occupation, finally. Who were they kidding anyway?

Day 14—It's the Independent Democrats' first meeting. We are waiting in the banqueting hall; it's large and very dark. It would help if we had night-vision glasses. A hodgepodge of people, many sheikhs, few women. We are participating in a democratic process. Michael says in yesterday's meeting of the Iraqi National Congress, Iraqi guards with Kalashnikovs and marines were on guard. Here there are no guns— excellent. It's started and the sound from the microphone comes and goes, freedom and frustration, democracy in the dark. Questions and suggestions all turn into speeches; they all think they are poets. The main issues: lack of security, robbing of cars and nothing is improving. It's rather sad but I guess it's a start. There is a new list of 250 wanted people circulating on the street. It's being sold for 250 dinars.

Day 15—Have now been here for two weeks and, just for the record, in the last three days we've had an average of two hours of electricity a day. Don't believe what's reported; it's all propaganda. There is no security, no telephone, no gas. Now they say gas will be imported from Kuwait, but nobody trusts that; they say it will be full of explosives. We got electricity for fifteen minutes this morning. I made toast. Sol says the museum theft looks like the wish list of some collector; a professional job, and there might have been some help from the inside. The Basitki Bronze was dragged down the stairs and broke every stair on the way down.

Day 16—My arms and legs are lacerated and bug-bitten, a disgusting sight. Cutting off the dead branches from the orange trees and the creepers that have grown all over them. Palms seem okay. The menagerie in the orchard: an alsatian and an Iraqi fawn-coloured pup, sweet-natured; twelve geese with seven babes—there were eleven to start out with, they are careless and stamp on their babies and kill them by accident.

Seventy-five thousand cluster bombs were dropped on Iraq during the war; twenty-five per cent of them didn't go off. That's a statistic. The stories of mass graves being found are never-ending, except now people are scrambling about and digging them up themselves and trying to identify their missing sons, fathers, daughters, etc. In some places cranes are digging up great tracts of earth. Forensic science down the drain. There is no help from the authorities.

Michael went to visit Adnan. The opposition is thwarting him from every direction and he has difficulty getting any hall for a meeting. Our neighbour Kubaisi told the marines that if they wanted to stop the car theft they should get Talibani and Barazani, the two Kurdish leaders, to pay for every theft. It would stop instantly, as the cars all get taken up to Kurdistan and from there to Turkey and Iran. Two days later they came back and told him he was right. They had just caught a bunch and they were peshmergas, Kurdish fighters.

Sheikh Zayed of Abu Dhabi sent his people to take over one of the hospitals. In a week he had it electrified, cleaned, and working for 1,000 patients a day. Ambulances, doctors, the lot. Queues are miles long beside it. Now if Abu Dhabi can do that, surely the US, in all its great might, can make something move. I don't think there has ever been a more inefficient takeover. Everyone has stories of robberies taking place under the eyes of the US Marines. They go to them for help and they refuse to lift a finger.

Since we are to learn the American way of life, and suing is a hundred per cent of it, we should start suing the US and the coalition for making war under false pretences. Weapons of mass destruction and Saddam have ceased to be an issue. They should pay for the reconstruction of Iraq. We don't owe anyone a penny. We should sue them in an international court in The Hague. Also, sue the UN for genocide for imposing the embargo for twelve years, killing more than one and a half million people.

Day 17—The fundamentalists are acting up in Basra, pestering Christians to wear headscarves, and in Baghdad an arak [liquor] factory was burnt. Amazing it's not worse in this vacuum of authority.

Qasr Adnan was not hit in any of the wars and its neighbours say that's because the US wanted to use the palace. True enough, Jay Garner is ensconced in it—not a very effective interim officer; better to have stayed retired. Just went to see a house which overlooks the palace. (It was hit by tank missiles, so depleted uranium aplenty.) On the first floor, the aluminium and thick glass of the windows had melted into puddles, and two inches of ash on the floor were all that remained of the furnishings. This precision bombing is extraordinary. The ground floor was intact, with all its heavy carvings. The owner was more upset about the loss of the decorations than the building itself. He said the house was once voted the most beautiful house in Baghdad.

Tonight is windy and cloudy, my candles keep blowing out. There is a small, delicate green bug sitting on my book. We're all agreed the US doesn't want the electricity to improve because they want to install a whole new American grid system, or to keep us worried about such matters, as opposed to the big issues of government.

I don't think any human being can be hated more at this moment than Saddam Hussein. Too many grisly stories about him and his sons. Next down the list are the Kurds, who do seem to be responsible for all the car thefts, though some say it could be Saddam loyalists making trouble. The Sunni and Shi'a haven't fought yet. Perhaps it's still too early, but everyone says we're one nation, no matter the religion. Miracles can happen.

Day 18—The BBC says the US is more successful at making war than peace. Our new minister of culture is going to be an Italian. Beautiful moon tonight. No electricity, so millions of stars and a grey blue sky with dark silhouettes of the palms.

Day 19—Most exciting morning. With Tomas and CNN went on a search of my art works—what used to be called ceramics. First to the Babylon Hotel, where they denied anything of mine had ever existed. Then, realizing what it might be, they took us upstairs. Originally it was a seven-piece sort of tapestry; five pieces were left and had been separated, one on every wall, and above each piece a three-pronged chandelier like a hat. First shock. Second, to the bank near Haifa Street. Bank was burnt. Black smoke has covered the panel, it looks absolutely charred. Then my fish net on a wall. That had fared better, just a few bullet holes. It had a black cloth strung across it announcing the death of someone in the district. Then we went to the palace area, which is now occupied by the US Army. It was a forbidden area then as it is now for us Iraqi mortals, but with a CNN car we managed to get in. A huge area full of Walt Disney palaces. Took a lot of searching to find the right one. Finally, there it was by the river. It had been bombed. The gates were open and we drove in. The bomb had fallen in the swimming pool; my panel had been one wall beside it. It wasn't grandiose as palaces go. So maybe that was why Saddam and family hadn't liked it and hadn't lived there. A German company was commissioned to construct it and I had made an effort to produce an earthly paradise on a fifteen-metre-long wall. It had taken a year of my life. Such a strange feeling. In history, one always reads of such-and-such a work being destroyed by flood, earthquake, war, and here it was. I am part of history.

Jane went to a demo in Kathum. They kept telling her to cover herself, so she told them, 'but you invited us, Sunnis, Christians, everyone.' They said, 'Yes, but not women.' I told her she should have said, 'Fine, then you don't get CNN coverage.'

It's an irony that for many years France, Russia and China have been wanting to lift the embargo, and the US and UK have said no, and now it's the US that wants it lifting and the others say not until the UN says no more weapons of mass destruction.

Went to see Adeeba today. She's in mourning, her husband died a few days before the war. She said, 'Two weeks ago, there was a knock on the front door.' She thought she recognized the voice, so she opened it. Hands were put on her mouth and throat and she was dragged in to the sitting room. She fought and fought till she finally managed to get her teeth into the hand that was holding her, and as it was removed she yelled for her son, Abdulla. The woman—it was a woman—made a quick getaway, out into a waiting car with two chaps in it and no number plate. Ma said, 'How did you manage to bite?' Adeeba said, 'It's a good thing I had my teeth in.'

Day 20—Last night there were huge explosions and lots of shooting. There is a big to-do about empty containers stolen from the old bombed nuclear plant site. They must have residue in them, and they are being used for water and washing clothes, etc. All sorts of rashes and blindness in certain districts. That's all we need, with the chemicals lying about from the war debris and no one cleaning up. Now we can have a nuclear disaster.

Helicopters overhead, they fly so low skimming the top of the palm trees. I see the marines, their legs hanging out, everyone boiling away in the sun. When Britain occupied India they invented the bush shirt as a uniform to cope with the weather. The US must invent something for these poor soldiers. I asked a marine yesterday whether there was a cooling substance in his helmet. 'No,' he said. 'It's hot.' As usual, the bosses are in air-conditioned splendour while the workers suffer. Amal has lost her two young guards. The Iraqi National Congress is handing out huge salaries, so they have gone to join them. Amal thinks they are making a militia.

The traffic has taken on a life of its own, barricades appear at will and one-way streets don't exist any more. Any direction goes. They call it democracy. Supposedly, the British police are going to come and train some of ours, but so far there is nothing on the streets. Hussein told me he keeps my car dirty because of the robbers. Though my Toyota is ancient, 1980, it's still sought after.

Going to see Ma and Needles with Jane, we passed by the orphanage near my house. There were four armoured cars with marines all on the alert, guns pointing. Jane said, 'Let's stop and see what's happening.' She came back. It seems they were just coming to visit the orphanage and give them sweets. Under the barrel of a gun? Just like our liberation, under the barrel of a gun.

We heard that Husb el Dawa and the Hawsa, two Shi'a parties, are accepting all the Ba'athies that are jobless. They also look after hospitals and help with food donations. So I can see this fundamentalist takeover and all of us being forced to wear scarves on our hair and stay at home.

Ahmed Chalabi, head of the Iraqi National Congress, has taken over the Hunting Club in Mansour, which is slowly becoming fortified with masses of guards. He's the Pentagon's man. Every party is making their own rules and lording it over the rest. Baghdad could easily become a hundred city-states, and no one will give up their illegally occupied territory.

Omar says Adnan is optimistic. As long as he is, I guess we can be too.

Day 21—Baghdad is like living theatre; you have to pinch yourself to see reality. The US does what it's doing and the Iraqis bumble about trying to make ends meet or make sense of the situation, because there is no communication, no dialogue, just separate camps miles apart.

Went to see the destruction at Amal's shop, and CNN was there filming her. Jane says she has interviewed some of the looters. They all say they were so deprived during Saddam's rule and that they are just releasing their anger. Maybe at the beginning, but now I feel it has become a way of life and bad sorts have just taken to the excitement of destroying everything. There are also pyromaniacs galore.

Meanwhile, each faction is building a little army and the more names they have on their platform, the better chance they have, in this so-called democracy, of getting a seat in the interim government. This is not going to get us anywhere, US tanks in the streets and nothing else visible. It's the strangest occupation in history, I think.

Today, two garbage trucks collecting. What a wonderful sight. The UN embargo is lifted... Wow.

The US occupation has also been legalized by the UN which now makes the US responsible for the mess. This is also a first in history, legalizing an invasion and occupation. On top of everything, under false pretences.

Day 22—Huge winds and sandstorm, palms swaying dangerously, chewed sand all night. Even so, it was better outside than inside with no electricity. In Saudi Arabia both the US and UK embassies have been closed for a few days due to terrorist threats.

The US is palling up with the Mujahedeen Khalk, the Iranian opposition, which had its base in Iraq. It's lovely now: the US is making a deal with a blacklisted terrorist organization in order to win a war against terror.

Petrol queuing has become a wage earner. Cars queue all day, finally get a tankful, then empty it into containers they sell for up to ten times the price. They say it's safer, because no one will steal your car if you're pushing it to the station. Plus, at the end of the day, you have some money. See how inventive Iraqis are?

The CNN taxi driver who brought me back home said, 'People are in an utterly dismal state. They are all wishing back Saddam's time.' I said, 'It can't be true.' 'Honestly,' he said, 'Everywhere we go, everybody says nothing could be worse than now.'

The appointment of the new Iraqi interim government has been postponed until July. The Kurds are upset and have gone up north. Everyone is upset.

The orchard is full of white feathers. Those geese shed a lot.

Day 23—There is a lot of black smoke and a lot of shooting. People are supposed to be giving up their arms, and no one wants to. Lots of ministries are being dissolved: the Information and Defence ministries, everything to do with the army. Bremer's orders. Bremer is our new boss. America's man, the pro-consul with his sweeping powers. There's much dissent; the whole country will be jobless.

The war against the Ba'ath has started in earnest and everyone who has anything to do with the party is out. That means the whole country, just about. First of all, most people are civil servants, one way or another. That's the way Saddam controlled everyone. You could not really get a job unless you were a Ba'athi, so most people just became Ba'athi to survive. Then, another fact: Saddam was never a real Ba'athi. He hijacked the party for his own means, so the poor real Ba'athies have suffered in both ways. They should be kicking out the Saddamies, not the Ba'athies. Also, the army was not loyal to Saddam and he never trusted them. That's why he made his own private army. But what about people who have been in the army their whole lives? Just as a job? Supposedly these people are not going to be even given their pensions. I don't think the Americans have a clue about this country or what to do with it. It seems they just listen to the opposition, those whom they brought with them from outside. It's all too bizarre and very sad.

Mohammad al Fartoos came out with a petition a week ago and today is the last day of his warning. No more alcohol, all shops that sell liquor will be burned, and all women not covered up will be killed. Imam Ubaida told 10,000 listeners the same thing and gave them licence to go ahead. Gangs are burning, looting and stealing cars at gunpoint. Of the 40,000 criminals Saddam let out of jail with his amnesty last year, 400 have been caught.

I guess getting rid of the army will allow the US to stay as long as it likes. Who can make a coup against them now?

I bet Iraq will never become another economic miracle like Japan or Korea, but I could be wrong. That's, of course, if the Americans encourage us to be. I am not certain that it's in their interest, or Israel's. We are certainly capable, but too individualistic and not an obedient lot. Very difficult to rule, as history has repeatedly shown.

Day 24—There is another meeting at the Alwiyah club, for the Free Democrats, and next Saturday will be a meeting for women. A few women have spoken. They are good and mostly say relevant things. Really, there is a great need to have women incorporated if anything is to become of this country. In fact, in the whole Arab world: we do consist of half the population.

Accountability is talked about. It's Iraqi money that is going to be spent on US companies, and they should check whether or not the work can be done by Iraqis. We should definitely try and help ourselves, because it doesn't look like the occupiers will. The US has offered twenty dollars a month to all civil servants and forty dollars a month to the retired. They will keep us at a servant level—a few crumbs here and there. Meanwhile Bremer and his guys, 700 of them, get $286 million in wages for six months. A billion a week to keep the US army in Iraq. The difference is staggering. Such humiliation.

Day 25—Um Hussein tells me that Saddam cleared out the Abu Ghraib prison because he was planning to put all the would-be captured marines there. In fact he held all his meetings underground in the prison. I don't know where she got this information.

The hospitals are in a very, very bad way. It's six weeks after the war. They still have no special electricity or water connections. They make do like the rest of the country.

There is much black smoke, shooting and many explosions. Everyone is supposed to be giving up their arms in two weeks, but who really will, with security being what it is? Nil. The arms black market is doing a thriving business. You can find anything you want.

Israel has accepted the road map. They must have been under

some pressure. I guess the US has its oil wells now. They can afford to put on pressure. I must say I can't see them exporting too much oil if the situation stays the same, with this total lack of security and unrest. They will blow up the pipelines. The Iraqi people have seen nothing but humiliation from the occupiers. Be warned.

The Kurds have been disarmed, all except for the Peshmergas who are defending the borders up north. They are very upset, as is Ahmed Chalabi, that there is not going to be an interim government. More fool them for being fooled and not knowing that this was an occupation from the beginning.

Schools are trying to open but it's difficult with the lack of security. Also, the books are full of Saddam so they have to cut out the pages that have things about him or pictures—which means they lose something important on the other side of the page. Some studies claim that thirty per cent of the books were made up of praise for Saddam. Our educational system is going to be like the Gulf's, apparently, but books haven't arrived yet.

We now know that three Tikritis, General Safwan and two other generals (all of them relatives of Saddam), were responsible for the collapse of Baghdad in a day. They gave the orders not to fight, and then they and their families were flown out of the country in a US plane and given new identities. This is the story. Saddam was going to do a Nero and let Baghdad burn. So, in a way, the generals saved it from further ruin, and saved a lot of people from death. I guess we have something to be thankful for.

Day 26—Rumours of Saddam. He was here, he was there, there were raids on houses by the marines, but he is not found. Many say he was flown out at the beginning, but I don't believe so. The US has no use for him any more. I wonder what has happened to his doubles? I think there were one or two left—maybe not all four. All these sightings could be one of them. There was a joke during the war about them, a bit macabre. They are called for a meeting and told there is good news and bad news. Saddam is still alive, that's the good news. The bad news is that he has lost both his arms and legs…

Day 27—Horrible last night, I had to stay inside. It rained twice in between the sandstorms. Bremer has told Ahmed Chalabi to leave the Hunting Club and get a place of his own. No more militias allowed, or arms, or occupying buildings. Big demonstrations against the abolition of the army. People were ready to do suicide bombing, talking publicly about it and showing their faces on television.

Yesterday there were two incidents, in Baghdad and Faluga. Two or three marines dead, five wounded. Also, a helicopter downed. They don't tell it straight. It seems there were four incidents, and in each, one or two died. In Kirkuk and Haditha, too. In Baquba, a woman was killed as she was coming towards the marines with grenades to blow them up. The US came with the message that they were coming to liberate, not occupy, so what happened? There is no guidance. You cannot expect a country that has had thirty years of dictatorship to get on its feet overnight. The infrastructure is totally gone thanks to the dismissal of everyone and everything Ba'athi. I am certainly not defending the Ba'ath, but that was what was there for thirty years. Rumsfeld says they won't allow Iraq to have a religious government like Iran. But I am afraid that's what's going to happen. They are the only ones that have both the organization and the money. They pay people wages and look after them in hospitals and at home and give them security. The lawyers' union just had an election and guess who won, a complete unknown with a beard, a pro-cleric.

I spent the day packing up the house again, closing all its orifices, though sand will get in anyway. Tonight, back at Ma and Needles', as Ma and I will leave from there tomorrow morning by car.

Day 28—We are already one hour on the road to Amman. Burnt-out cars and tanks have been removed from the outskirts of Baghdad. Farewell palm trees, this is the last of them, they're beautiful in this early light. Miles of lorries coming in full from Jordan and miles going out empty. At the Iraqi border a young marine talks to us in Arabic. In Jordan, long queues and much searching for looted antiquities; more than ever because of a Japanese reporter who took an unexploded cluster bomb from Baghdad as a souvenir. It was discovered in Amman airport. It killed two people in the airport as it exploded. The security guards remind me not to try and leave without a permit from the palace. They have not forgotten me.

Amman—Sure enough, I am not allowed out. This time we will do things properly. I hope to get the right permit. I find Wisam living in Amman. He was summoned back to Baghdad for questioning when the UN inspectors were there last year, because he was the one blamed for the uranium from the Niger episode. At the time he was Iraqi ambassador to the Vatican. Later, the whole thing turned out to have been caused by a forged letter—it had neither his letterhead nor his signature. This was acknowledged by the UN, but he had a hard time convincing them. He had been sent to Niger to extend an invitation to visit Baghdad, and that was all. He said he was given a camel saddle as a parting present but had left it behind, too big to carry. Absolutely nothing to do with uranium. So who was responsible for the forgery? And how many more untruths are slowly coming out of the woodwork. Rumsfeld says that weapons of mass destruction were the only thing all parties agreed on before the war and that's why this became the main issue to start the war. Meanwhile, Blair bleats on that they will be found. And Bush says everyone should work together now and put differences aside. See how everyone is backtracking? But no one talks of helping the Iraqi people.

Another helicopter was downed and four marines are dead. Naila says marines caught Syrians and Palestinians in Fallujah. They are being paid by Saddam, as he certainly took enough cash with him. They are the ones making all this disruption. Because I don't think too many Iraqis would still be fighting for him. Maybe only his lot, who have nothing else to lose and, by now, have had time to regroup.

June 2—Beirut—I finally made it out of Jordan but my name is still on the banned list on the computer. No wonder nothing moves forward in the Arab world. The Iraq story will not finish, and I can see myself updating this diary forever.

I will end this episode with a quote from Rumsfeld, because it shows perfectly the dithering, the lack of knowledge and planning that we have been, and will be, subject to (though miracles can happen). In an ABC interview on March 30, 2003, regarding weapons of mass destruction, Rumsfeld said: 'We know where they are. They're in the area around Tikrit and Baghdad and east, west, south and north somewhat.'

To be continued. □

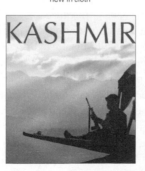

NOTES ON CONTRIBUTORS

Nuha al-Radi's *Baghdad Diaries* appeared in *Granta* 42 and have since been published as a book (Saqi/Vintage). Trained as an artist, she lives in Lebanon.

Christopher de Bellaigue is a reporter currently living in Tehran. His book on Iran since the Islamic Revolution will be published by HarperCollins in 2004.

Edward Burtynsky's photography appears in *Manufactured Landscapes* (Yale University Press). A mid-career retrospective organized by the National Gallery of Canada is touring the US and Europe until 2005.

Marian Botsford Fraser is a writer, critic and broadcaster living in Canada. Her most recent book is *Solitaire: The Intimate Lives of Single Women* (Random House/Macfarlane Walter & Ross).

James Hamilton-Paterson's books include *Playing with Water* and the novel, *Loving Monsters* (Granta Books). His next novel, *Cooking with Fernet Branca*, will be published by Faber. He is a Fellow of the Royal Geographical Society.

Matthew Hart's most recent book is *Diamond; the History of a Cold-Blooded Affair* (Fourth Estate/Plume/Penguin Canada). He lives in London.

Thomas Keneally's *Schindler's Ark* won the Booker Prize in 1982. His most recent novel is *The Office of Innocence* (Sceptre/Doubleday). He lives in New South Wales where, on his occasional trips to town he is driven by Manly Cabs, which has the highest regional Granta-readership of any cab company on earth.

Mark Lynas is a journalist and campaigner specializing in climate change. His book *High Tide: News from a Warming World* is forthcoming from Flamingo.

Philip Marsden's most recent book is a novel, *The Main Cages* (Flamingo). He is currently working on a book about Ethiopia and a novel set in the Caucasus.

Jon McGregor was born in Bermuda in 1976 and now lives in Nottingham. His first novel, *If Nobody Speaks of Remarkable Things*, was published last year (Bloomsbury/Mariner). He is currently working on a second.

Bill McKibben is the author of *The End of Nature* (Bloomsbury/Anchor) and, most recently, *Enough: Genetic Engineering and the End of Human Nature* (Bloomsbury/Times). He is scholar-in-residence at Middlebury College.

Wayne McLennan has been a professional boxer in Australia, mined for gold in Costa Rica and skippered a fishing boat in Nicaragua. Further accounts of his travels will be published by Granta Books.

James Meek has reported from several conflicts, most recently the Iraq war. He is a writer with the *Guardian*. His latest book is *The Museum of Doubt* (Rebel Inc.).

Maarten 't Hart is the author of thirteen novels, most recently *The Sun Dial* (Arcadia/Toby Press). Trained in zoology and ethology, he was the 'technical adviser on rats' when Werner Herzog remade the film *Nosferatu*. He lives in the Netherlands.